aspect of taming your brain gremlins. If you want to start at the first page and work through the prompts as they come, follow that bliss. But if you need some of the later pages right now, skip on ahead. It's *your* mental health, so you get to pick how to unfuck your mind.

Most of all, know that feeling like garbage is not the end. Mental health is an ongoing struggle, but you have the strength to build your resilience, manage your stress, and bring wellness into your life. Go ahead, lose your shit, then come back to this journal to dust yourself off and move forward.

forks really are simply the end of your patience. But maybe you're at your wits' end because you are already spending a shit-ton of energy to get out of bed in the morning, to put a smile on, to figure out why you feel so bad...and the forks are just one more unexpected wrench in your plan.

No matter where you are in your journey, there will be bad days. And this journal will be here for you when shit is really hitting the fan. Sometimes, just screaming into the void, or onto the page, is enough. Other times you'll need to call in the heavy hitters from your support network. Either way, the prompts in this book will help you manage the tough times and achieve actual wellness.

Scary as it may seem, you're embarking on a kick-ass journey here. Getting your mental health on track can make all the difference in your life. How much can you accomplish without anxiety whispering in your ear about everything that could go wrong? What opportunities will you be able to take on when you're not trapped thinking about your past mistakes? Not to mention, when you make space for self-care and self-love, you teach yourself and the world that you're worthy and down-right deserving of good things. You're expected to spend all kinds of time and energy on getting your body in shape. How about devoting some of that attention to your mental state?

As you work your way through this journal, don't stress

INTRODUCTION

So Maybe It Isn't So Fine Right Now (but It Will Be)

So...things are kind of a shit show right now, huh?

Welcome!

To start things off, you should know that managing your mental health is damn hard. The world sucks sometimes, and it's easy to feel like you're all alone, trying to get it together. But you're *not* alone. Everyone has days (or weeks or months) where they don't feel all right. It's not a fun place to be, and it can feel overwhelming. Don't worry! You're doing the right thing by starting this journal, the first of many steps in a more positive, productive direction.

This journal is designed to help you identify the warning signs of a shit storm and gather the tools you need to weather it. If you're in a state where opening your kitchen drawer and finding zero clean forks has you on the verge of tears, it's not about the forks. The better you get at checking in with your-self, the better you'll get at identifying your triggers big and

Published by Sourcebooks
P.O. Box 4410, Naperville, Illinois 60567-4410
(630) 961-3900
sourcebooks.com

THE ANXIETY CHECK-IN

A Guided Journal to Support Your Mental Health and Help You Through the Hard Days

BREE CARTWRIGHT

Routledge Philosophers

Edited by Brian Leiter

University of Chicago

Routledge Philosophers is a major series of introductions to the great Western philosophers. Each book places a major philosopher or thinker in historical context, explains and assesses their key arguments, and considers their legacy. Additional features include a chronology of major dates and events, chapter summaries, annotated suggestions for further reading and a glossary of technical terms.

An ideal starting point for those new to philosophy, they are also essential reading for those interested in the subject at any level.

Available:

Hobbes
A P Martinich

Leibniz
Nicholas Jolley

Locke
E J Lowe

Hegel
Frederick Beiser

Rousseau
Nicholas Dent

Schopenhauer
Julian Young

Darwin
Tim Lewens

Rawls
Samuel Freeman

Spinoza
Michael Della Rocca

Merleau-Ponty
Taylor Carman

Russell
Gregory Landini

Wittgenstein
William Child

Heidegger
John Richardson

Adorno
Brian O'Connor

Husserl, second edition
David Woodruff Smith

Aristotle, second edition
Christopher Shields

Kant, second edition
Paul Guyer

Hume
Don Garrett

Dewey
Steven Fesmire

Freud, second edition
Jonathan Lear

Habermas
Kenneth Baynes

Peirce
Albert Atkin

Forthcoming:

Nietzsche
Maudemarie Clark

Mill
Daniel Jacobson

Einstein
Thomas Ryckman and Arthur Fine

Plotinus
Eyjólfur Emilsson

Plato

In this engaging introduction, Constance Meinwald shows how Plato has shaped the landscape of Western philosophy. She provides much-needed historical context, and helps readers grapple with Plato's distinctive use of highly crafted literary masterpieces for philosophical purposes.

Meinwald examines some of Plato's most famous discussions of human questions, concerning *erōs*, the capacities and immortality of our *psychē*, human excellence and the good life, and Plato's controversial ideas about culture, society, and political organization. She shows how Plato makes a sketch of his theory of Forms foundational in this work, and she offers illuminating readings of texts concerned with the development of the theory and its relationship to Greek science and mathematics.

Throughout, Meinwald draws expertly on Plato's dialogues to present a lively and accessible picture of his philosophy.

Including a chronology, glossary of terms, and suggestions for further reading, *Plato* is an ideal introduction to arguably the greatest of all Western philosophers, and is essential reading for students of ancient philosophy and classics.

Constance Meinwald is Professor of Philosophy at the University of Illinois at Chicago, USA. She is the author of *Plato's Parmenides* as well as many articles on ancient philosophy.

Constance Meinwald

Plato

Routledge
Taylor & Francis Group

LONDON AND NEW YORK

First published 2016
by Routledge
2 Park Square, Milton Park, Abingdon, Oxon OX14 4RN

Simultaneously published in the USA and Canada
by Routledge
711 Third Avenue, New York, NY 10017

Routledge is an imprint of the Taylor & Francis Group, an informa business

British Library Cataloguing in Publication Data
A catalogue record for this book is available from the British Library

Library of Congress Cataloging in Publication Data
A catalog record for this book has been requested

ISBN: 978-0-415-37910-6 (hbk)
ISBN: 978-0-415-37911-3 (pbk)
ISBN: 978-0-203-08332-1 (ebk)

Typeset in Joanna MT and Din
by FiSH Books Ltd, Enfield

To Pamela Joan Meinwald

Contents

Acknowledgements

In view of the unusually diverse audience envisaged for this volume, I have an unusually diverse group of test readers to thank. The book is meant to be of use to (among others) those no longer at school who are interested in learning more about Plato. I am grateful for the reactions of Alison Edwards, the intrepid canary in the mine of my earliest attempts, and of Henri Frischer. My sister Pam helped me improve my discussions of several crucial points. Jeffrey Donnell worked through several drafts of the entire manuscript, bringing both the point of view of an interested scholar from an outside discipline and his invaluable expertise in opening up academic work to a broad readership. Many students in my courses have also tried out draft chapters on topics they wanted to explore.

I've taken colleagues in my department as paradigm cases of working philosophers who don't specialize in ancient. Thanks especially to Mahrad Almotahari, Colin Klein, Sam Fleischacker, David Hilbert, Tony Laden, Marya Schechtman, and Sally Sedgwick for commenting on draft chapters and discussing them with me. Walter Edelberg read multiple drafts of every single chapter, showing incredible generosity with his attention.

I have had much expert advice from scholars of ancient philosophy as the manuscript developed. Sandra Peterson, always my most faithful reader, commented on every single chapter when it was new – as well as looking at later versions of many. For reactions to parts of the manuscript I am grateful to Elizabeth Asmis, Elizabeth Belfiore, Pat Curd, Nick Denyer, David Ebrey, Gail Fine, Paula

Gottlieb, Richard Kraut, Jan van Ophuijsen, Wolfgang Mann, Chiara Robbiano, and Franco Trivigno. I have benefited from the comments solicited at various stages by the press, especially those of Dominic Bailey and Katja Vogt.

I have enjoyed and profited greatly from invitations to present ideas that I was testing for the book to the Symposium Megarense, the Philosophy Department of the University of Indiana at Bloomington, the Thirteenth Arizona Plato Colloquium, the Northwestern Ancient Philosophy Workshop, the University of Chicago Ancient Philosophy Workshop, the University of Illinois at Chicago Department of Classics, the University of Illinois at Chicago Institute for the Humanities, the "2nd Saturdays" Chicago ancient phil work-in-progress group (especially Agnes Callard, Dhananjay Jagannathan, Gabriel Lear, John Schaefer, and John Wynne), the International Conference on Ancient Greek Philosophy: Plato's *Parmenides*, the Purdue University Ancient Philosophy seminar, the Midwest Seminar on Ancient and Medieval Philosophy, the International Plato Society Symposium on the *Symposium*, the Notre Dame Workshop on Ancient Philosophy, the subtly named Minnestoa, and the Phi Club, University College, and Department of Philosophy of the University of Utrecht.

I am grateful to the University of Illinois at Chicago for research support during a sabbatical leave and during a year as a fellow of the Institute for the Humanities. I would like to thank the Routledge team for their invitation to the series (without which I would never have written such a book), and all those involved in production (especially Hamish Ironside) for their cooperativeness and understanding.

Texts and translations

I generally base myself on the Greek of the Oxford Classical Texts (for Plato these are the original series in five volumes ed. Burnet 1900–1907, together with the new vol. 1 ed. Duke et al. 1995, and the Slings 2003 edition of the *Republic*). I also rely on *Plato:"Symposium"* (ed. Dover 1980).

In order that readers may be able to locate quotations in this book within the context of a complete translation, I have taken them from *Plato: Complete Works* (ed. John M. Cooper, 1997, Hackett Publishing Company) as much as possible, by the permission of the publisher. When that is not possible, I refer to other published work by the names of the translators (or make clear that I am translating myself).

Chronology

(Information typically conjectural; all dates BC.)

ca. 570–500	Life of Pythagoras.
ca. 500	Parmenides of Elea "floruit" (i.e. maturity, high point of activity).
ca. 500	Heraclitus floruit.
495–29	Life of Pericles.
ca. 492–32	Life of Empedocles.
ca. 465	Anaxagoras floruit.
ca. 470–390	Life of Philolaus.
469–399	Life of Socrates.
460–03	Life of Critias.
451–04	Life of Alcibiades.
446–03	Life of Charmides.
444–393	Life of Phaedrus.
431–04	Peloponnesian War.
427	Plato's birth.
423	Aristophanes *Clouds*.
405–354	Life of Dion.
404	Thirty Tyrants rule Athens.
403	Athenian democracy restored.
380s	Plato visits Sicily (two more trips in 360s).
383	Plato establishes Academy.
384–22	Life of Aristotle (comes to Academy around 367).
348	Plato's death.

Introduction

A young woman on *Doctor Who*, struggling to make her "mum's soufflé," faces a challenge from one of the children in her charge about how this is even possible. "How can it be your *mum's* soufflé if *you're* making it?" Her response is the superficially paradoxical quote: "The soufflé isn't the soufflé; the soufflé is the recipe."[1] For this claim to function on a widely popular TV program indicates the broad accessibility of a thought we might gloss by saying that the recipe is the *real* soufflé. A quick initial characterization of Plato's philosophy is that he takes tremendously seriously and follows up in a magnificently fruitful way the thought that the real soufflé is the recipe, or rather whatever it is that the soufflés we can eat all have in common and which accounts for them; and that the corresponding thing holds for all other cases. Over the course of his compositional career, he goes back and forth between treatment of special topics (done by trying to find and study the *real* thing relevant to each case) and his ever-evolving discussions of the status of those real things and of what the best method is if we wish properly to come to grips with them.

Plato's works range extremely widely. He provides discussions of erōs; the immortality of the soul and the divided character of the psychē; the good life, ethics, pleasure, and the virtues; aesthetics; politics; rhetoric; language; metaphysics; epistemology; and cosmology. Often several topics are intertwined, yet the combinations are different in different works.

These works are engaging and highly crafted. They have genuinely dramatic form. The literary elements of these compositions, the cultural context and the philosophical context of Plato's time all have bearing on the discussions within his dramas. And if "'Platonism' is the name of a debate ... not a fixed unvarying essence" (Burnyeat 1987: 216), this is largely because Plato's own works represent continuing exploration of a research program. In fact, Plato is orchestrating all of this as a way of drawing us readers into philosophical activity: we are meant to enter the discussions portrayed in his texts. The interest of doing this accounts for the perennial popularity and importance of the dialogues. One profits from the engagement both when one agrees with what one reads and when one is provoked to develop reasons for one's disagreement.

All of this makes it impossible for one person to write down for everyone else a simple takeaway from Plato's body of work. Nor did he himself approve of that kind of project. If we can credit the Seventh Letter, he considered that Dionysius II (the tyrant of Syracuse) showed by attempting to produce an epitome of Plato that he was not a philosopher! I have therefore designed this book to be used by those who want to learn to fish; I don't wish to offer a pack of frozen fillets. My goal corresponds to what one does for a course on Plato that has a broad constituency. One selects some widely appealing works that can be arranged in a meaningful way, and spends considerable time on selected passages that need and repay special attention, though everyone should read the entire works from which these are taken. The main purpose of the course is to help students develop the skills involved in doing philosophy with Plato. Yet sometimes colleagues sit in on each other's classes—perhaps as a way into topics they don't work on themselves, or to engage with the parts of the presentation that represent fresh thinking, or just to see how someone else presents things. For these sorts of reasons, professional philosophers and classicists may find the book of interest.

I believe that what newcomers need help with in reading Plato varies with different dialogues. Usually, some background information makes a real difference. Sometimes, as with the Socratic dialogues of definition, an interpretative framework can enable people to organize their own reading of the works. Often, people unfamiliar with Plato feel unsure about the philosophical relevance of the literary elements. With many dialogues, the overall structure is clear but help is needed in reconstructing and engaging with the arguments of certain brief but important passages. Oppositely, with the ethics and politics of the *Republic*, the primary initial difficulty is to track how the sub-arguments of particular passages fit together.

In light of all that is involved, the procedure of the book cannot be uniform. Some stretches will be comparatively easy going for readers. Other parts will require more effort. While I give quotes from Plato and paraphrase as much as is practicable, often turning to the texts will be desirable. And sometimes independent thinking will be called for! The purpose of the book is to help readers get more from engagement with Plato, not to provide a cheap substitute for that activity.

Part I contains three chapters each providing a distinctive kind of lead-in to the body of the work. Chapter One is a gathering-place for non-philosophical preliminaries. It assembles some history and some legends about Plato's life for those who are interested, and provides information concerning his texts that is necessary if one is to engage with them in an intellectually sophisticated way. Chapter Two takes up Plato's discussions of art and writing. This chapter presents selected passages in an unusual position that is useful because the topic is foundational in a special way. After all, the aspect of Plato that can be hardest for us to come to grips with is that he makes written dramas the vehicle of philosophy. And famous passages in the *Republic* and the *Phaedrus* seem at first to make this choice even more perplexing: they contain criticisms of art and of writing as seriously dangerous. By addressing these discussions, we will develop a nuanced understanding of Plato's views on these matters that will guide us in reading his own written dramas. Chapter Three completes Part One by treating Plato's Socratic works. It lays out aspects of these early works that prepare for the project whose development we will study in the body of the book. We will see how Plato's portrait of the historical Socrates shows him engaging with people who might be supposed to understand what is real in a series of areas central to human life. In each case the supposed authorities turn out not to possess the understanding in question. Since that understanding is called for if we are to live well, these works show the need for more philosophical inquiry.

In Part II of the book, we turn to that inquiry in some of Plato's most famous works. The character Socrates in the *Symposium*, *Phaedo*, and *Republic* offers positive views due to Plato himself on topics of central importance for us as humans: *erōs*, the immortality of the soul and signature capacities of the *psychē*, the human excellences that are necessary if we are to live well. These topics are foregrounded in the works themselves, and account for the broad interest of these dialogues. While our focus in Part Two will be the way these works treat their human questions, we will also take note of the fact that these treatments make explicit commitments on the foundational issue of what sort of things have the status of the *really real*—the items known today as "Platonic Forms." In these works we get a sketch—but only a sketch—of these entities. Thus these elaborate masterpieces function not only to advance our understanding of their human questions, but also to indicate to us the importance of turning to further study of Plato's Forms.

Part III of the book addresses that theme. We start with the programmatic remarks about Forms in the *Phaedo* and *Republic*, which I will locate within the context of previous work in Greek philosophy concerning the real. Next we will see how Plato proceeds in the *Parmenides* to shine a spotlight on issues about Forms that haven't yet been adequately specified. In that dialogue, he is giving us an exercise that will help us to come to a viable understanding. Then in the later works he continues to experiment with ways of developing this further. We can identify a kind of division of labor among dialogues so that while not repeating the same thing over and over, neither is Plato giving up on his program. Rather, in different ways throughout his career, Plato is always exploring aspects of his study of Forms.

Note

1 "The Name of the Doctor," *Doctor Who*, series 7 season finale, broadcast 2013 (writer: Steven Moffatt).

Part I

One
Life and works

Plato, the son of Ariston, was born around 427 BC, probably at Athens. (The ancient Greeks did not have "last names" in our sense. They had patronymics specifying a person's father; these could be used either in combination with an individual's given name or alone.) We know his brothers Glaucon and Adeimantus through Plato's portrayal of them in the *Republic*. Their mother Perictione was married after the death of Ariston to her uncle—commonly done at the time to keep property in the family. The offspring of this marriage, Antiphon, figures briefly as a character along with Adeimantus and Glaucon in the introductory action with which Plato frames the *Parmenides*. Plato's father and mother both belonged to aristocratic and distinguished families: his mother was related to the great lawgiver Solon. The offspring of such a house would normally have taken a leading role in the life of his city. Plato did not.

In this chapter we will first consider Plato's life in historical context to get some sense of why this was and what he did instead. In fact, almost no information can be definitely established about Plato's biography. It is not even certain if "Plato" was his real name! Many families named a son after the grandfather, and none of the sons of Ariston seems to have the expected name "Aristocles." An ancient report has it that this was Plato's real name, the nickname "Plato" then referring to the breadth of his shoulders, his forehead, or his prose style. We will look briefly at some ancient anecdotes and legends concerning Plato because even when their content cannot be credited, the fact that people put these things about is a historical fact of some interest. If historical information about Plato is scanty, his body of work is not; this corpus of compositions has come down to us remarkably intact. Indeed, for us, Plato is essentially the author of these works. The second half of the chapter will provide information about these writings that is needed if one wants to engage with them in an intellectually sophisticated way.

Some history

Largely as a result of reforms due to Plato's kinsman Solon in the sixth century BC, a democracy of a quite fundamental sort was established at Athens. The scale of a modern state has us making do with a form of democracy in which ordinary people vote for our representatives, who then make the actual decisions. The scale of the Greek city-state, however, allowed direct democracy: all adult male citizens could gather in the Assembly. Leading politicians were men who were able to persuade others to support their recommendations in this setting. Many leaders of the Athenian democracy were in fact from aristocratic families, as was Pericles, the "first citizen of Athens" during what many regard as the Golden Age.

Some today assume Plato lived at the glorious high point of Greek civilization, and find him villainous for not taking an active role in the Athenian democracy. But the picture becomes very different if we consider it in detail. First of all, while Plato depicts fifth-century leisured society in such works as the *Protagoras* and *Charmides*, this is not his own actual world at the time of composition. Plato was not even born until after the fictional date of those two works; indeed his birth was after the death of Pericles (of whom Plato's great-uncle/step-father had been a close associate). At the time of Plato's birth, the Peloponnesian War was already ongoing. This conflict was to continue with some lulls from 431 through 404 BC; it was a Great War of the time with Greek states divided between allies of Athens and those of Sparta. When Plato was born, the war had already led to a plague when the Athenians were confined defensively within their city walls; over a quarter of them died. While the city had originally been confident, the war ultimately proved costly in almost every possible way. Athens lost fleet, empire, and prestige, having refused several offers of peace when temporarily victorious.

In the immediate aftermath of the war, an oligarchy came briefly to power; Plato's relative Critias was among its leading members. Critias involved his ward Charmides in this project, and according to the Seventh Letter the much younger Plato too was invited.[1] But he did not accept. In the event, anyone who may have hoped the rule of the few would be better than the rule of the many was disappointed. The "Thirty Tyrants" proved violent and grossly self-interested. They had people killed for their property, and they forced as many citizens as they could to be implicated in their acts. Less violently they were hostile to Socrates, whose habit of public questioning they found an embarrassment and tried to restrain. But the democracy when it was restored had nothing to boast in that regard: it was under their system that Socrates was sentenced to death.

Plato in his formative years lived through a series of disasters at Athens. In such times, a conscientious person *should* have wondered if the city had made wrong choices, and if so why that was. The best and the brightest of the period had failed to live up to their early promise and ended badly to their own cost and to the cost of the city. Alcibiades, the ward of Pericles and brilliant darling of the democracy, persuaded Athens to the Sicilian Expedition only to have his personal scandals result in his being recalled from leading it. The hyper-ambitious expedition turned into a landmark disaster in the war; Alcibiades fled abroad, betraying the city, only to be murdered. Plato's relatives Critias and Charmides figured in the most hated regime in Athenian history; both were killed in the fighting that restored the democracy. Within a short space of time, oligarchs and democrats alike fell disastrously short.

In this context, Socrates' long-standing program of questioning men of note about human excellence (or "virtue," that which enables us to live well) must have seemed to have clear diagnostic relevance, for all his interlocutors had failed the test. Plato and others in antiquity pursued philosophy as having a valuable contribution to make in this area. Philosophy was needed to identify the good life (the natural goal of human flourishing is called in Greek *eudaimonia*, conventionally translated "happiness") and to help us live it. Plato and others saw this program as a more fundamental way of advancing the goal that ordinary political activity also has.

Philosophical inquiry into human questions is something that Plato took up as a result of his youthful association with Socrates. Plato as a young man may have known other philosophers as well. Aristotle mentions one Cratylus, a follower of Heraclitus of "all is flux" fame (*Metaphysics* 987a). After the death of Socrates, Plato may have traveled extensively in Greece, among the Greek colonies of Italy, and even to Egypt. Readers should be warned though that our evidence concerning these trips abroad leaves us far short of certainty. Pythagorean thought on mathematics and harmony influenced Plato, but his knowledge of it could have been through its written form. Their written works account for Plato's engagement with the ideas of Parmenides the Eleatic and the natural philosopher Anaxagoras, who round out his most important Presocratic influences.

A series of trips to Sicily seems to have been connected with a passionate attachment to Dion, brother-in-law to Dionysius I, the tyrant of Syracuse. Plato and Dion apparently tried to influence Dionysius II for good, but without success. According to some stories, Dionysius II sold Plato into slavery from which he was saved by one Anniceris, and at another time confined him so that he was only released after the intervention of the mathematician Archytas of Tarentum (I rely throughout on Riginos 1976 for all anecdotes and legends about Plato.) Again, it is impossible to know whether to credit these reports.

We are accustomed to say that Plato "founded the Academy" at Athens. But we should not be unthinkingly anachronistic in what we take that to mean (information on the Academy from Dillon 2003: ch. 1). Even before Plato's foundation, the Academy had existed as a grove with a place for exercise (*gymnasion*) outside the city walls; this public space had already been frequented by philosophers of an earlier generation. Plato purchased a garden of several acres where he lived near this site, and dedicated a temple of the Muses, establishing an identification with himself in the area and providing a focus that attracted others of like interests. Much of the philosophical activity of "Plato's Academy" was conducted in the park or in a part of the *gymnasion* building. On their way home, people might stop by Plato's house and might have dinner with him; and the private property must have been the location of whatever library there was. There was a lecture hall in the private garden by the time of Polemo (head of the Academy 314–276 BC), and some pupils lived in structures there.

Members of the Academy were not necessarily students in our sense, but often fellow researchers: Aristotle remained there for twenty years, leaving only on Plato's death. We do not know how much the institution offered formal instruction. The range of research interests associated with the members was much wider than that of philosophers today; it included mathematical and scientific activity. Our term "academic" marks appropriately the fact that the modern university is the descendant of Plato's foundation. Yet in size the original Academy was closer to a school, a philosophy department, or a small research institute.

On Plato's death around 348 BC, his nephew Speusippus became head of the Academy. While Aristotle too had distinguished himself philosophically, his connections to the court of Macedon were against him because of the extreme unpopularity of Macedonian military aggression. Plato's school for centuries fulfilled his wish to draw others into the activity of doing philosophy. His writings do that to this day—and we'll be joining that tradition in this book.

Anecdotes and legends

This section will take up some of the legends that circulated about Plato in the centuries after his death. While these are typically not credible, their *existence* is a historical fact that can give insight into Plato's reception in antiquity. Numerous legends concern in an intertwined way Plato's relationships to Apollo and to Socrates, and his outstanding literary gifts. Diogenes Laertius (*Lives of Eminent Philosophers* 3. 2) and others write that Plato's nephew Speusippus transmitted a report about "a story at Athens" according to which Plato's mother was a virgin when she gave birth to him, and his real father was not Ariston but Apollo. (In antiquity, descent from a god seemed explanatory of the "super-human" abilities of outstanding individuals, usually heroes of the legendary past.) In another story, bees deposit honey in the mouth of the infant Plato. A third legend concerns a dream Socrates is supposed to have had the night before he met Plato: a baby swan nestled in his lap, immediately put forth full plumage, and flew away enchanting everyone with his song. The next day on meeting Plato, Socrates supposedly identified the young man with the cygnet of his dream.

We of course cannot credit the legend concerning Plato's birth. But even the claim that there was such a report is of some interest. Here we find in its strongest form the motif seen in our other legends of a special connection with Apollo. If Plato was going to be credited with a divine forebear, the leader of the Muses and father of Asclepius (whose medical art addressed the health of the body as Plato's philosophy did the health of the soul) fits the role well.

The legend about the bees is not only implausible in itself, but is a stock report about poets in antiquity. It is told of Homer, Pindar, and Virgil; the honey in the baby's mouth prefigures and symbolizes the sweetness of his verses. Transferring the story to a philosopher appropriates for him this traditional recognition of eloquence. Further touches in some versions of the story create more ties to Apollo. Ariston and Perictione are sacrificing to him in some; he is the leader of the Muses with whom the bees of others are associated.

The dream of Socrates could have occurred, though it seems too good to be true. The swan is another connection with Apollo. And the dream symbolizes in charming form both what Plato's development owed to Socrates and how unusual it was: the cygnet's turning instantaneously into a full-fledged swan and flying away shows both how readily he profited from his philosophical nurturing and how independent he quickly became.

Our first cluster of anecdotes had their source among those who wanted to glorify Plato. It will now be interesting to consider for a moment two kinds of report that come from detractors. An example of one family of negative anecdotes is a variant of the dream of Socrates we have already considered. In this variant, Socrates' dream concerns a crow, which flies up onto his head and starts pecking, while croaking away. To drive home the point, Socrates then supposedly announces that the dream symbolizes how Plato represented him falsely. Less colorful stories exist in which other people claim Plato had depicted them incorrectly. A different family of stories accuses Plato, oppositely, of plagiarism. He is said to have copied from "such diverse figures as his fellow Socratics Aristippus and Antisthenes, the obscure Bryson of Megara, Protagoras, Epicharmus, certain Pythagoreans, and Zoroaster" (Riginos 1976: 166).

While such negative reports are palpable fabrications intended to diminish Plato, they incidentally provide confirmation on some points of interest. The charge of falsification indicates that people at the time were aware that the historical originals of Plato's characters had not said exactly the things his literary figures based on them do. This point actually supports the present mainstream belief that Plato is not setting up to be a mere recorder; his activity is that of a creative and original thinker. The supposed repudiation of "their" speeches by the originals of his characters is no more concerning than if the historical Hamlet could somehow have protested that he never said "To be or not to be."

Plato's characters are typically based on real people, and in many cases he relies on readers bringing knowledge of the characters' real-life careers to his works. A straightforward example of this is a character we will meet in Chapter Seven, Cephalus in the *Republic*. By the time of composition it was well known that the real Cephalus had lost both his shield factory and his son Polemarchus to the violence of the Thirty. Plato counts on our knowledge of this to color our view of the wealthy old man he presents fictively at an earlier time. We readers know as the character does not what disasters are about to befall him.

The opposite charge of plagiarism goes in another way to the character of Plato's project. In some cases the texts on which he is supposedly dependent are later forgeries, but it is interesting to consider the general issue because Plato certainly did think about other people's work. In this book we will see how, when taking on ideas from his predecessors and contemporaries, Plato transformed them by incorporating them into his program. The tag of Archilochus that "the fox knows many things; the hedgehog one big thing" is often quoted to distinguish two kinds of thinker. Plato's interests have a foxlike range. They extend from the inquiry into virtue and ethics of Socrates through the austere metaphysical pronouncements of Parmenides the Eleatic; they encompass a Heraclitean appreciation of the flux of sensibles and the explanatory scheme of the philosopher of nature Anaxagoras; they incorporate the reverence for mathematical harmony and the immortal soul of the Pythagoreans. Yet everyone takes Plato to be a star case of a hedgehog. His blending of diverse influences into a distinctive and unified project is an unmistakable personal characteristic of his own.

Transmission and translation

We now turn to Plato's body of works. There is reason to believe that none of Plato's genuine works has been lost: all the compositions mentioned in ancient sources have been handed down to us in their entirety. Besides the dialogues that are widely agreed to be genuine, we have a few miscellaneous items. These include some dialogues of contested authenticity, and some letters and verses that may be Plato's.

Awareness of the causal chain that connects us to ancient authors is important for understanding the status of what we have. Initially Plato probably wrote on wax, which was used for drafts because of the ease of making changes. Finished texts were written on papyrus rolls. The Academy probably had a library containing the founder's works among others; we don't know to what extent these were also available through booksellers. In any case, readers in antiquity who wanted to own any text had to have a copy made by hand from an existing version. Since by now the originals have long perished, the survival of classical texts has depended on the copying process being done over and over again. Those that survived have been copied first as papyrus rolls and then eventually, much later, in the codex form of a book; the pages of books too were originally made from papyrus, later from parchment or paper.[2]

In the Greek-speaking world throughout the Byzantine period, Plato's high prestige as an author ensured the continued copying of his works. Knowledge of Greek was widespread in imperial Rome, but declined with the empire except in parts of the south of Italy and Sicily that had originated as Greek colonies; Greek all but died out in Western Europe in the Middle Ages. During this period the West had little access to Plato, though there was a fourth-century translation of the *Timaeus* and a twelfth-century one of the *Phaedo* and *Meno*. In the fourteenth and fifteenth centuries, however, the residence in Italy of such Greek men of learning as Cardinal Bessarion, combined with the revival of interest in classical antiquity that had started in Petrarch's generation, brought about a whirlwind of activity in acquiring and reading Greek manuscripts. By around the turn of the nineteenth century, all the great manuscripts of Plato had come abroad. We can get a sense of the vicissitudes that result in their present locations by tracing a famous and important one. The work of John the Calligrapher, it was apparently the first volume of a two-volume complete Plato, made in the ninth century for one Arethas, Byzantine scholar and future archbishop of Caesarea. (Arethas was so engaged as to correct the manuscript against the exemplar himself; he also copied variant readings and a large amount of commentary into the margins in his own hand.) This handsome production arrived at the library of the Monastery of the Apocalypse on the island of Patmos sometime between 1201 and 1355, was discovered there in 1801 by the Cambridge mineralogist E. D. Clarke, and came finally to the Bodleian Library—hence it is known today as the Clarkianus or B.

Originally and for a long time, manuscripts were written wholly in capital letters, without punctuation, accents, or word division; later they came to be written in a variety of scripts. So scribes were faced with copying from cryptic exemplars possibly written in scripts with which they were not terribly familiar. Classical scholarship has come to recognize a repertoire of types of mistake whose occurrence one can confirm informally in one's own experience. Common mistakes occur when people trying to resume their place in an exemplar after copying a phrase go to the wrong occurrence of the word they are using as a marker, saying to themselves something along the lines of "I was up to 'Nevermore.'" They may copy the same letters twice, or if they have skipped ahead in the exemplar, letters will be left out of the copy. Letters also drop out just through simple inattention or outright mechanical damage to manuscripts. They can unconsciously be changed to others more acceptable on a superficial reading, a type of error counteracted by editors under the rubric of *lectio difficilior* (a reason for choosing the more difficult of two readings, the idea being that an innovative idea or phrase that is beyond the understanding of copyists is apt to be corrupted to something that seems normal to them). Complications also result, ironically, from the efforts of early scholars: a guess, a gloss, a note giving a reading culled from a different manuscript tradition is sometimes copied into a manuscript in place of what its proper reading would have been.

Starting with the activity of Aldo Manuzio, publisher of the first printed editions of most of Greek literature, Greek texts of Plato were more widely available. The Aldine Plato was published in 1513. Early printed editions had significance primarily as a technology for diffusion. Such editions of ancient texts cannot have the kind of authority that modern first editions enjoy in virtue of the direct involvement of authors. And Renaissance editors carried out much less systematic study of the manuscript tradition than classicists are able to do today. The early edition of Henri Étienne (Lat. Stephanus) is immortalized for a different reason, through the continuing use of its page numbers and system of marking parts of a page of text with letters. Stephanus page numbers and letters are still printed in the margins of texts and translations of Plato today, so that readers may share a common way of referring to passages. I will be using them when quoting and citing passages in this book.

A modern edition of a classical text represents an attempt to do all that is possible to counteract the depredations age has wreaked, with the conveniences of word division and punctuation added. We have seen that the chain of copying copies of copies tends to produce corruption. Because of this, manuscripts fall into families representing traditions that diverge from each other; these then stand as independent lines of evidence concerning the original composition. Ideally scholars compare all manuscripts of a given text and arrange them in a stemma, a diagram showing which derive from which. This allows them, where an ancestor of copies survives, to eliminate the copies as competitors with their own ancestor, to collect the readings of the independent lines, and to choose among them where they disagree. Where this still leaves something impossible or manifestly unsatisfactory, scholars try to emend the text. A modern edition lists important variant readings and a selection of the suggestions of scholars at the bottom of each page in the *apparatus criticus*, and employs a system of markings to make clear where its editor is making additions to or deletions from the received text.

The preparation of an edition of Plato requires enormous judgment: technical expertise in varieties of scribal error must be weighed with knowledge of prose style and with reflection on the philosophical force of what one prints. For textual critics generally embrace a self-conception according to which careful recension and command of paleography are only part of their art. Thus the flamboyant proclamation of Haupt, endorsed by Houseman, "If the sense requires it I am prepared to write *Constantinopolitanus* where the MSS have the monosyllabic interjection *o*" (Reynolds and Wilson 1991: 233). What the sense does require is a matter on which people can disagree, and so, even after good editions come out, debate can continue about passages of special interest.

While for most editorial choices only one decision is possible, there are still many instances where several courses are viable, and where the choice among them makes a great deal of difference. The way we read an entire Platonic dialogue can depend on as small a matter as the choice between a smooth or a rough breathing (marks indicating aspiration's absence or presence, neither of which would have been in the original). In the case of the theme question of the *Lysis*, this choice determines whether or not the dialogue is a search for a definition (Sedley 1989). In the analogous case of the Bible, the ninth-century Photius and later the Renaissance humanist Erasmus of Rotterdam observed independently that incorrect punctuation is enough to give rise to heresy (Reynolds and Wilson 1991: 64, 279)!

The work of a translator requires a further round of difficult judgments and compromises. Ancient Greek does not line up with any modern language in such a way that a given sentence of Plato's has exactly one correct translation. Some sentences admit of fundamentally different grammatical construals resulting in widely differing sense, and some words have no ready-made equivalent in our terms. This makes it impossible to maintain a one-to-one correspondence between Greek words and the English that renders them, even though doing so is an obvious desideratum—or would be if it were possible. Moreover, the practice of some English-speaking scholars of using initial capitalization to produce such expressions as "Form," "Justice," or "the Good" is wholly due to interpretative activity. This can be helpful, and indeed I often do it myself: sometimes it is the best way to show readers of the English that something universal is in view; sometimes it is desirable to mark the special status Plato gives Forms. But it is misleading if readers take it to reflect Plato's own compositional practice.

In recent centuries there have been changes of fashion in the purpose and style of translations of Plato. The nineteenth-century work of Jowett was not a vehicle for research; anyone who would undertake that knew ancient Greek. The translation made Plato easily accessible for non-specialist purposes, in English prose of some merit. At the other extreme from Jowett we find a type of translation that had a vogue in the second half of the twentieth century. Exemplars of this are the Clarendon series and also, in a radically different tradition, the translations made by followers of Leo Strauss. By that time many serious students and working philosophers were not prepared to engage with the original language, creating a demand for translations which could be used in an ambitious way by Greekless readers. The goal of this type of translation was to indicate all and exactly the philosophical potentialities of the original text. This led to a strained and artificial form of English that has received the nicknames "translationese" and "Eek." The gains envisioned from this attempt at fidelity proved elusive, though there is a small number of exceptional cases. By now, the pendulum has begun moving back. Exemplars of the present mode make up *Plato: Complete Works* (ed. Cooper 1997), the compendium translated by various hands and published by Hackett. This will be the default translation for passages quoted in this book.

We've traced the route that Plato's texts take on their way to us. This explains why there can be significant disagreement between editors, translators, and commentators without any one of them being simply right or simply wrong. Now let us turn from how Plato's works reach us to some issues concerning the works themselves.

Groupings of Plato's works

We do not know the dates of composition of Plato's individual works. But they are so numerous that we need some way of organizing them for ourselves—and no such scheme as "comedies, histories, and tragedies" is available. Nor are the dialogues easy to group by topic treated, since many consider a variety of issues in an intertwined way, and the combinations shift from one work to another. In fact it has become quite standard today to divide Plato's dialogues into three groups. Unfortunately, the membership of the groups varies, and there is widespread misunderstanding about the basis on which the division is made.

The grouping has sometimes been supposed to be definitely established by "hard" scientific evidence. The discipline of stylometry (quantitative study of features of style) has produced masses of numbers from the nineteenth century to the computer era. But it is one thing to generate numbers and another to establish that they measure something one cares about, as one sees with putative "assessments" of what students learn in school. We must regard as unjustified any dogmatic belief that stylometry has scientifically established a linear chronological ordering of Plato's works (Keyser 1991, 1992; Young 1994).[3]

Three clusters of works grouped by stylistic affinities do tend to emerge (see Kahn 2002). In fact, the late group *is* definitely established. This comprises long, advanced works of considerable gravitas, typically revisiting issues treated in the other dialogues. To put it anachronistically, Plato's late works represent the sort of thing one might do in an advanced metaphysics or epistemology seminar, or when treating ethical, aesthetic, and political questions in a way that presupposes that members of the class have done the technical subjects already. Like advanced seminar work, they tend to presuppose that readers are already motivated to undertake the study in question.

At the other stylometric extreme, there appears to be a cluster containing all, but not only, "Socratic" works (i.e. those representing the activity of the historical Socrates). In such Socratic dialogues as the *Euthyphro*, Socrates is shown primarily questioning others who are putative experts about vital human concerns, but who nevertheless fall short when trying to defend their understanding. It has plausibility that the earliest works in the corpus were these short, comparatively accessible depictions of this great man: a huge influence on Plato, recently (on this chronology) put to death by Athens as a corrupter of the youth.

In between is a group anchored by the *Republic* (on justice); the *Phaedrus* and *Parmenides* are in this stylistic cluster as well. The *Republic* is long, but leavened by both conversational byplay and a series of great images and turns of phrase. The character Socrates now holds

forth with considerable confidence. He develops ethical and political doctrines and declares that they require foundational work in
metaphysics; thus he embraces special entities that constitute fundamental reality—what we have come to call "Platonic Forms."
Discussion of the special status of these entities has been identified—in a tradition going back to Aristotle's reports—as a
distinctive Platonic departure from the historical Socrates.

It is natural to assume that the widespread talk of the "early,"
"middle," and "late" dialogues tags the three stylistic/chronological
clusters. That is a mistake! To the extent that an early cluster is indicated by stylometry, the *Symposium* and *Phaedo* are in it. But these are
members, with the *Republic*, in what at a certain point mainstream
scholarship converged on designating as the "middle" group.[4] One
can see what the motivation for talking about these works together
was: all three feature a Socrates who offers more positive views of
his own than he had in the Socratic works. All three are longer and
more elaborate than the Socratic dialogues of definition had been.
And all three connect the treatment of human questions with a
sketch of the Forms, even if this is less developed in the *Symposium*
than in the other two.

At the end of the day, it is pointless to fight over whether to call
the *Symposium* and *Phaedo* "late early" or "early middle" dialogues: only
over-reification of the groups can seem to give such labels meaning.
Nor do we need to associate each exclusively with one group or the
other. Consider how a pick-up works in music: a note or a few notes
in the previous measure lead into and indeed are part of the phrase
that follows over the bar line. So a dialogue that is
stylistically/chronologically in one time period may have content
that leads into a "phrase" in the next. Mentions of Forms in the
Symposium and *Phaedo* lead in well to the discussions of them in the
Republic. Likewise, the description of dialectic in the *Phaedrus* and the
main exercise of the *Parmenides* (both of which belong stylometrically
with the *Republic*) lead naturally into the work of the clearly late *Sophist*,
Statesman, and *Philebus*. Nothing prevents dialogues containing such
"pick-ups" from also having some philosophical affinities with their
own stylometric cluster. In a case like the *Symposium*, realizing its position in the early stylistic cluster is especially illuminating, and so the
practice of calling it a "middle" dialogue is particularly unfortunate.

It is still useful—and indeed justified, if only to a degree—to organize Plato's dialogues chronologically. One must simply be careful not to give any such scheme more scientific status, fine-graining, or developmental force than it has. The first would require further investigation. The second, especially if manifested as a wish to fix a linear ordering of Plato's works (or something very close to that), is misguided because the character of the available evidence will never support such an ordering. And the third can come only from *interpretation* of the works once ordered. For chronological groupings do not automatically enable us to read off the state of Plato's mind at the different times of composition. Unless one is obsessed with dating for its own sake, chronology is primarily of interest to the extent that it underlies theses about the development of Plato's thought. Yet such theses, to be well grounded, require considerable additional work. As we will see in the chapters to come, Plato's use of dialogue form frustrates the agenda of anyone who wants mechanically to cull simple dogmas to attribute to him. Most serious readers eventually find themselves with views about Plato's philosophy, which can then be combined with the chronology to tell developmental stories. But we should be aware of how much these accounts owe to interpretation, and so of how far from automatic their production must be.

Speaking of Forms

We've touched on the circumstance that Plato's works show increasing interest in entities that today are called "Platonic Forms." In the course of this book, we will build up an increasing under-standing on the topic. It will be useful to start now with a basic sense of how some of the vocabulary in play works, and of how Plato's usage develops out of ordinary speech. It may come as a surprise to recognize that Plato does not rely on dedicated technical terms to name what we call "Platonic Forms."

One or the other of two words established in ordinary Greek usage before Plato commonly lies behind the translation "Form": these are *eidos* and *idea*.[5] In very early usage, these refer to an aspect of a thing that can be presented to our vision. (The two terms *eidos* and *idea* are etymologically related to each other, being both derived from an archaic word meaning to look; because of this common ancestor, "idea" and "video" are actually related too!) Over time the semantic range is extended so that the characteristics *eidos* and *idea* pick out needn't literally meet the eye. And each word comes to have occurrences in which it refers to something general, which can be common to a number of things as redness is common to red objects and cathood to particular cats. (This is what I shall mean in this book by a "universal" or a "property.")

Since it is normal usage to speak of a single thing that can be common to many cases as an *eidos* or *idea*, to do so does not require any explicitly metaphysical discussion or self-consciously philosophical theory about the status of these entities. One need not take a position on such questions as whether they are "immanent in" or "separate from" particulars—indeed the very habit of asking such questions and the special vocabulary for doing so belong to a later point in the history of philosophy.

Let's now turn briefly to the language for naming particular Forms. Here too Plato's usage grows out of a metaphysically unloaded history. This starts with the sort of expression rendered in translations along the lines of "the beautiful." The ancient Greek originals of these expressions are in fact importantly ambiguous. On the one hand, the Greek may refer to something or some things or everything that happens to be beautiful: an urn, Helen, and so on. On the other hand, it may pick out what it is about such things that is beautiful: not their hair or their shape, but in English their *beauty*. Abstract nouns came into increasing use in Plato's time in order to disambiguate. Again, there need be no commitment on the part of ordinary users of the language to any philosophical theory about the items referred to in this way.

Nor are the Greek originals of English formulations along the lines of "the F itself" consecrated to picking out Platonic Forms. "Itself" (*auto*) in this usage lets us know we are to pick out a thing "free from some kind of clutter … that is indicated in the context" (Denyer 2007a: 304). Because it is the context that lets us know what is the "clutter" in question, it is the context that determines what is left after the isolation process; the results can vary widely in different cases.

There are famous cases where the result is the isolation of

Platonic Forms. Of course, an ordinary person could use the phrases "the equal itself" and "the beautiful itself" and even call what each designates a "form" (*eidos* or *idea*) without necessarily being committed to some big metaphysical theory. But, as we will see in subsequent chapters, both the *Republic* and *Phaedo* contain explicit discussions that show that Plato is developing such a theory. I will follow a convention of using initial capitalization when it is important to mark this.

Thus we can now trace in a preliminary way a special strand of usages of the vocabulary we have been considering, which is of thematic importance in Plato's work. In the earliest, Socratic dialogues, the characters are interested in human questions. Socrates typically leads his interlocutors into discussion of the single common thing that is the same in "the many Fs" and that makes them F. The discussion we have just had lets us see why calling this an *eidos* or *idea* is straightforward, and not yet metaphysically controversial. Ditto with particular names for these forms.

Plato's special theorizing about Forms comes about because he at some point starts to wonder explicitly what the status of these entities really is. (There is no useful way to decide between the possibilities that Plato had no thoughts on these points when he wrote the Socratic dialogues, and that he already had the thoughts he would write up elsewhere but for presentational reasons did not include them.) In the *Symposium*, *Phaedo*, and *Republic*, these entities continue to play the functional role of universals each of which can be common to and is explanatory of many participants. But in addition, Plato now explicitly draws attention to a big difference in standing between Forms and "sensibles" (a term that in Plato can refer broadly to what is patent to superficial observation). Over the rest of his writing career, Plato explores how we should think of Forms: how they do their jobs, how exactly they relate to sensibles, and how they relate to each other.

What sort of entities are Platonic Forms? Must each be the kind of perfect exemplar that such present-day expressions as "the Platonic ideal of the banana split" have in view? Does Plato really think that Courage is some perfectly courageous object, while Largeness performs its function by being bigger than the galaxy? In this book, we will see that he composed texts that explore the intractable problems that come from thinking of Forms that way, and that he provided resources for us to come to a better interpretation of his theory.

Notes

1 This letter is widely judged to be authentic if any of the letters attributed to Plato is, and to show contemporary awareness of the events of Plato's life even if by another hand.
2 Information in this section on transmission and editing is based on Reynolds and Wilson (1991) and Dodds (1959).
3 Keyser's background in mathematical and scientific disciplines as well as in classics makes him uniquely suited to evaluate this work. While the sheer bulk and quantitative presentation of stylometric data can have a bullying effect, Keyser declares that "The news seems bad—a survey of all the work done to date more or less proves that no one knew what he was doing" (Keyser 1992: 72). In many individual cases, the feature selected is not as it should be independent of content, or the inquiry is question-begging, or the results are not statistically significant. He also mentions a point discussed at greater length in the interesting and less technical Young 1994: the illicit assumption that stylistic features change over time in a linear (i.e. monotonic) fashion.
4 This usage became established as a result of the influence of Cornford, Guthrie, and Vlastos.
5 The Greek *idea* is the source of the alternative translation "Idea," which has now fallen from favor because of the mentalistic connotation it has for us.

Two
Philosophy, drama, and writing

Plato's philosophical works are remarkable in receiving admiration as literature. While J. L. Austin, say, wrote in a way that was beautiful and beautifully adapted to the task at hand, his works have so little to offer to non-philosophical readers that he is virtually unknown to the general public. Other monumental figures have made philosophical contributions without being great prose stylists at all. In the context of classical antiquity, Plato is one of the three exemplars of the different levels of Greek prose: in between the simulated everyday idiom of the speeches Lysias wrote for his clients to deliver in the Athenian law courts and the high-flown mode of Thucydides' *History of the Peloponnesian War*.

Plato's works are prose dramas animated by the interchange of vigorous characters and by literary tropes of great imaginative power. This is why they continue to affect even readers who are not philosophers. TV shows and the musical theater today still reference Aristophanes' story in the *Symposium*. This tells of original creatures who were punished by being cut in two, resulting in our present selves: *erōs* is the consequent drive we feel to be reunited with our literal other half. The legend of Atlantis, which first appears in Plato, is refracted throughout the popular culture of today. Many other Platonic creations have a legacy in high art and serious thought.

Thus one might assume that Plato highly valued artistic achievement, and writing in particular. Yet his attitude to literature is more complex than that. Diogenes Laertius (*Lives of Eminent Philosophers* 3.5) transmits a report that, before Plato met Socrates, he had composed poetry including tragedies. Whether or not this is literally true, it encapsulates something symbolically: Plato possessed significant poetic ability, but instead of devoting himself to this kind of composition, he turned to philosophy. Given his own talent, the criticisms Plato developed of the poetic canon come not from insensibility but from real appreciation of its attraction and its power. It is far from obvious that Aristotle, who will seek to rehabilitate Greek tragedy after this critique, understands it better than Plato does.

Extended passages in the *Republic* contain discussions of the harms that can come from the theater and the rest of poetry, and have sometimes been taken to constitute a wholesale rejection of the creative arts. Yet this very discussion is carried out by characters within an artistic composition! Thus we need to ask whether the criticisms the *Republic* contains rule out the dialogue itself—along with the rest of Plato's works. In this chapter, we will see that the arguments in our text, while indicating deep reasons for giving up much great art, still leave room not just for harmless but indeed for positively beneficial works. There is room for the powers of drama to be used for good.

Beyond the *Republic*'s "condemnation of the poets," a well-known passage in the *Phaedrus* is widely taken to disparage writing as such. This passage must apply to Plato's compositions since they are all in writing. Because of this, the "Tübingen school" of interpretation holds that Plato transmitted his serious thought only orally, as "Unwritten Doctrines." Within the drama of the *Phaedrus*, it is not impossible to take the character Socrates as a pure exponent of spoken interchange. He is depicted strolling at leisure to a lovely spot in the country-side with his conversation partner, to whose interests and abilities he masterfully adapts his discourse so as to win the youth away from the initially attractive writing of the famous Lysias.

However, we are not primarily concerned with the character Socrates but rather with his author, Plato. It is ultimately he who develops the criticism of writing we are considering: criticism made in the very medium itself that it warns against! Do these remarks really tell against the natural response of readers through the centuries who have supposed that Plato means to offer us something of philosophical value in his written works? His output is on a scale that would be prodigious even in our own publish-or-perish times. Given the criticisms of writing the *Phaedrus* contains, why did Plato produce so much of it, with such depth, rigor, detail, and polish?

Socrates tells young Phaedrus that one ought to consider not so much the source of a report as whether it is true (275b–c). In this case as often, Plato's text contains considerations both pro and con, to start us on an active process of thought. And we shouldn't confine our attention just to its most obviously philosophical parts. A famous simile likens a good speech to a living creature, with each part having a fitting relation to the others and to the whole; the point seems applicable to written works as well (*Phaedrus* 264c). Thus we should attend to literary detail and explicit argumentation alike as we engage with Plato's writing. In the case of our *Phaedrus* passage we will see that some of its literary details have considerable philosophical import. Once we've worked through the passage as a whole, we will see that ultimately there is no need to be simply for or against all engagement with writing—or to think that Plato was. Rather he advances considerations that can help us understand its potential both to help and to limit us.

The circumstance that the discussions in view will bear on our approach to Plato's compositions drives the positioning of this chapter. Of course, just taken by themselves, Plato's treatments of drama and of writing are of considerable complexity and interest. Because of this we will initially think about each of the individual discussions on its own, sometimes noting how a local consideration applies to Plato's own work. Then having worked through the individual passages, we will in the chapter's final section draw together the individual threads. We will develop a sense of why Plato writes works of the special sort he does. Our consolidated understanding will both forewarn us about the dangers we face as consumers of written compositions and prepare us to get the benefits that are still possible.

The *Republic* on dramatic art

The discussion of art in the *Republic* is wide-ranging.[1] It occurs in the context of constructing an ideal city in thought. But many of the considerations we find in this text apply to us in our present circumstances as well, since we have the psychology on which they are based. Also, while the tag "Plato's condemnation of the poets" is conventionally used for our present theme, the discussion applies much more broadly than just to poetry in the narrow sense of metrical verse. The topic is the presentation of stories or discussions with or without meter. Later forms including the novel, opera, movies and TV fall within the scope of the discussion (Nehamas 1988; Burnyeat 1999).

Criticism of the great poets as a bad influence challenged a culturally dominant group in Plato's time, for poetry in ancient Greece occupied a position very different from that it has today. Far from being a marginalized recreation of a few, poetry was central to civic and religious experience. Traditional education consisted largely in the mastery of literature, centrally of Homer. In Plato's Athens, both tragic and comic poets took on important issues of the day before the widest possible public. Great authors were taken to have insight into the human condition, making natural the thought that literature was a guide to life. Thus, to challenge the cultural hegemony of the poets was a tremendous undertaking. The *Republic* does this in two extended discussions (once in Books 2–3 and once in Book 10). In each, the cognitive inadequacy of the poets turns out to be subtly connected with their pernicious moral effect. We will now consider in some detail several important lines of thought from each discussion.

The earlier discussion forms part of the treatment of the education and upbringing of the future guardians of the projected city: consideration of stories leads into consideration of music and applied arts like architecture and weaving (376e–403c). Our main interest now is the discussion of stories between Socrates and Adeimantus. The first main criticism within it works by pointing to certain problematic passages in the existing canon of great works. Examples according to which gods do and say unworthy things can't be correct. Such passages and ones showing heroes behaving badly have a bad influence (376e–392c). And the harm in question is not simply an occasional false belief. Because gods and heroes are taken to be exemplary, these passages will influence consumers of the art in the direction of vice.

The second main criticism (392c–398b) in the exchange with

Adeimantus turns on considering people's involvement as *performers* of art. Socrates draws attention to a difference in impact on the performer between reporting without quoting someone else's speech and actual imitation of a character done by saying their lines (*mimēsis* and cognate words are used here to pick out this impersonation). Because impersonation tends to cause assimilation in the character and understanding of the imitator, impersonation of characters behaving badly will have a problematic impact on one's own personality (395d). This does not rule out *all* impersonation—we don't yet know how pervasive the problematic kind is. But we should note that impersonation in this passage's sense would in antiquity have occurred far more than just in the "school play" and public performance of works with embedded quotation, because reading was typically done aloud. The process of memorizing and reciting quantities of poetry that was central to elite acculturation in Plato's time would already cause the sort of assimilation in question. (Indeed, the role of poetry in elite education was due precisely to recognition of its habituating the young to the ways of thinking and feeling of characters the society took to be exemplary.)

A common initial reaction among us is to disagree with the idea about the impact of taking on roles that is offered here. Yet reflect what a commonplace it has become for actors to access their own emotions in playing a part, and for even performers cast as bad or problematic characters to see and feel from their character's point of view. Professional performers from opera singers to Marlon Brando have reported the huge cost to their own well-being of taking on certain roles. (And strictly speaking, our present passage is about the young, who will plausibly be even more open to influence.) The concern Plato has developed could well be correct, even if we don't want it to be.

The criticisms developed here with Adeimantus have limited impact. So far it looks as if all we might need to do is correct or expurgate selected passages. In fact, the importance of art as an influence even suggests that art of some kind could be an important influence *for good*, as Plato's culture had recognized even if it was wrong in its construction of the canon. The end of the discussion encourages this idea (once all art forms have been canvassed with the aid of Glaucon):

Is it, then, only the poets that we must supervise and compel to embody in their poems the semblance of the good character ... or must we keep watch over the other craftsmen, and forbid them to represent the evil disposition, the licentious, the illiberal, the graceless, either in the likeness of living creatures or in buildings or in any other product of their art ... [w]e must look for those craftsmen who ... are capable of following the trail of true beauty and grace [*tēn tou kalou te kai euschēmonos phusin*], that our young men, dwelling as it were in a salubrious region, may receive benefit from all things about them, whence the influence that emanates from works of beauty may waft itself to eye or ear like a breeze that brings from wholesome places health, and so from earliest childhood insensibly guide them to likeness, to friendship, to harmony with beautiful reason.

(401b–d, tr. Shorey 1930; on *kalon* see Glossary)

Republic Book 10 returns to and deepens Plato's discussion of the arts (595a–608b). Socrates in partnership with Glaucon brings out the general point that what makes people artists and what makes their art pleasurable and powerful has nothing to do with actual understanding of the truth. And he develops at length ways in which engaging with artistic works can corrupt our own ways of feeling and thinking. We will now consider in detail two of Book 10's famous criticisms.

First let's take up the claim that artists damage the understanding of their audience because of their own limited cognitive attainments (595a–602c). It cannot be stressed enough that the point here is not that artists can never be accurate about specific matters of fact on the order of who did what when. Nor is the claim that poets cannot be accurate in portraying how someone feels. The sort of cognitive limitation in view in our passage is that of, for example, someone who represents what are supposed to be courageous actions without being able to relate this to an adequate understanding of the nature of courage. To take another example, consider how a movie or novel can show us what is supposed to be a great love, and how that representation can have a huge role in forming our own expectations and responses in that domain. But what if the movie-maker himself has no idea of what love really is?

The psychology of the *Republic* has it that one part of us—the rational part—is concerned to engage with fundamental realities (such as the nature of courage). Other potentially competing psychological elements just go with how things strike them and may be importantly mistaken, as they often are when it comes to appearances of value. The problem with artists is that they typically lack an adequate general understanding of F-ness, which is what makes F things F; this renders them liable to make unreliable and even deceptive depictions of particular things that appear F. A practice given to excessive representation and the copying of appearances in ignorance of the associated reality is what Book 10 criticizes as *mimētikē* (mimetic).

Let's unpack this line of thought further and assess it. To start first with an example outside the domain of value, let us suppose that there are such things as the natures of a sunflower, of a lily, and so on—perhaps in each case the constitution and functioning characteristic of members of the kind. Then that is what someone with understanding of the plant forms in question would have to grasp. We ourselves accept such matters as possible objects of expertise, that of botanists. In addition, we can plausibly say that individual plants are what they are because they have the relevant forms, and that the plants in our gardens are intelligible by reference to these.

Now consider paintings of flowers. They may be contrived to capture the way some particular flowers look to the artists or the public, each of which may in turn have been influenced by other artworks showing similar subjects or the general canons of beauty of the time. Usually, artists proceed without bothering about scientific understanding of the species in question. Consider van Gogh's sunflowers: the last thing he and his viewers are after is scientific information about plants. Artists of this kind operate at the level of visual impression and their genius has to do with the composition and purpose of their picture on its own terms.

However, while this may be the typical case, the considerations in our text have done nothing to rule out the possibility of exceptions. The artist Pierre-Joseph Redouté collaborated closely with botanists in many of his projects; in *Les Roses* he contributed to science by making known more than ten times as many kinds of roses as Linnaeus had identified. Those responsible for the *Flora Danica* encyclopedia undertook a high level of study and made renditions designed to convey real understanding. Similar programs motivated Audubon (on birds of America) and Stubbs (on horses).

596a–602c makes essentially the claim that poets are generally like van Gogh. The greatness of such artists is a supreme talent in handling the elements of their compositions (601a–b). In antiquity visual art forms were all representational, making it natural to think of painters as trying to give the appearance of different kinds of flowers, horses, or whatever. Socrates and Glaucon in our passage take the case of poets to be parallel—they show what is going to strike their ignorant audience as a brave action, a great love, etc. (Belfiore 1983; Moss 2007). Like the public at large, poets operate from the generally inadequate conceptions present in the surrounding society, which are themselves the cultural product of previous generations of poets and others. Myles Burnyeat's Tanner Lectures (1999) show how our conception of ourselves and our world is gradually and imperceptibly shaped by "the total culture" and in turn influences cultural production. He provides the model of a marriage to illustrate this mutual shaping of development (Burnyeat 1999: 253–4, 276).

Poets typically don't have the time or the ability to engage with fundamental research to guide their artistic production, any more than most painters do to master botany, veterinary science, anatomy, astronomy, metallurgy, etc. It has become clear to us that it is dangerous to take Mario Sorrenti's images of Kate Moss for Calvin Klein's Obsession campaign as a guide to our physical development. (The pace at which popular culture moves may have rendered this example completely out of date—but readers can surely come up with one of their own to do the job!) The criticism we are now considering trades in the analogous thought: the productions of poets as a class are just as questionable as guides to our life. These representations influence our understanding and character—typically for ill.

But this argument does leave a loophole for exceptions, as we noted in the case of visual representation. It does nothing to rule out the possibility of artists like Redouté, Audubon, and Stubbs, who really are concerned with a scientific understanding. This type of exception requires considerable specialization on the part of the artist. Painting in general does not require or even encourage this, but if some individual renounces the greater scope of his fellows and has a special clientele to support him, the medium itself does nothing to rule it out. And the situation is analogous with the literary case. Thus there is room for artistic works that escape the criticism we are considering. There is room for Plato's own philosophical dramas to function as so to speak the Audubon prints of literature: designed to help readers come to a deep understanding of a kind that the canonical great poets did not attempt. Of course I do not mean that reading a dialogue or looking at a print could automatically result in knowledge acquisition, but that it can at least be an orienting part of the process for learners and perhaps play a recording/stabilizing role for those who have had some success. (We will take up these issues when we turn to the *Phaedrus*.)

The final idea from the *Republic* for us to examine now is that the dramatists, by trading in fictive outbursts of emotion, demoralize audience members by undermining our emotional stability (602c–607a). Here as with the line of thinking we just looked at, a foundational role is played by the dialogue's study of the *psychē* (conventionally translated as the "soul"). Corresponding to the characteristic and potentially competing ways of viewing the world I mentioned above, there are different and potentially conflicting types of human motivation. What is highest in us loves truth, that is, it wants to achieve the general understanding (of bravery, of goodness, etc.) we were just discussing; this part is motivated to secure the good of the entire soul in light of its fundamental understanding. But we have other sources of motivation (typically rendered in English as spirit and appetite) focused on other types of gratification. Our text does not suggest that the healthy soul is one in which the lower forms of desire are extirpated: to take an obvious example, it is natural and good for the person as a whole to feel and satisfy appetite for healthy food. The healthy *psychē* is one in which the lower desires are directed to what is in fact healthy and good for the person overall. Thus the person with "psychic harmony" or the excellent state of the soul is neither some miserable dieter who chokes down steamed broccoli while longing to devour a mountain of greasy chips, nor someone who eats solely out of duty without any appetitive desire. Rather the virtuous person would on appropriate occasions enjoy without conflict moderate portions of delicious, sustainably sourced, and healthy food: perhaps this person's favorite is leek and potato soup. (Again, readers for whom this example does not work should construct one of their own.)

While some desire and desire satisfaction of the lower parts is healthy, it is very unhealthy to let these parts of the soul get overdeveloped or fixed on inappropriate objects. Sweets are attractive but one mustn't form a habit of eating a box of chocolates every evening. Similarly, it is natural to grieve at the loss of those one loves, but to give in to exaggerated public wailing is wrong. We have a tendency to give rein to these impulses; the *Republic* suggests that an important project in life must be to counteract this. Now we can see the basis of our final main criticism of drama: far from helping in this project, the greatest poets lead us in the wrong direction.

This is because they cater for the pleasure we take in indulging vicariously in the emotional outbursts of their characters. This is necessary for popular success with a broad audience (604e–605a). Even audience members who are decent people find it sweet to see on stage expressions of extreme emotion they would find shameful in real life and would struggle against. Is this harmless because it is after all not real life? Plato offers the insight that while one tells oneself this, it is not really so. Rather, when one reacts with sympathy—*sumpaschontes* (605d), which I take to have its full and basic force: *feeling along with the character*—what one feels is real even if the dramatic situation as a whole is not realized around oneself. This is the very reaction we prize most in our consumption of art. But by that reaction itself, the part of us that yearns to express lamentation, lust, and so on is strengthened, to our real harm. (This is the "most serious charge" at 605c–607a.)

To repeat the bottom line here: the very thing we prize most in our engagement with art is to be swept up in the emotions the characters express. Yet, when this happens, we are insidiously assimilating their ways of seeing and responding to the world. This inevitably affects our own psychology, strengthening the part of us that tends to experience like emotions, and affecting our own ways of feeling and thinking in our real lives. Comedy is just as bad (606c), and will be analyzed further in Plato's *Philebus*. Even in social contexts one may have noticed how people, under cover of the excuse that "it's just a joke" are actually expressing real hostility and so fostering something unhealthy in their hearers as well.

While the idea that the *psychē* has parts with characteristically different kinds of motivation lends itself to the development of this point, a version of this criticism is available even if we bracket this particular psychology. Indeed, the basic idea here anticipates one familiar now in the context of such debates as that over violence on TV; empirical evidence is now piling up that is friendly to the position Plato developed.[2] Viewers' characteristic ways of feeling, thinking, and behaving *can* be affected by exposure to media fictions; people *do* become more apt to experience and act on the kind of emotions given voice on stage and screen.[3] While this idea was once associated primarily with a certain strand of feminism, it has now percolated much further through society. The Dean of West Point and a group of expert military and FBI interrogators actually met with the creative team behind the television drama 24 (famous for the protagonist Jack Bauer's resorting to torture and in general "whatever it takes" in the fight against terrorism) because, in their view, "the show promoted unethical and illegal behavior and had adversely affected the training and performance of real American soldiers" (Mayer 2007: esp. 72).

Today we are familiar with the countervailing idea that freedom to create and engage with works of art has such great value as to outweigh or make us bracket almost any harm that could come from it. What though if we consider the parallel case of an industry which, let's say, provides some benefits, but also causes water pollution that seriously compromises our physical health? Here most of us would want to avoid the pollution. The present argument in the *Republic* challenges us to say why the situation should not be the same with this threat to the well-being of the *psychē*—more precious after all than that of the body.

Again, having noted this challenge, we should also ask how much of literature it operates against. Even if it is true that a poet who wants to achieve popular success on the tragic stage (or in today's analogue, filming blockbusters) will concentrate on expressions of the extreme and problematic kind of emotion, will this criticism apply to all possible works? *Anna Karenina* and *Kill Bill* may have to go, but Jane Austen's *Persuasion* or *The Warden* of Trollope may be all right or close. Anne in *Persuasion* and Mr Harding in *The Warden* are good candidates for Plato's prescribed representation of a good person displaying measured reactions—and so elude the objection from "drama queens."[4] Works as varied as poems of Pindar and adventure stories have also been suggested (Burnyeat 1999: 276–8, 280, 311).

What about the *Republic*? Does the dialogue rule itself out? It is possible to maintain that the text does not directly present shameful emotions for our vicarious enjoyment. Strictly speaking the *Republic* is a one-man show for Socrates, who presents as our narrator. So we must ask when he directly quotes/impersonates the other participants in the discussion he is recounting. The most violent and emotional one is Thrasymachus. It is possible to maintain that Socrates draws the veil of narrative discretion over the truly problematic outbursts of Thrasymachus (not his surface rudeness, interestingly), shielding us from their direct expression (Meinwald 2011). Plato's long-term use of the character Socrates seems largely to fit the agenda we are considering. Indeed, some see this character as offered to us by Plato as a hero to replace those of the dramatists and Homer—a "new Achilles." Readers can consider when engaging with individual dialogues to what extent each passes this test, and whether any change in Plato's compositional practice took place as a result of this line of thinking.

More generally, we have seen that the *Republic*'s criticisms of art do not necessarily apply to every single artistic effort. They turn on features of some passages, or features that art typically has. Thus these arguments leave loopholes for some literary efforts that are free from these problematic features. Plato's dialogues in particular would escape these criticisms if they help create a desire for philosophical progress, and contain useful sketches or images of the truth. For dangers that are still inherent in the project, we turn to the *Phaedrus*.

Writing in the *Phaedrus*

A well-known passage in the *Phaedrus* is widely taken to disparage writing as such. It contains the suggestions that far from being a technology for the transmission of knowledge, writing leads to intellectual passivity and a false conceit of wisdom; writing is also problematically unresponsive and indiscriminate with respect to readers. These criticisms do not turn on the content of the writing, but on its inability to respond individually to readers, and on problematic ways that readers may receive it—no matter how wise the author.

The *Republic* had mentioned briefly, by contrast with Homer, the case of someone who is genuinely expert and able to bring about progress in his real-life students (599a–600e). The claim was that such a person, given his relation to originals, would not attach great weight to the production of copies (that is, to written depiction), or organize his life around that as the most important thing. This is perfectly compatible with producing the copies in question: consider the parallel case of how many snapshots parents take! Our passage in the *Phaedrus* will actually take up this scenario, exploring reasons for which even such an author cannot simply transmit knowledge to readers via writing. But the news is not all bad, as is perhaps signaled by the way Socrates introduces the topic: "What feature makes writing good, and what inept?" (274b).

Socrates begins by telling a story of origins to Phaedrus, who is immediately aware that he has manufactured the tale (275b). However, by convention an origin story does claim to reveal something deep about the capacities of what it concerns. The story Socrates retails is that the ancient Egyptians had a divinity called Theuth, who discovered number, reckoning, geometry, astronomy, checkers and dice, and writing. Theuth brought these gifts to Thamus at Egyptian Thebes. Concerning writing, Socrates reports,

> Theuth said: "O King, here is something that, once learned, will make the Egyptians wiser and will improve their memory; I have discovered a potion for memory and for wisdom." Thamus, however, replied, "... In fact, it will induce forgetfulness into the soul of those who learn it: they will not practice using their memory because they will put their trust in writing ... You have not discovered a potion for remembering, but for reminding; you provide your students with the appearance of wisdom, not with its reality. Your invention will enable them to hear many things without being properly taught, and they will imagine that they have come to know much while for the most part they will know nothing."

> (274e–275b)

We will return later to the detailed mention of reminding. A starting large-scale observation: we have here a pro and con pattern. One figure takes writing to be a huge benefit, the other points out drawbacks. Before we get carried away by censure of the invention, we should remember that Theuth was explicitly introduced as a god. This has some tendency to suggest that his gift of writing—at least if rightly used—is a good of some kind. While Thamus may well have insight into ways in which mortals may misuse it, we should not assume prematurely that his criticism must induce wholesale rejection of Theuth's invention.

Let's evaluate the claim of Thamus, that writing can lead to a certain kind of intellectual passivity. Is there anything in what he says? Consider the more recent invention of GPS. People often rely on this to the point of having significantly less sense of direction than was once cultivated. This can be problematic, even dangerous, as when for example those out hiking or climbing are making no attempt to keep track of where they are, and then discover that their technological aids are lost or malfunctioning (see Whittaker 2007, an op-ed piece by the first American to climb Mount Everest). But the equipment of course does not *necessarily* degrade our abilities; it only does that if we give ourselves over to reliance on it. The ideal is probably a person who does cultivate awareness of location, and who also has the technology to use when appropriate.

Actually, two sub-kinds of case fall within the family of drawbacks we are considering. In one, individuals possess an ability which they allow to atrophy through reliance on technology. In the other, people are made so confident by their possession of what is really only an aid that they take themselves already to possess the knowledge in question, and never actually acquire it. Consider the attempts of people without medical training to figure out, when ill, what is wrong with themselves by googling their symptoms. One may fall into supposing that calling up such information constitutes knowledge, without realizing that except for someone skilled at interpreting and applying the information, it can be useless or actually misleading. The point here is *not* the difficulty of how to tell which sources to trust. Even if one had access to a database of reliable information, one would need to be a doctor to interpret and apply it reliably. No doubt someone skilled may become even more effective when able to access all the information in the world through the internet, but the technology on its own cannot substitute for expertise.

So our own review of technical innovation suggests that while naively to rely on it threatens our abilities, a sophisticated user can be helped when able to make appropriate use of external aid. Thamus has not said anything to indicate that the situation is not analogous with the invention of Theuth. Socrates goes on from here with a summary that also brings out that the problem is not with writing as such but with a certain attitude to it: "those who think they can leave written instructions for an art, as well as those who accept them, *thinking that writing can yield results that are clear or certain*, must be quite naïve" (275c; emphasis added).

Next Socrates uses a comparison with painting to bring out additional defects writing has. Just as figures in a painting seem as if they can speak, but when questioned remain silent, so too whatever is once written down cannot make any new remark, whatever readers may ask of it. Moreover writing has no ability to discern which readers to address and how, but must go on always saying the same thing indiscriminately: it is unable even to defend itself when unfairly attacked (275d–e).

Here we may note that while writing of course cannot add anything new, it is not automatic that all speakers can do so. The real action at a philosophy talk is in the question period precisely because this is a chance to probe whether the speaker can respond to apparent objections, say more on appropriately related points, and avoid falling into confusion. Speakers who cannot do this cannot claim philosophical knowledge on the topic they've staked out, even if some of their views happen to be true.

Socrates' phrasing is appropriately nuanced in this very regard when he contrasts the written imitation of speech with another kind of discourse. What he endorses is not any and all oral communication: "It is a discourse that is written down, *with knowledge*, in the soul of the listener; it can defend itself" (276a; emphasis added; cf. Phaedrus' gloss in his immediately following reply). Socrates returns to this idea at the end of our passage:

The dialectician chooses a proper soul and plants and sows within it discourse *accompanied by knowledge*—discourse capable of helping itself as well as the man who planted it, which is not barren but produces a seed from which more discourse grows in the character of others.

(276e–277a; emphasis added)

These passages concern a "best-case scenario." The comparison is not between reading and all speech; we are only considering the case in which the listener actually achieves knowledge. Obviously this will be better than the general case of reading; indeed it will be better than the general case of listening! So far we have been given no reason to think that every case of listening, even by a talented listener, is a case in which the listener achieves knowledge.

Now our text actually makes the very contrast that figured only briefly in the *Republic*: between projects a hypothetical expert would be most serious about and those of lesser standing. Here the idea is developed through the rich analogy of the comparative attitudes a sensible farmer would take to "gardens of Adonis" and his crop-bearing agricultural practice. Gardens of Adonis were associated with a summer festival, and involved the forcing of plants. Seeds were planted indoors in pots and kept in the dark for seven days; plants developed quickly and were brought outdoors for the festival where they quickly wilted in the sun and died without yielding fruit/seeds.

No doubt part of the point here is that these plants come up quickly and do not have the substantial development a farmer looks for in his real crops. This—taken together with the idea that participating in the festival is only recreational in contrast to the serious business of farming—has led some to think that the contrast is wholly derogatory to the Adonis-gardens. The idea as applied to writing would be that it is quick and showy, but causally unconnected with the process, available only through living speech, that has a valuable intellectual yield.

To think this is to ignore part of the richness of this extraordinary figure. Let's look now at how Socrates puts it to Phaedrus:

And tell me this. Would a sensible farmer plant the seeds he was serious about and wanted to yield fruit in the gardens of Adonis in the middle of the summer and enjoy watching them bear fruit within seven days? Or would he do this as an amusement and for the festival, if he did it at all? Wouldn't he use his knowledge of farming to plant the seeds he cared for when it was appropriate and be content if they bore fruit seven months later? ... Now what about the man who knows what is just, *kalon* [beautiful/splendid/fine/admirable], and good? Shall we say that he is less sensible with his seeds than the farmer is with his?

(276b–c; my translation, based on Nehamas and Woodruff in Cooper, ed., 1997)

Let's start by registering that the distinction in the farming case is not between a sensible and a foolish farmer. It is between how the sensible farmer (the only one in view) handles seeds he is serious about and cares for, as opposed to something else he does.

How should we understand the reference to seeds the farmer is serious about, which is so emphasized in the passage? I would like to suggest that this actually connects up with the Adonis-garden image. Research has made clear that these little gardens, as they originated in Egypt and were used in other parts of the ancient Mediterranean world, had their grounding in sound agricultural practice (Baudy 1986).[5] One planted *a variety* of seeds in a pot, forced them for quick development, and exposed the plants to the sun so as to see which withstood the heat the best. In other words, the practice was a way of comparing seeds with respect to fitness, so as to select which ones to use in the next cycle of planting. The practice was in fact for the purpose of finding out which seeds to be serious about and care for.

This indicates that the original gardens of Adonis were far from being causally unconnected with the serious business of agriculture. At a distinct stage from the crop-bearing planting, they were importantly preparatory to it. This additional stage improved the ultimate yield by saving farmers from planting inferior seeds on a large scale. What might it mean to see writing as serving an analogous purpose? Is there any sense in which "seeds" of discourse might be developed quickly and tested for fitness in the medium of writing by an author who regarded the ultimate goal as something further that only occurs when they germinate and bear fruit in the minds of talented people?

Writing functions in this way in our own lives! Working philosophers and researchers of many other kinds obviously prepare a lot of manuscripts. While this production can almost seem to be the ultimate goal of academic activity, a simple thought experiment shows that it is not. If a manuscript will never be read with any sympathy and so will have no impact on living minds, it surely loses much if not all of its point—however polished, beautiful, and deep it may be. The reason authors work so much on their writings is because these have a special role to play in reaching other minds.

Let's grant that the ideal way for people to achieve philosophical understanding is through discussion in a series of tutorial, seminar, or workshop meetings, or other serious conversations. These are the modern venues for the best-case scenario for spoken interchanges that we were previously considering. (Indeed, the name "seminar" is based on the very metaphor of seeds that Plato used in the *Phaedrus*.) Even so, just tossing out questions to be debated from scratch is not the best way to proceed. That would be extremely inefficient: it can take hours before someone comes up with a thought that could have cleared matters up a lot sooner—if they ever do. Besides the inefficiency of the naturally occurring discussion process, there is a danger in discussing ideas pointed out at *Protagoras* 314a–b: such wares must be received directly in one's soul so that one is immediately exposed to any risk they may pose. And keep in mind that one can be significantly harmed if one comes to believe thoughts that aren't really correct: consider the difference it makes in life whether one thinks that all that matters is getting ahead, or that the most important thing is relationships with others.

A well-crafted piece of writing can be an instrument both for rendering the dialectical process safer and for speeding it up. The potentialities of various lines of thought are developed and explored in simulated discussion so that on future occasions the author and readers too can go much faster in their real-life thinking. In Plato's case the way in which writing simulates discussion is obvious—his written works are dramas within which the primary action is discussion (or narration of such occasions). But even philosophers who don't write dialogues preserve the element in question: the interplay of ideas. Nothing is more characteristic of philosophy from Aristotle to the present day than the use of the phrase "someone might say" to introduce a line of thought one does not oneself hold, to be followed by the development of one's own thoughts about why this hypothetical someone's idea though suggestive is not right, or at least not the whole truth. So our review has suggested that even if the ultimate fruits of philosophy do require living discussion for their full development, a written stage can play a valuable preparatory role.

A final observation to prepare us for our return to the text: another obvious advantage of writing is that it helps both authors and readers transcend our locations in space and time. While each of us must be limited when it comes to personal communication, writing allows readers to enjoy the efforts of authors we may not have met, just as it gives authors a chance to have an impact beyond their own immediate circle. This benefit of writing is analogous to what recording offers in the case of musical performance: the downside of musical recordings is obviously that they can only provide a fixed version reproducing a live performance, further diminished by being without the visual component. Yet despite the loss of the immediacy of live performance, the opportunity for those of us who did not overlap with them in time and space to hear such musicians as Louis Armstrong or Arthur Rubinstein is obviously a great good. In a case like this, mediated and inflexible contact with an extraordinary artist is of such great value that it must be prized alongside the direct and living contact that one can only have with one's spatiotemporal neighbors.

We are now ready to look at Socrates' further remarks on the motivation of the "man who knows" discussed above:

> When he writes, it's likely he will sow gardens of letters for the sake of play, storing up reminders for himself "when he reaches forgetful old age" and for everyone who wants to follow in his footsteps, and will enjoy seeing them sweetly blooming. And when others are at play in other ways, watering themselves with drinking parties and everything else that goes along with them, he will rather spend his time in the play which I have just described.
>
> (276d; my translation, based on Nehamas and Woodruff in Cooper, ed., 1997)

Let's go through this bit by bit. The notions of play, reminders, and drinking parties all strike us as trivial, but all will have had resonance for Plato. I've modified the translation to include the word "play" to bring out the connection with passages in other works where Plato identifies play (*paidia*) as a crucial early stage for significant intellectual projects. *Laws* 819a–c discusses with approval Egyptian educational methods that introduce mathematical lessons to children as part of play. And the venerable Parmenides in his namesake dialogue designates as play (137b) the massive 30-page dialectical demonstration that he gives as a necessary prerequisite if one is ever to reach the truth in philosophy. To overdraw the contrast between play and serious work to the detriment of play would be an unsophisticated way of reading Plato.

In a different way, "reminders" are a resonant notion. We now return to the point reserved from the original exchange between Theuth and Thamus. Here as our passage concludes Socrates fills out the earlier remark that writing will be a potion for reminding, saying that the knowledgeable author will be storing up reminders both for his own old age and for everyone who wants to follow in his footsteps. The first case perhaps gets separate mention because it makes the quoted tag possible. The thinking we have done on our own now helps us see that "everyone" who wants to follow in an author's footsteps can include, importantly, people in other times and places. Not everyone who wants to follow in someone's footsteps can necessarily take lessons from him, but a much wider group can obtain his written works.

How significant a thing is reminding? Very significant indeed, in the context of the *Phaedrus*. Reminding in this dialogue can hardly be limited to the sense in which what we are reminded of is everyday information that we once knew and then lost track of, for the *Phaedrus* is one of the works featuring Platonic recollection. In outline this view is that we are born with innate knowledge of fundamental matters (not, of course, of contingent matters of fact), which Plato represents in the *Phaedrus* as a matter of our soul's having seen the Forms. Our soul has had this knowledge from a time prior to its being in our present body, but we are born without conscious awareness of it: it is only latent due to forgetting. For our knowledge to become active again our recollection needs to be triggered. The presentation of this view in the *Phaedrus* gives special application to the repeated assertions of Socrates in both his own person and in his fictive report of the ancient Egyptians to the effect that in writing one stores up reminders. We must be intended to see that writing in storing up treasuries of reminders can serve philosophical recollection (i.e. can help us recover knowledge of Forms).

Finally, the comparison of writing with attendance at *symposia* (rendered above as "drinking parties"). These were by no means *mere* drinking parties. They were the central site for training and confirming members of the Athenian elite both by socializing them into distinguished company and through the pervasive recitation of poetry/song that itself was a repository of attitudes and beliefs constituting the culture. So with this remark Socrates is in a sense coming back to the theme we considered in connection with the *Republic*. A man who knows what is just, *kalon* (beautiful/splendid/fine/admirable), and good will avoid gatherings that feature the canonical poetry that presumes to acculturate us in these matters—he will rather do his own writing, which can help readers towards the truth, even if for reasons the *Phaedrus* has made clear it cannot simply convey it wholesale.

In this chapter so far, we've seen how the criticisms of the *Republic* and the *Phaedrus* leave room for some beneficial drama and some valuable engagement with writing. Our final task is to consider how Plato's use of dialogue form connects with all this.

Plato and dialogue form

The main warning that emerged from our consideration of the discussion of writing in the *Phaedrus* is that ultimately it is on us to save ourselves from falling into the trap of taking ourselves to be wise just because we've read through a book—whether an ancient text or a contemporary work such as the present effort. But we can now appreciate that Plato has done all he can to help us. He not only writes in such a way as to develop and test ideas. His compositions are dramas whose primary action is philosophical conversation. These works not only mimic but are designed to draw us into the real-life activity whose high value the *Phaedrus* has emphasized. The interest the represented interchanges hold for the participants, our identification with some of the characters and their views, our disagreement with others, and the open-ended character of the discussions all combine to spark philosophical engagement in a reader with any aptitude for it. We ourselves come up with an objection, imagine how we might maintain a thesis better than its exponent in the text, try out a slightly different account, work towards an understanding of how the truths established in the text can be correct, and so on.

If we do all this, then we are launched on philosophical activity of our own. It will take hard work, and a lot of it, if we are to attain wisdom. If we do that work, we can avoid the drawbacks of writing developed in the *Phaedrus*. In that case, Plato will have succeeded in the aims left by the loopholes we identified earlier in the *Republic*'s criticisms. While a typical literary artist may be indifferent to research and may cater for an unhealthy *psychē*, Plato has designed his own creations to foster the passion for understanding in readers, and to help us on the way to it.

This overall purpose is compatible either with Plato depicting sound characters giving correct accounts, or with his leaving what is correct for us to discover. Indeed, he might proceed in different ways at different times. But even when a character presents thinking that is on the right lines, we have to make it our own by our personal engagement in a process of dialectical activity. Success is not guaranteed for this activity—whether or not it is inspired by reading—but no success will be possible without it. Only so can we win the wisdom at which philosophy aims. In the chapters to come, we will engage with the dialogues in the spirit in which the present chapter leads us to believe they were intended. We should reanimate the dialectic Plato portrays and do some philosophy ourselves.

Further reading

The Seventh Letter (Epistle). Like all the letters attributed to Plato, of controversial authenticity. This document purports to explain Plato's involvement over the decades in the political affairs of Syracuse; repudiation of the intellectual pretensions of the tyrant Dionysius II leads to famous remarks on writing (340b–345c).

Secondary literature

See Bibliography for full details of the works listed below.

E. Asmis (1992) "Plato on Poetic Creativity."

E. Belfiore (1983) "Plato's Greatest Accusation Against Poetry."

M. Burnyeat (1999) "Culture and Society in Plato's *Republic*." Lectures
  that present great scholarship combined with big-picture
  thinking in a way that is lively and accessible.

G.Ferrari (1989) "Plato and Poetry."

M. Frede (1992) "Plato's Arguments and the Dialogue Form."

C. Griswold, ed. (1988) *Platonic Writings/Platonic Readings*. A dialectically
  productive assemblage of essays by scholars displaying an unusually wide range of interpretive styles.

C. Meinwald (2011) "Reason v. Literature in Plato's *Republic*."

J. Moss (2007) "What is Imitative Poetry and Why is it Bad?"

A. Nehamas (1988) "Plato and the Mass Media."

K. Sayre (1995) *Plato's Literary Garden: How to Read a Platonic Dialogue*. Starts
  from interesting discussions of the Seventh Letter and the *Phaedrus*.

T. Szlezák (1999) *Reading Plato*. Accessible exposition from the
  Tübingen school of interpretation.

K. Vogt (2012) *Belief and Truth: A Sceptic Reading of Plato*.

Notes

1 This section draws from Meinwald (2011). For fuller treatment see that and
   other suggestions for further reading at end of chapter; the agenda of the present
   inquiry shapes which aspects of the passages in question I emphasize here.

2 See www.apa.org/about/policy/media.aspx (accessed January 20, 2016).

3 See Eaton 2012 on cases in which good art can be immoral not only in the
   sense of portraying bad characters but also of having a bad influence on us.
   Eaton does not suggest that we should give up such art; reading Plato makes
   us ask why not.

4 Does Anne's wish for marriage with Capt. Wentworth make her a bad character
   by Plato's lights? In Socrates' Kallipolis, marriage, private families and private
   property are forbidden to the guardians so as to remove common sources of
   conflict of interest. But it doesn't follow from this that all marriages are bad,
   even for people who aren't guardians in Kallipolis. The case of Mr Harding and
   private property is parallel.

5 Slezák 1999: 42 and fn 34 cites Baudy, but refuses to use this historical nugget
   for understanding the *Phaedrus* as he thinks nothing in the passage makes it
   relevant. In my view the passage does make it relevant.

Three
Testing authority
The legacy of Socrates

Background and context

Well before Plato's day trade had brought the Greeks into contact with Near Eastern peoples and their cultures, notably those of Egypt, Babylon, and Persia. With time, awareness of these cultures spread throughout the Greek world. It became apparent that one's own traditional beliefs about the cosmos, the divine, and human life were not the only possible ones—others were the basis of these tremendous civilizations. Herodotus' *History of the Persian Wars*—whether or not it is accurate—shows the fascination the beliefs and practices of other cultures held for the Greeks.

Then as now, awareness of such matters threw into question traditional ways of living and believing. How could one be sure that one's own ways were correct? Or was some other, perhaps unknown, possibility really the one? Something in us longs to get these things right, and applying one's reason is an attractive way to proceed. In this climate, individuals made novel contributions to medicine, to history, and to political institutions. The innovators, who by definition lacked the authority of tradition, needed to give reasons to others for taking their suggestions seriously. Thus they characteristically offered justificatory argument. Traditional beliefs and practices too could be approached in the new spirit of inquiry, and could in some cases be vindicated with new justification.

The subjects and institutions in play varied tremendously, as did the temperaments and motivations of those who emerged in this intellectual ferment. Thus the value of their contributions varied as well. And because so much came to be questioned, the stakes were very high. At best innovators could point to better and better-grounded ways of understanding the world and of living within it. But at worst they were tearing down a viable way of life in favor of who knows what. This conflict is at the heart of Aristophanes' play the *Clouds*, which was composed and staged during the lifetime of Socrates. The old ways were not immune to criticism and ridicule: the speech of the personification of the old education (*Clouds* 961–83) is hardly the portrait of a wholly sound and healthy tradition. Yet the old education had bred the men who fought at Marathon (*Clouds* 985–6). The primary threat in the eyes of Aristophanes comes from the new fashions; the primary target of the play as a whole is the tide of innovators.

To us it can look as if Aristophanes lumps together very disparate types when he targets this entire class. We automatically wield classifications according to which scientists are one group, lawyers another, philosophers yet another and so on. Thus we tend to classify the ancients into groups that are proto-versions of ours: natural philosophers, sophists, philosophers, etc. But in antiquity, natural science had not yet split off from philosophy, and the distinction between sophists and philosophers would be due largely to the polemical activity of Plato himself. So the contemporaries of Aristophanes and Socrates would not have divided up their fellows in the way we do.

Comedy standardly employed composite characters so as to make fun of a whole class under the guise of a single individual on stage. Now we can see how the character at the center of the *Clouds* came about. He stands for the newfangled motley: proto-scientists as well as teachers of law-court trickery, proto-logicians as well as early philologists; the character combines ascetic elements with encouragements to petty thievery, and operates a school for attendance at which he demands exorbitant fees. This character bears the name "Socrates."

Many elements in this portrait are foreign to Socrates as philosophers think of him. When one concentrates solely on the intellectual aspect of what he was doing, one sees the good side of Socrates. This made him the hero of almost all the ancient philosophical schools, a veritable patron saint of inquiry. And he continues to inspire many individuals to this day. The composite nature of Aristophanes' Socrates explains to some extent why this character need not have been offered as faithful in all particulars to the historical individual of the same name. But what the historical Socrates was doing must have struck people in such a way as to make the comic composite viable. Even within a practice of forming composite characters, one would not combine, say, Mahatma Gandhi and George W. Bush. In fact, the historical Socrates was put to death as a harmful influence by his fellow-citizens in a city we admire—and that admired herself—for her culture and for her openness.

In this chapter, we will consider the huge impact the life and death of Socrates had on his younger associate, Plato. While Plato's rendering of the figure of Socrates has been the main source for all that is admired in the Socratic legacy, it includes touches that allow us to see what went wrong as well. Our understanding of the large-scale framework of Socratic activity as Plato represented it will prepare us to go on to the main body of Plato's work.

Plato and the death of Socrates

One of the most striking features of Plato's corpus of works when one reads through them all together is how frequently they represent and refer to the trial and death of Socrates. Plato recurs to these events throughout his compositional career. Indeed, he continues to do this even in works whose philosophical content is not "Socratic" in the narrow sense we will develop in the next section.

Let's start with works often bundled in present-day compilations with titles along the lines of *The Trial and Death of Socrates*. As the *Euthyphro* opens, Socrates runs into the title character by the king-archon's court. They proceed to discuss the indictment of Socrates for corrupting the youth and introducing new gods while not believing in the old ones; this leads on in turn to discussion of the case in which Euthyphro is involved, and his supposed expertise in piety. The *Apology* represents Socrates' trial—the Greek word *apologia* means defense speech. We get the remarks of Socrates addressing the jurors, and he briefly examines his accuser Meletus. The *Crito* is set in the time between Socrates' conviction and execution: he converses with an old friend who is trying to persuade him to save his life by escaping. The *Phaedo*'s frame represents two friends, one of whom recounts to the other the conversation between Socrates and his visitors in prison on the last day of his life. Socrates and his comrades discuss the apposite theme of the immortality of the soul; then our narrator actually recounts the death scene of our hero. This is given a final twist of pathos in the closing words of the text when the more conventionally human and emotional narrator calls the person we may have come to see as cold "a man who, we would say, was of all those we have known the best, and also the wisest and the most upright" (118a). (For parallels in popular fiction, consider Dr Watson's narration of the death of Sherlock Holmes and Captain Kirk's reaction to the death of Spock.)

Yet these works are not the only ones whose primary content Plato sets fictively at that time. The inner dialogue of the *Theaetetus* and hence, by implication, the *Sophist* and *Statesman* are also set then. The *Theaetetus* ends with Socrates saying, "And now I must go to the King's Porch to meet the indictment that Meletus has brought against me; but let us meet here again in the morning, Theodorus" (210d). That is, as the *Theaetetus* ends Socrates is on his way to court on the very occasion on which, according to the opening of the *Euthyphro*, the meeting depicted there will take place. The conversation of the *Sophist* will be the next morning, and the *Statesman* is its sequel.

The themes, method, and general tone of, for instance, the *Euthyphro* and the *Sophist* differ markedly. (The seven works on the present list come from each of the three stylometric clusters.) The *Theaetetus*, *Sophist* and *Statesman* are extremely advanced in subject-matter and mode of presentation; these dialogues require a great deal of philosophical effort if readers are to get anything from them. This is surely why those three are not nowadays bound in the "last days" volumes we noted, despite their fictive dates. For a related reason, the *Phaedo* sometimes has its more taxing content removed to leave just the death scene for this type of volume.

Was Plato trying to get us to read the *Theaetetus*, *Euthyphro*, *Sophist*, *Statesman*, *Apology*, *Crito*, and *Phaedo* as a series ordered by the fictive time sequence? To try to do so is disconcerting. Tone and difficulty jump discontinuously from one dialogue to another; themes and discussions which on other orderings have been prepared for pop up here unmanageably naked. The series presents a bizarre appearance if considered as aiming at representation of a stretch in the life of the character Socrates: an ancient analogue of television's 24 or a secular version of Haydn's *Seven Last Words of Christ*.

Indeed, the most standard present-day way of reading the complete corpus puts the *Euthyphro*, *Apology*, and *Crito* together with other works such as the *Laches* and *Charmides* that do not feature the trial. All these works are allied in other ways that, as we will see in the next section, make us think they are intended to give Plato's portrait of the historical Socrates; such dialogues as the *Sophist* come in much later in one's reading career. But the function of the fictive date need not be to set the ordering of the episodes in a biographical mini-series. Rather, the death of Socrates is relevant philosophically to each of the seven dialogues whose primary philosophical conversation is temporally located by reference to the trial. Plato, writing before the age of footnotes, has developed other means of making references than those we employ.

Setting the *Sophist* and *Statesman* at the time of Socrates' trial—even if their main conversations are no longer primarily depictions of the "historical Socrates"—points up how their topics bear on the issue the famous trial turned on. These works take up the questions what expertise sophists, statesmen, and philosophers possess: whether and how they differ from each other. This was directly relevant to understanding and deciding what to do with this unusual man.

Indeed, the fictive timeframe is not the only way in which a work can make reference to the crisis in the career of Socrates. The so-called "digression" in the *Theaetetus*—concerning how a philosopher appears ridiculous in the context of a law court—is generally read as concerning the clash of cultures at Socrates' trial, when he himself contributed to his conviction and death sentence by his unwillingness to make the sort of appeal that was expected. Also relevant is a dark touch in the famous image of the Cave in the *Republic*. That introduces a figure who in terms of the image is trying to release people imprisoned underground from engaging only with shadows of artifacts, and to force them up so that they can see natural objects in the full light of the sun. We are told that people returning from the upper region to the cave would at first have trouble seeing, and that the others would turn on the one who was trying to free them and would try to kill him (517a). This too, as many think, is a comment by Plato on the fate of the historical Socrates.

His treatment at the hands of his fellow citizens is alluded to more directly in a number of dialogues. We hear from Anytus (whose historical original was one of the three accusers who brought Socrates to trial) after Socrates in the *Meno* has drawn attention to the fact that Pericles and other eminent Athenians were unable to teach virtue to their own sons. The future accuser says: "I think, Socrates, that you easily speak ill of people. I would advise you, if you will listen to me, to be careful" (94e).

A much more extended warning is given to Socrates by the possibly fictional Callicles in the *Gorgias*:

> ... don't you think it's shameful to be the way I take you to be, and others who ever press on too far in philosophy? As it is, if someone got hold of you or of anyone else like you and took you off to prison on the charge that you're doing something unjust when in fact you aren't, be assured that you wouldn't have any use for yourself. ... You'd come up for trial and face some no good wretch of an accuser and be put to death, if death is what he'd want to condemn you to ...
>
> (486a–b)

Plato's preoccupation with the death of Socrates must have been connected with wanting to determine what led to it, and of course to convince others that the verdict of the Athenian jury had been a mistake. The final dimension in Plato's reaction to the death of Socrates is perhaps his wish to deny or overcome it. This may contribute to his general interest in the immortality of the soul—a topic that people often come to when it is relevant to someone in their own circle. More particularly, Plato's compositions confer literary immortality on Socrates. As we will see in the next section, the character Socrates is initially closely based on Plato's notion of the real individual—and within Plato's texts he is of course alive and philosophizing.

The famous beauty Helen in the *Iliad* speaks to Hector of undergoing woes "so that hereafter / we shall be made into things of song for the men of the future" (6.357–8, tr. Lattimore 1951); in remarks of the hero Sarpedon in the same work, we find the idea that winning glory is an approximation of immortality (12.322–8). Plato in the *Symposium* will develop at length the thought that artistic and intellectual achievements are humans' best bid for immortality. Thus he may well have conceived that in his dialogues, he was preserving the life and lineage of his teacher.

In fact, almost all of Plato's works contain a character named "Socrates"—and in most, that character has a leading role. But the relation between the character "Socrates" and the historical individual is not necessarily always the same. While the character of Socrates is initially closely based on the author's understanding of the activity of his senior associate, over time Plato comes to use the character (among others) to explore his own innovations. Nevertheless, the continued use of the character signals Plato's acknowledgement of the legacy. Let us now turn to how Plato saw Socrates' own activity.

Plato's reception of Socrates

Our primary focus for the major portion of this chapter will be a cluster of dialogues that are widely considered "Socratic." The sense of the tag is not just that they feature a character called "Socrates"— that is true of a much broader class of works. Rather the tag reflects the belief that these works are Plato's literary versions of the sort of thing he took the historical Socrates to have been doing. Let's see why this belief is quite safe, even if going all the way to think we have detailed information about the actual person is less secure.

The identification of Plato's Socratic dialogues rests on ancient support. Aristotle in particular provides a handful of useful assertions about what Socrates the historical man was doing.[1] This characterization of the activity of the historical Socrates matches some—but only some—of Plato's dialogues. So to go by Aristotle's evidence, a subset of Plato's works shows us the characteristic activity of the historical person. Many today believe Aristotle must be correct about this. After all, Aristotle spent twenty years in Plato's Academy and so had plenty of opportunities to hear about his teacher's teacher.

How secure was Aristotle's knowledge of the historical Socrates? First, let us observe how varied in length three-generation teacher's-teacher bridges can be. To take some musical cases, the cellist Janos Starker as a child already had students, one of whom beat him in the Geneva Competition of 1946. This student's students could themselves have been close to Starker in age, and gone on in turn to compete against, study with, or play in an orchestra alongside him. At the other extreme is the case of the violinist Joshua Bell, a youngish man even today. He studied as a boy at Indiana with the former Cleveland concertmaster Joseph Gingold, who had in turn been a student of the great Belgian violinist Eugène Ysaÿe, musically a man of the nineteenth century. Here the middle generation links two people from completely different worlds.

Since Socrates, Plato, and Aristotle all lived long lives, with the overlaps at the ends of the older men's careers, Aristotle's case resembles that of Joshua Bell. His time in the Academy—around 368–48 BC—was well after the period in which Socrates was alive. Socrates' philosophical activity had been in roughly the period 450–399 BC. Thus his death was already thirty years in the past when Aristotle arrived in the Academy, and there is a space of roughly a century between the start of Socrates' activity and the end of Aristotle's.

Of course, everyone knows that Aristotle did not have direct contact with Socrates, but what is at issue is what he learned from those who did: from Plato and other members of the Socratic circle. In some musical cases the middle generation does pass on intact a well-formed legacy of the oldest one. This probably depends on considerable insulation from other influences, as with the preservation of the Russian violin tradition during the Soviet period. But Plato's case was not like this. Far from being an insular follower of Socrates, he was deeply influenced by Parmenides, Anaxagoras, Heracliteanism, Pythagoreanism, and contemporary mathematics.

Moreover, both Plato and Aristotle were primarily interested in the development of their own philosophy, not biography or even history of philosophy. By Aristotle's time Plato would have been an elderly man recalling Socrates as a philosophical influence of his youth—and without any possibility of rereading original texts, since Socrates had written nothing. Plato would likely have long since concretized his view of what Socrates had been doing. Since even the composition of his own Socratic works would by then have been well in the past, Plato would quite likely have thought of "Socrates" primarily in terms of his own long-held interpretation. And Plato's understanding of Socrates would have been a strong influence on many others Aristotle could have consulted (if he even bothered to investigate in this way).

So it is hard to eliminate skepticism about our access to the historical Socrates. But note that a primary reason for this skepticism is Aristotle's dependence on a tradition dominated by Plato. What Aristotle had good access to is *how Plato thought of Socrates*. (Or perhaps, to put it even more carefully: what Aristotle was in a good position to know is *which works of Plato's* were supposed to represent the activity of Socrates.) Thus Aristotle is a good source, if what we are interested in is not so much the historical Socrates as Plato's reception of him.[2] We can quite securely read the works that match Aristotle's description of the activity of Socrates as giving us Plato's representation of the legacy of his teacher. And that's what is relevant for the purposes of this book. In this chapter we will consider the general framework of the philosophical activity Plato attributed to Socrates.

Aristotle tells us that Socrates confined himself to questioning others, and for a characteristic reason: "Socrates used to ask questions and not answer them—for he used to confess that he did not know" (*Sophistical Refutations* 183b[3]). What was the subject matter of these questions? Aristotle says:

> Socrates ... was busying himself about ethical matters and neglecting the world of nature as a whole but seeking the universal in these ethical matters, and fixed thought for the first time on definitions ...
>
> (*Metaphysics* 987b)

While the beginning of this description is reasonably straightforward, there is some danger of confusion when Aristotle speaks of the Socratic search for definitions. Socrates was not searching for the sort of definitions sometimes found in dictionaries, which paraphrase so as to give the sense associated with linguistic items (and so specify the meanings of words in one sense of "meaning"). In that case he presumably would not have found all his fellow-citizens lacking! Definitions/accounts of the sort that Socrates was searching for derive explanatory power from capturing what the thing in question really is.[4]

To illustrate the contrast, let's say that, in the extremely distant past, the sense of "gold" and its analogues in other languages could have been given by lexicographers—if there had been any then—by a definition along the lines of "yellow metal." Obviously, knowing that definition would have been compatible with further scientific inquiry into what the nature of gold really is. We now believe we have the scientific account of gold: an account in terms of atomic structure. (In fact, dictionaries today include this information about gold.) That very thing is present in all cases of gold, and makes them what they are.

A correct account of this sort may quite possibly identify some underlying structure not evident to superficial observation. Understanding this enables one to be somewhat revisionist in one's way of viewing the world. Some lumps that might have satisfied the "yellow metal" paraphrase are relegated by the scientific understanding to the status of fool's gold (iron pyrites). Considered as a way of understanding gold, the paraphrase giving the sense associated with its name can be superficial. The scientific definition is obviously deeper; it comes to grips not just with linguistic usage but with reality. Certainly when we want to *acquire* gold we want metal that satisfies the scientific account. The hope ancient ethics had to benefit people was derived largely from the thought that the good human life is analogous. Discovering what it *really is* and not just what we associate with the words is an intellectual project whose result everyone has a stake in: without it we could waste our lives pursuing fools' goals.

The what-is-it question

We now have an overview of the philosophical activity of Socrates. He focused on ethics; he confined himself to inquiring of others as he himself claimed not to know; he was seeking the universal and wanted definitions. We will next examine in detail the proprietary question associated with these inquiries. The Euthyphro will serve us as a continuing thread in this section (and in the next one, on how Socrates evaluated those he questioned).

As mentioned earlier, the discussion featured in the Euthyphro arises out of the court cases in which its two characters are involved. Socrates is charged with impiety among other things (5c). And Euthyphro is charging his own father with murder; that is, Euthyphro is doing something that in antiquity was considered to be impious. The huge stake and unorthodox character of this action mean that the bar is set very high for the knowledge he must bring to the pursuit (4e–5a). By contrast, someone might try an unorthodox way of strapping on her sandals as a whim. No problem, since hardly anything turns on it. But if her novelty is on the order of the Golden Gate Bridge, she had better have real technical expertise to back her up: the harm invited by faulty engineering in this case raises the bar for how expert one must be to undertake the innovation. Since knowledge is called for in Euthyphro's present case, Socrates at least affects to wish to learn from Euthyphro about the pious (5a–6e).

Socratic questioning is not just garden-variety conversation. Nor is it like a normal interview. We will now see Socrates doing what Aristotle reported when he told us that Socrates fixed thought for the first time on definitions. Socrates repeatedly poses a question, sometimes called "the Socratic question" to mark his special use of it or "the ti esti (What is it?) question" to show its content. The respondent is supposed to answer by specifying the relevant ousia (being/reality/nature; ousia is a substantive derived from "to be" in ancient Greek).

Let's trace how this goes on a particular occasion. Socrates asks Euthyphro: What is the pious? We saw at the end of Chapter One that this does not sound odd in the original, as it does in the English parallel. Yet the original of "the pious" is multiply ambiguous. It can refer among other things to pious actions or to piety itself. Indeed, when Euthyphro initially claims to know about the pious and the impious, he may only have in mind pious and impious actions (4e–5a). But Socrates interprets his interlocutor as a putative expert on the pious where that is equivalent to piety in general, and Euthyphro does not protest.

We can see this when Socrates elicits from Euthyphro assent to the idea that the pious should be something the same in every pious action. The impious should be its opposite, such that everything that is going to be impious has that single form (5c–d). At 14b–c when recapitulating his what-is-it question, Socrates treats the unambiguous abstract noun form corresponding to "piety" interchangeably with "the pious." He is after a universal as I am using the term: something general, which can be common to a number of things. And at 11a Socrates says explicitly that Euthyphro was supposed to answer the question what the pious is by making clear its nature (*ousia*).

Euthyphro's first answer to the question posed to him starts from one case of pious behavior and uses an obvious, surface description of it to gesture at a bunch of very closely related cases. "I say that the pious is just what I'm doing now, prosecuting the wrongdoer, be it about murder or temple robbery or anything else, whether the wrongdoer is your father or your mother or anyone else" (5d–e my translation, based on Gallop 1997 and Grube in Cooper, ed., 1997). Whatever exactly we take the roles of the token (his own action) and the type (prosecuting a wrongdoer) in this answer to be, Euthyphro is open to the objection Socrates makes: his answer violates the demand to give something the same in *all* pious actions.

Socrates says explicitly that looking to the form he seeks will enable him to determine which actions are pious (6e); he makes clear (and Euthyphro accepts) that the common thing he was asking for is that *by which* all pious actions are pious:

> Bear in mind that I did not bid you tell me one or two of the many pious actions but that form itself *that makes* all pious actions pious, for you agreed that all impious actions are impious and all pious actions pious *through* one form.
>
> (6d–e; emphasis added).

Compare the *Charmides*, where Socrates tells his young interlocutor: "when you have decided what effect the presence of temperance [*sōphrosunē*] has upon you and *what sort of thing it must be to have this effect* … tell me … what does it appear to you to be?" (160d–e; emphasis added). Generally, when Socrates asks in some ethical domain "What is F-ness?", he is seeking an account of the nature that is common to and explanatory of F things, the nature that makes them F.

Euthyphro's first answer has betrayed how dominated his thought is by his own situation: how else could someone think of piety solely in terms of prosecutions? Other dialogues depict parallels. The initial answer of Laches concerning courage is: "if a man is willing to remain at his post and to defend himself against the enemy without running away, then you may rest assured that he is a man of courage" (*Laches* 190e). This earns a rebuke from Socrates:

> I wanted to learn from you not only what constitutes courage for a hoplite but for a horseman as well and for every sort of warrior. And I wanted to include not only those who are coura-geous in warfare but also those who are brave in dangers at sea, and the ones who show courage in illness and poverty and affairs of state; and then again I wanted to include not only those who are brave in the face of pain and fear but also those who are clever at fighting desire and pleasure ... try again to state ... what is the courage *that is the same in all these cases* ... What power is it which, because it is the same in ... all the ... cases in which we were just saying it occurred, is therefore called courage?
>
> (191d–192b; emphasis added)

Lest we think it is impossible to satisfy this sort of demand, Socrates within this very passage, where I elided, takes the example of quick-ness. He points out that while there are many contexts in which one may display quickness, quickness itself may be given a unitary defi-nition as the power of doing much in little time.

Socratic *elenchos*

Once interlocutors get coaching about providing some one thing, F-ness, that is common to all cases of F things, they typically offer formulas of appropriate generality. Indeed, they typically make a series of such attempts. How can Socrates tell if what his interlocu-tors offer him is adequate, given that he himself claims not to know?

We now turn to his special way of evaluating them, known as "Socratic *elenchos*" (testing or, in view of the test's typically negative result, refutation).

Here we come to an important difference between the Socratic method in Plato and what passes under that name today. "Socratic" instruction as practiced in law schools and elsewhere is *generically* Socratic in that it involves questioning. But law school professors are invested with authority and hold themselves out as having knowledge of the matters in question. A teacher of this type is all too free crushingly to reject answers for being wrong whether or not others can see why. The teacher already knows the correct answer, and compares what the student says with it.

By contrast, Socrates professes not to know. In the opening of the *Euthyphro*, there was considerable by-play concerning how eager Socrates was to learn about piety from his interlocutor, so that he might defend himself against the charge of impiety brought against him (5a–c). He is not in a position to reject any of Euthyphro's proposals simply by consulting his own expertise.

How then does he proceed? Socratic *elenchos* is based on the interlocutor's being a putative expert on the subject matter in question.[5] This is what gives testing his account interest as a way of approaching inquiry into the subject. Now knowledge as this was understood in antiquity is not (just) a matter of being certain, possibly about a single isolated statement. Rather, expert knowledge in some field involves understanding of the explanatory principles of the field and of their application to lower-level facts. Thus, a person with expert knowledge must be able to give answers to a series of questions appropriately related to his initial claim. This is foundational for the Socratic procedure; it is what licenses Socrates to collect each interlocutor's answers to a series of related questions.

The problem Socrates reveals over and over again is tension within the putative expert's belief system. Over and over again the skill of Socrates elicits from the interlocutor a set of beliefs associated with the topic of his supposed knowledge, which appears inconsistent. Let's consider the exchange with Euthyphro at 12e–13d. In response to Socrates' suggestion that Euthyphro try to say what part of justice piety is, Euthyphro gives as his account that piety is the part of justice that is concerned with service/assistance (*therapeia*) to the gods. Socrates then institutes a line of questioning in the course of which Euthyphro assents to proposed characterizations of a series of cases of the kind of *therapeia* he means. In each case there is a special expertise that some people have (e.g. as a horseman knows how to care for horses), and in all these cases the aim of this service is to benefit the animals and make them better. Can we then be the gods' "therapists" in the sense that we are able to benefit them and make them better? What he has said so far commits him to this, but Euthyphro rejects it vehemently. He thus agrees that he should revisit the issue of what the *therapeia* in question is, and is thereby embarked on the next stage of the discussion.

Or consider Nicias in the *Laches*. He suggests that courage is knowledge of the fearful and the hopeful in war and every other situation (195a). Socrates then brings out tension between Nicias' handling of this claim and his belief that courage is a proper part of virtue as follows (198a–199e). Nicias agrees to an analysis of the fearful as future evils, and of the hopeful as future goods. ("Evil" here has its broadest use where pain e.g. could be one; it's not limited to cases of malign agency; "goods" are good things.) This makes knowledge of the fearful and hopeful amount to knowledge of future evils and goods. He also accepts that kinds of knowledge are not demarcated temporally. So knowledge of future evils and goods is indistinguishable from knowledge of evils and goods in general. And someone with this knowledge seems to Nicias to have *eo ipso* all of virtue: this knowledge will make the person who has it temperate, just, and holy. This is in apparent tension with the claim, which he had already accepted, that courage is a proper part of virtue. In a case like this, it may be inevident where the mistake was. Nevertheless, if the interlocutor accepts that contradiction has emerged within his position, he has failed to sustain any claim to expertise.

This aspect of the procedure makes it essential that all the commitments in play are those of the interlocutor. This is why the contributions of Socrates, formally speaking, are questions. It is for the respondent to accept or reject the suggestions made in those questions, since he is the one being tested. If he falls into contradiction, unacceptably even to himself, then he does not after all have deep understanding of his subject matter, and is not the guide we might otherwise have hoped he would be.

What is the relation between Socratic *elenchos* as a test of the interlocutor and Socrates' program of inquiry into the definitions of ethical terms? The way in which Socrates was investigating ethical matters was by approaching those who were supposed to be experts in the matters in question. He asked them to give accounts. After all, we are surrounded in society by people who hold themselves out as knowing how we should live—if not our parents, perhaps politicians, teachers, religious leaders, and writers. And there are others whose apparent excellence suggests they have understanding of the relevant virtue. So a natural starting-point is to see if any such person really does have understanding. The Socratic *elenchos* is a test of that.

This sort of activity is represented by Socrates in the *Apology* as the grounding for his interpretation of the pronouncement of the oracle at Delphi that there was no one wiser than Socrates. This oracle was typically enigmatic, as in the case of Croesus, the proverbially rich king of Lydia. To his inquiry concerning the duration of his reign, Croesus received a reply describing the time when he would have to flee as when a "mule" should be king over the Medes; he took this to mean he was permanently secure (Herodotus, *History of the Persian Wars* 1.55–6). Only after his defeat at the hands of Cyrus did Croesus see that the oracle referred figuratively to the mixed parentage of his conqueror. So Socrates is doing nothing unusual in taking the oracle as having a hidden meaning requiring interpretation, and the one he offers is that while no humans have actual knowledge, Socrates is wisest because he is free from the false conceit of wisdom. In the *Apology*, Socrates tells us that there is actually a group whose claim to expertise survives his examination. The craftsmen do have some knowledge—but only of their proprietary arts. Nevertheless, he diagnoses, even in them, the mistake of taking themselves wrongly to be experts on other matters.

Given his much-vaunted disavowal of knowledge, what are we to make of assertions Socrates sometimes makes, such as that while he doesn't know if death is a bad thing or not, he does know that to do something unjust and disobey one's superior whether god or man is bad and shameful (29b)? Perhaps the knowledge he disavows is only the highest-grade sort of knowledge (which some commentators designate as expert knowledge, or definitional knowledge). And perhaps when he says he knows various things he has more modest attainments in mind.

These could of course include some impressions he came by in an ordinary way. But there are indications that he gives some a higher status than that. In the *Crito*, Socrates is represented as facing the decision whether or not to flee before the execution to which he has been lawfully sentenced. He says the decision about what to do should be made on the basis of principles he has developed unless better arguments recommend themselves (46b–c). This seems to indicate that, while these principles may still be discredited, and so must fall short of knowledge of the highest-grade sort, they have more standing than just random beliefs he happens to have.

How could Socrates have developed principles? We can now extend the understanding we have been developing of the Socratic *elenchos* by considering not only its immediate but also its cumulative results. The immediate result is what we have studied so far: when a putative expert, asked for full views on his area of supposed expertise, falls into contradiction, we can conclude that he is after all not an expert. Notice that if someone survived questioning for five minutes, or for fifteen, or for fifteen hours or fifteen days or fifteen years, this would not necessarily show that he had knowledge. There could be a contradiction lurking which the questioner had not yet managed to bring out. Still, a position that survives over many occasions might be thought to gain some status.

Also, there are several ways a thesis can survive even if the interlocutor's position as a whole does not. For there are occasions when the interlocutor's failure can be assimilated to a *reductio ad absurdum* of one of the claims he has committed himself to. (Only "assimilated to" because this strategy strictly speaking requires that the inferences be valid and the other claims known to be safe: then one would have an indirect proof of the denial of the targeted, vulnerable premise.) There are some episodes of Socratic *elenchos* in which we may feel that all but one of the claims in play are safe and the reasoning good, so that when contradiction emerges it is clear which claim we need to give up. If certain claims are never given up—especially if in play over a long time with a variety of participants—they might be thought to gain some status. Similarly for the denials of the ones that are given up.

When we consider the numerous occasions on which Socrates has taken part in discussion of human concerns—it has been the primary activity of his entire adult life which was a long one at that—it is not surprising that a cluster of tenets is associated with him by the tradition. (For the literary version of one such attribution in a Socratic dialogue, see Laches 194.) We have now seen how it is possible to regard these as having acquired their status in the course of the elenctic process, even if Socrates did not consider himself to have expert knowledge of them strictly speaking.

The downside of Socratic testing

As we noted in the beginning of this chapter, Socrates' contemporaries were confronted by an embarras de richesses—not only surrounded by people holding themselves out as authorities, but surrounded by competing and incompatible claims. When these were all subjected to the Socratic elenchos, however, complete impoverishment resulted: no one passed the test when the subject got beyond the craft knowledge of tradesmen to the larger issues of human life.

One important function of Plato's choice of characters who serve as interlocutors in the Socratic dialogues is as we have seen that they are people who were expected to have expertise on important aspects of human life. The precise subject matters of individual dialogues match up with their interlocutors. We have looked at Euthyphro and his claims concerning his knowledge of piety. Similarly Laches and Nicias, Socrates' main interlocutors on courage, were well-known generals—men who were expected to have an understanding of the virtue in question.

Now we should take note of the number of characters shown in our dialogues to be intimates of Socrates—indeed, often shown in a moment of glamour and promise—who were widely known to have turned out badly by the time of composition (Rutherford 1995). Laches and Nicias had significant failures in war. Perhaps most notably of all, the young and attractive Charmides and his guardian Critias are Socrates' two interlocutors on sōphrosunē (this untranslatable word is rendered as "temperance," "moderation," "soberness," and "self-discipline" among others: the root idea is sound-mindedness). Both Critias and Charmides were to figure in the oligarchy which came briefly to power when Athenian democracy was overthrown; Critias proved one of the most extreme and most violent of them. Also maximally famous was Alcibiades, who is identified as Socrates' beloved at *Protagoras* 309a and *Gorgias* 481d, and who at *Symposium* 215a–222b gives a drunken and ambivalent speech about Socrates and the latter's influence on him. Here we have a man whose career trajectory showed a brilliant beginning before an abrupt crash. Responsible for the disastrous Sicilian Expedition, embroiled in scandals, traitor to Athens, he died murdered abroad. Plato in his works is hinting that the practical failures of these men were due to their not having the knowledge that is necessary for virtue.

But more familiar to Socrates' own contemporaries than this philosophical diagnosis was the simple fact that Socrates was associated "on both sides of the aisle" with prominent men who, at least with hindsight, were disasters. This association played a large role in the animus against Socrates that led to his prosecution, and was the real meaning behind the charge of corrupting the youth. Yet while even a politically insightful author such as I. F. Stone accuses Plato of not reproaching Socrates for this and of covering it up (Stone 1988), it seems clear to me that by his use of characters Plato was precisely *not* covering it up. The use of these characters at all must immediately have put readers in mind of their well-known careers and violent deaths. The general technique of relying on one's audience to bring well-known facts to bear on one's presentation is common in Plato. To see how it works, just reflect that if one made a movie today showing John F. Kennedy as a boy, or preparing for the trip to Dallas, the actions of one's work would be seen through the lens of audience awareness of subsequent events.

Plato shows each of these characters at a time in the past: each was a talented person from whom much was expected. This choice makes our view of them bittersweet. One thinks back on the lost days of the promise of these brilliant men, while already knowing that it is not to be realized. In fact, to be aware of the association of Socrates with these figures is only a starting point. It might be that Socrates was a bad influence; another possibility is of course that the people in question turned out badly not because of their association with him but in spite of it. And note that it is quite wrong to think that Socrates' view that virtue is knowledge made him favor the oligarchy. Critias and Charmides are shown failing the *elenchos* and so *not* having knowledge: Socrates was an equal-opportunity pest (*contra* Stone 1988).

This historical context in which so many of the best and the brightest failed to live up to their promise motivates the repeated querying in Plato's works why even the sons of great fathers so often do not turn out well (*Laches* 179c ff; *Meno* 93b–94e; *Protagoras* 319e–320b). The general issue of how to help people develop so that they can live well is one of the most enduring themes throughout Plato's career. As far as concerns the particular effect Socrates was having on people, Plato presents a complete enough—and mixed enough—portrait for us to see how complicated the issue is.

On the one hand, calling people to an examination of their lives and helping to see whether they had an adequate understanding of basic matters was potentially helpful. But Plato frequently represents participants in the dialogues getting frustrated at the hands of Socrates. A famous place is in the *Meno* when the title character says:

> Socrates, before I even met you I used to hear that you are always in a state of perplexity and that you bring others to the same state, and now I think you are bewitching and beguiling me, simply putting me under a spell, so that I am quite perplexed. Indeed, if a joke is in order, you seem, in appearance and in every other way, to be like the broad torpedo fish, for it too makes anyone who comes close and touches it feel numb, and you now seem to have had that kind of effect on me, for both my mind and my tongue are numb, and I have no answer to give you. Yet I have made many speeches about virtue before large audiences on a thousand occasions, very good speeches as I thought, but now I cannot even say what it is. I think you are wise not to sail away from Athens to go and stay elsewhere, for if you were to behave like this as a stranger in another city, you would be driven away for practicing sorcery.
>
> (80a–b)

Here is a good moment to consider a complaint that many readers have against Socrates. The complaint is that the confusion and lack of resource (*aporia*) in which interlocutors typically end up is his fault: he traps them with tricks and fallacies, or misleads them when he might have offered salutary instruction. If we keep in mind though that the *elenchos* is a test of expertise, we can see what this thought misses. Assuming that the truth is free from contradiction, someone who is in a position to consult the real state of affairs in giving his answers will always stick to the truth, and so will avoid contradiction. Socrates is not responsible for the set of beliefs being tested, but is merely eliciting it. The sense that something goes wrong in certain places though is still a valuable one. We can use our perceptions of these moments to go back and consider how the interlocutor (or we in his place) could answer better. Perhaps also we can go back and consider whether Socrates handles his exposure of the interlocutor's inadequacy in the most helpful way.

In the *Apology*, Socrates shows that he is aware that his elenctic engagement with people has led to hostility (e.g. at 21d–e, 22e– 23a). Here I think it is important to distinguish two aspects in what he was doing. When we concentrate on the result just in terms of the intellectual achievement, his procedure is an undeniable boon: if people think they have knowledge when they don't, of course becoming aware of that is a precondition for improvement.

But what this official philosophy major's defense of Socrates leaves out is the emotional reality. Plato's portrait contains touches showing that Socrates humiliated his distinguished interlocutors with his irony and his often-public examinations of them. The interlocutors then could easily become defensive and react against Socrates, instead of relishing the chance now uncovered to make intellectual progress (Robinson 1953). Of course Plato thought that Socrates, by his heroically persistent questioning, had performed an immeasurable intellectual service in establishing that outstanding contemporaries did not have the wisdom they might have been supposed to command. But the younger man also showed how the way Socrates went about demonstrating this was counterproductive: in testing the expertise of his distinguished fellow citizens, he tested their patience too far.

Plato in the *Parmenides* gives a portrait of the (highly fictionalized)

Eleatic subjecting to elenctic examination a young "Socrates" who is (in that dialogue) a confident theorist about Platonic Forms. Parmenides' pedagogic style is different in the extreme from that of Socrates in the elenctic dialogues we have been considering. Parmenides is encouraging and supportive of his interlocutor. Once he has established the shortcomings of Socrates, the venerable Eleatic offers a program of instruction that will set the young man on the road to realizing the truth.

By contrast, Plato's portrayal of the way Socrates typically administered the *elenchos* shows that it often turned out to be threatening: those examined reacted defensively instead of with delight. Of course, some members of the audience found the result delightful. Yet the circumstance that the effect of these examinations was publicly to discredit existing authority figures meant that it destroyed the foundations of the ongoing lives of all who were aware of this activity. Socrates' contemporaries lived through his project of realizing we know nothing in real time, and associated it with moral and political upheaval. Little wonder that some of them felt ill done by.

Plato himself follows a strategy that now stands out as careful and carefully less aggressive. In composing exchanges that we can enter imaginatively, he invites us to self-administer the *elenchos*: if we cannot do better than the interlocutors in the texts, we discover that in the privacy of our studies, and at least have the dignity of discovering it for ourselves. This very control we have over the discovery disposes us to experience delight in our intellectual progress rather than register the humiliation of those who failed with Socrates in public space. And if, as we read along, we think we can do better than the characters in the text, then we are already launched on the positive activity that defensiveness and hostility to the questioner may have derailed in them. Moreover, in longer (non-"Socratic") dialogues, Plato typically devotes considerable time to the development of positive views, thus helping with the progress for which the Socratic *elenchos* was an indispensable preliminary.

Prospect

We now have a sense of how Plato saw his Socratic legacy that will serve us in the body of this book. The activity of Socrates showed that neither outstanding individuals nor authority figures in contemporary society understood key human issues—indicating the need for research. Plato himself will continue to make central Socrates' practice of seeking answers to the "what-is-it" question, though he will engage us in his development of suggestions that go beyond those Socrates explored. Moreover, while Plato will continue to explore human questions, he will also broaden his inquiry to all other domains. And he will reflect explicitly on the sort of thing one is engaging with when one seeks to give this type of account, leading to the development of his "theory of Forms."

Further reading

Ancient literature

Aristophanes, *Clouds*. Available in many translations; Henderson is especially good.

Xenophon, *Memorabilia, Symposium*, and *Oeconomicus*. These works all represent Socrates. Unlike Plato, Xenophon does not have his own philosophical program; on the other hand he tilts his picture in ways that he thinks makes Socrates more acceptable.

Secondary literature

See Bibliography for full details of the works listed below.

H. Benson, ed. (1992) *Essays in the Philosophy of Socrates.*

G. Fine, ed. (1999) *Plato 1* and *Plato 2*. Each volume contains some papers on Socrates.

T. Irwin (1995) *Plato's Ethics*. Revised and accessible version of *Plato's Moral Theory* (below).

T. Irwin (1977a) *Plato's Moral Theory*. This and *Plato's Ethics* (above) both concern themselves in their early chapters with Plato's Socratic dialogues; Irwin takes Plato's portrait as giving us the historical Socrates, and takes that figure to be a constructive ethical theorist.

C. Kahn (1996) *Plato and the Socratic Dialogue*. Useful on the context of the Socratic discourses of other ancient authors.

R. Kraut (1984) *Socrates and the State.*

S. Peterson (2011) *Socrates and Philosophy in the Dialogues of Plato*. Takes the position of Vlastos's *Socrates: Ironist and Moral Philosopher* (below) as a foil and develops the opposite hypothesis: that the figure of Socrates (like his author Plato) is never doctrinal in any of the dialogues; rather he is always examining others. Different dialogues present different phases in such examination: throughout a text like the *Republic*, he is *eliciting* the views that appeal to the interlocutors.

G. Vlastos (1983) "The Socratic Elenchus."

G. Vlastos (1991) *Socrates: Ironist and Moral Philosopher*. Holds that Plato throughout his compositional career uses the figure of Socrates to put forward the views and methods he himself at the time espouses.

Notes

1 See Ross (1924: xxxix–xli) for defense of "Fitzgerald's canon," according to which when Aristotle uses "Socrates" without the definite article and puts the verb in the past tense, he is speaking of the historical man; by contrast the name with the definite article is to be classed with such locutions as "the Socrates in the *Republic*," and so refers to the character Socrates in whatever texts are relevant. Ross draws both on general prose usage and on Aristotle's practice in other cases in which a literary character is based on (what the Greeks took to be) a historical person.

2 Kahn (1996) argues for the dependence of Aristotle on Plato in service of his claim that Aristotle has no value as an independent source for the historical Socrates. But he does not take up the further question of Aristotle as an indicator of when we are getting Plato's reception of Socrates. And while he mentions briefly that Aristotle does not use the middle dialogues in forming his conception of "Socrates," he has no explanation for this. As Irwin has pointed out (2008: 83), the best explanation for why Aristotle takes only certain dialogues as giving the views of Socrates (as opposed to others whose positions he attributes to Plato) is that he uses some evidence from outside the dialogues. While Irwin then goes all the way to believe that Aristotle has obtained evidence about the real Socrates, one need suppose no more than that he knows from the Academy which dialogues Plato meant to represent the tradition of Socrates.

3 The default for translations of Aristotle in this book will be *Complete Works of Aristotle* (The Revised Oxford Translation) (ed. Barnes 1984).

4 I am intentionally not relying on the phrase "real definition" because people mean too many different things by it. But, depending how you think of real definitions, Socrates is pursuing either them or a proto-version of them.

5 The interlocutor does not always claim this status for himself. The hope of Socrates that Charmides will have insight into what temperance is derives from Critias' having put the youth forward as outstanding in his possession of the virtue (157d–159a).

Part II

Four

Platonic love

Mysteries of *erōs* in the *Symposium*

The *Symposium* offers a theory of *erōs* as the force behind the creativity needed if we are to fulfill our most fundamental motivation. Presented by the fictional priestess Diotima as narrated by Socrates at the drinking party of the title, this theory shows why *erōs* expresses itself in sexual activity and the production of physical offspring. But Diotima also indicates that the very same force can in some people lead to a better sort of consummation and the production of a better sort of offspring. On this theory, erotic energy is responsible for the greatest forms of creativity. It leads to artistic works, law codes, progress in technical forms of expertise, scientific and mathematical discoveries, and above all philosophy. The priestess ultimately invokes the Eleusinian Mysteries in metaphor as a culturally familiar parallel for the progression she recommends for those who are "pregnant in soul."

This text has led to our current idiom of a relationship's being "Platonic." However, by some historic irony, what a "Platonic relationship" has come to mean is so watered down as to leave out the fundamental point. While for us to say that a relationship is "Platonic" is to say that it has no erotic component, real Platonic love is a form of *erōs*. What distinguishes it from the more common sort is not its basis but its expression. Platonic love is a manifestation of the tremendous motivating force of *erōs*, directed in a distinctive way.[1]

The paragraphs above have to do with the content of a fraction of the dialogue. There is a lot more to the text as a whole. This most literary of Plato's works employs multiple frames for the story of the namesake drinking party. We learn what happened at the long-ago symposium, when each of a series of men gave a speech about *erōs*. The character of this highly complex text requires us to bring diverse kinds of activity to reading it.

Because of the theme and setting, information about the cultural context is particularly useful in understanding where the speakers are "coming from," so we will take that up first. We will then go on to study how Plato's handling of the elaborate framing sets us in subtly different relations to different parts of the text. In particular, it works to privilege one portion of Socrates' turn—not his elenctic exchange at the symposium with the host, Agathon, which Plato handles like the rest of the exchanges at the party, but Socrates' report to his fellow-guests of an encounter he claims to have had.

Plato privileges this story, of Socrates' supposed lessons from Diotima, because he is offering it for our primary philosophical engagement. Everything up to this point is in a sense background for it. We will look at the preliminary, background passages with this role in mind. Next we will be in a position to note by contrast some characteristics of the highlighted Diotima–Socrates endeavor. Seeing its special characteristics will prepare us for the special kind of activity that reading it is designed to elicit in us. We will engage in that activity to reanimate the dialectic of Diotima's lessons and create for ourselves an understanding of *erōs* from them. Finally we will see how, by providing a challenge to this, the intervention of the party-crashing Alcibiades is there to make each reader of Plato's text continue to think further.

Cultural context: erōs in antiquity, Greek homosexuality, and sympotic culture

The ancients recognized *erōs* as holding great sway over human beings (Skinner 2005). Typically a response to perceived beauty, in archaic poetry it is an invasive force. The desire *erōs* imparts is not necessarily for sex (in Homer it can be directed to food and drink), nor is all sex occasioned by *erōs*, whose mark is an intensity that can cross over into obsession. However, *erōs* is typically for a person and typically drives us to seek satisfaction in sexual release. Prodicus, the fifth-century arch-distinguisher, specifies that *erōs* is desire doubled, while *erōs* doubled is insanity. *Erōs* is also spoken of as a deity, as are justice, victory, shame, terror, etc. But because the orthographic conventions of the time did not use the distinction between initial capital vs. lowercase letters to mark proper names as is done today in English, there is nothing except our understanding of context to determine whether speakers are referring to the "youthful winged deity or … an aspect of human feeling and behaviour" (Dover 1980: 1) or, indeed, sliding between the two. Readers of the *Symposium* should not attach more significance to the presence or absence of capitalization than it merits.

The effects of *erōs* are notoriously complex. Erotic pleasures are well known, but to be in the grip of *erōs* can be experienced as disconcerting, disorienting, and disabling (a theme of poets throughout antiquity: see Anacreon, Archilochus, Sappho, and, in Latin, Catullus). *Erōs* not only occasions suffering but can drive a person to behavior ordinarily considered shameful; tragedy often deals with this destructive aspect. (See the *Medea* or *Hippolytus*; again readers can no doubt come up with more current examples of their own!) Yet the force of *erōs* also operates for good: Thucydides' Pericles in his Funeral Oration (*History of the Peloponnesian War* 2.43.1) exhorts his fellow citizens to gaze on the city and become her lovers (*erastai*), and the sexual activity to which *erōs* urges us plays a key role in contributing to the continuation of our kind. The translation "lover" for *erastēs* renders appropriately the intense and focused desire that *erōs* imparts. It also suitably parallels the existence of a narrow usage (in which *erōs* is oriented to sex with our love object) together with a wider application (in which one can be a lover of power say).

It was commonplace for Athenian upper-class men to assume that the most emotionally intense and rewarding erotic relationships were homosexual (Dover 1978; Skinner 2005). This attitude was reinforced by several features of the society. Concern for the purity of patrilineal descent and the honor of their house led men of the upper classes to keep their daughters and wives at home, in segregated women's quarters. Moreover, women had no scope to develop and exercise the attainments that were most admired in the culture.

Male homosexual activity was not thought of as involving an identity that excluded marriage to women: this was of great practical importance to leading citizens for the sake of offspring to continue their house and their city. In fact, women were available to men as wives, prostitutes, and slaves. But these involvements were not necessarily the emotionally absorbing relationships of those who were in a position to devote themselves to love as a leisure pursuit. Of course, only the wealthy were in such a position. The ordinary man, absorbed in working for his living, married as part of practical life, and relied on his wife as household agent and principal sexual partner. Hostility to homosexual affairs as a practice of the elite is reflected in comedy and law court speeches—two maximally populist forms (Hubbard 1998, 2005). The dual circumstances that the practice was seen as a Doric (Spartan) import and as characteristic of leisured, decadent, aristocratic life made it increasingly suspect in the eyes of the subsistence-level citizens of the democracy.

How did privileged men see homosexual attachments? These relationships were often asymmetric not with regard to gender or class, but with regard to age and attributes. In each such pair, the elder of the two is the lover, and the younger the beloved. The beloved is beautiful (*kalos*): his beauty is what has attracted the attention of his lover, who longs for sexual contact and release—feelings the beloved is too innocent to feel on his own account. (The beauty of the beloved was, if not literally ephemeral, thought to be at its height before the growth of his beard; thus the affair was typically an episode, one in a series of attachments.) An affair offered something with a different kind of value to the beloved: the example and connections of his lover helped him in coming to take on the role of a leading citizen.

Because of the complexity of the attitudes in the society as a whole, a love affair was a two-edged matter. There was the possibility for enemies to assimilate the receiving of gifts within a relationship to prostitution, which was a disgrace. One who sold his own body was thought not to be worthy of the trust citizens needed to have in each other. Because of this, prostitution was actually grounds for stripping men of rights—such as speaking in the Assembly—they would otherwise exercise as citizens. Thus clearly one would have wanted to avoid any such imputation.

Independently of any financial transaction, to have any part of one's body penetrated by another was thought to be shameful, since this was to occupy the inferior role of the passive rather than the active partner; yet more shameful would be to come to enjoy this role.

But as we can see from vase painting, a socially acceptable compromise was available. The intercrural (between-the-thighs) position allowed sexual release to the lover and preserved the beloved in the condition of a technical virgin: he was not penetrated. This possibility may of course not have received universal approbation, nor do we have any way of knowing to what extent people in practice violated what they took to be norms. But one way or another, the extensive concern in contemporary society to assess sexual behavior in terms of the notions of penetration and passivity, where certain configurations were thought to be threats to the proper development of the junior partner, must have made people's feelings about their practices highly charged.

We have seen that love affairs provided elite youth with a special entrée into adult society. Indeed, symposia themselves had cultural significance as venues for this aspect of socialization: as drinking parties they were obviously occasions for bonding. Moreover, symposia were a typical venue for the reciting of poetry—including poetry about how to comport oneself at symposia and beyond. Thus the symposium functioned as:

> a central site for the transmission of a shared cultural and intellectual heritage, in other words for (male) education in the broadest social and political sense ... for example, much of the elegiac poetry of Theognis of Megara ... is set at a symposium and offers moralizing social, sexual, and political advice to a young man. It is at symposia that membership in a privileged group is both tested and acted out.
>
> (Hunter 2004: 15)

So the symposium, literally a drinking party, was that and more: it was a venue in which both erotic attachment and cultural transmission were central. Our drinking-party's constituency and the evening's program of going around with each guest in turn giving an encomium of Erōs makes sense within sympotic culture.

While it was the elitist aspect of symposia that attracted disapproval from populist elements in society, we can already see that Plato will have other causes for concern: he cannot regard the work of the canonical great poets as a sufficient guide to life[2]—nor would a prominent career among "the great and the good" of the existing aristocracy be his ideal of what the young should be initiated into. The speech Socrates gives at this fictional symposium will be the occasion to envisage a way in which erotic energy is responsible for the greatest forms of creativity, culminating above all in philosophy. Let's look now at how the way the dialogue is composed affects our reception of the contributions of the various speakers at the party.

Compositional form of the Symposium

This dialogue is composed in an extremely elaborate way. By contrast, the dialogues we looked at in Chapter Three exhibit one of two forms. Some (e.g. the Euthyphro) are dramas in which we see Socrates and the other participants in the dialogue speaking in turn just as characters in a tragedy or a comedy do. For us the effect is of being present at their conversation. The other form is exemplified by the Charmides. While the philosophical exchange represented in it is in many ways similar to that in the Euthyphro, the mode of presentation is different: Socrates functions like the narrator in a novel, and reports to readers a conversation in which he represents himself as having taken part.

Now we can understand why the narrated/dramatic distinction does not bulk very large in the experience of many readers of the Socratic dialogues. The ones that are narrated are told to us by Socrates, who after some initial scene-setting recounts complete conversations. A charming recent description of Socrates as narrator applies:

> He is presenting ... a philosophic conversation that he had ... as we ourselves might convey to an acqaintance the substance of a ... conversation by reporting the actual words, interspersed with many a "and then I said ...," "and then he goes ..."
>
> (Ferrari 2010: 19)[3]

Socrates when reporting never seems at a loss; we tend to trust him and assimilate him to the "omniscient narrator" of a novel. And his extensive use of direct quotation gives us the vivid experience of hearing the original conversation.

The *Symposium* too is a narrated dialogue with much reported speech. But its effect is very different from that of the *Charmides*. As we will now see, this results from its construction being far more elaborate. For one thing, and quite possibly for the first time, our narrator is not Socrates. And the work draws attention to the difficulties of transmission from its start. Our narrator Apollodorus in his first speech recounts a request that was made to him recently by someone named Glaucon (about whom we know nothing, not even whether he is Plato's brother or another person of the same name). This Glaucon had heard an unclear report of the dinner party from someone who had gotten it from a certain Phoenix, who as we will learn was himself dependent on the report of another. While Glaucon hoped to get a better—even first-hand—report from Apollodorus, our narrator can still do no better than pass on what he heard from Phoenix's source—one Aristodemus, who was present on the occasion of the famous party.

Not only does this work raise at the start the question of our problematic access to what is retailed within it, but the chain of reporting has manifestly weak links. Both Aristodemus and Apollodorus admit that they have forgotten some of what was said (178a, 180c, 223d). Aristodemus seems to think that being a philosopher is a matter of imitating the dress of one's master; he affects Socratic shoelessness (173b). Yet Plato himself was known for his personal elegance, and so must have thought imitation of such surface characteristics beside the point. And Aristodemus is so negligible in the eyes of the symposiasts that when it should have been his turn based on spatial position, Aristophanes speaks as if Agathon and Socrates are the only remaining speakers (Dover 1980: 121).

A notable feature of the *Symposium* derives from its use of distancing forms of mediation. To develop parallels for these in English, let's start with an extract from P. G. Wodehouse (corresponding to the "novelistic" presentation of the *Charmides*), and compare it with versions produced by applying distancing techniques that, as we will see, are employed to significant effect in the *Symposium*. In the Wodehouse original ("Sir Roderick Comes to Lunch"), Bertie Wooster recounts his welcome of the intimidating Sir Roderick Glossop as follows:

> "What ho! What ho! What ho!" I said, trying to strike the genial note, and then had a sudden feeling that that was just the sort of thing I had been warned not to say.

At another extreme, a narrator might report an episode in what I will call "description style":

> I greeted him trying to strike the genial note, and then had a sudden feeling that that was just the sort of thing I had been warned not to say.

Notice how through the quotation in the genuine Wodehouse, we seem to hear the silly voice of Bertie nervously greeting his guest, and in the description-style version we do not—even though he is himself the narrator. The original Wodehouse with its direct quotation makes us feel we have direct access to the episode narrated.

Now consider the case in which a non-participant narrator relays to us the message of another source, along some such lines as:

> He [the source] reported Sir Roderick to have entered, then Bertie to have said, "What ho! What ho! What ho!" and then Jeeves to have told them that luncheon was served.

This last demonstrates the way in which, in much of the *Symposium*, the chain of reporting makes itself felt. While the words that were spoken at the symposium are generally quoted, the actions of the guests and the "he said"s that introduce their quoted words have been thrown into indirect discourse. The infinitive forms so introduced are a reminder—often what I will call "instrusive"—to us that the words of the inner narrator are now transformed in the outer narrator's report. This phenomenon, a striking feature of the Greek text, usually goes missing from translations, which may be aiming to make everything as vivid and lively as possible.

Like jewels in a darkened setting or a photograph in a tarnished frame, quoted speech, however intrinsically vivid and bright, is affected by being set this way. Yet since the effect is due to our awareness of the setting, the setting's intrusiveness determines the effect. A portrait miniature carried in an antique locket can hardly be viewed without awareness of the darkened metal, while a large-scale painting affords us the possibility of ignoring its frame: we may focus on the picture alone, and even have the illusion that we enter the world seen within it.

In our text, as I have said, the conversation among the party guests is set in such a way as intrusively to remind us of the multiple mediation and so of our distance from the occasion. The machinery of the telltale infinitives of indirect discourse is in abeyance only during the speeches that each guest gives in turn. Socrates' speech after his examination of Agathon is the longest of these; he launches into a narrative that takes up all of 201e8–212a7. Socrates' own narration (quoted in the text) presents, using primarily direct quotation, his conversation with Diotima. So Plato has handled the nesting of speakers in such a way that the conversation Socrates reports between himself and Diotima is free at its opening, at its closing, and throughout from any of the telltale infinitives of mediation. This is the longest such stretch in the dialogue. The stretch of text from the semicolon in 201d1 through 212c3 could be removed from the *Symposium* and be a lively "novelistic" dialogue on its own!

Alcibiades' seven-page account of his relationship with Socrates is the second-longest stretch without telltale infinitives betraying the mediation of Aristodemus and Apollodorus. Although Alciabiades also in a sense treats of conversation and indeed sometimes of philosophy, he is at the opposite extreme from Socrates as a reporter, relying almost exclusively on what I called "description style." Thus—with the exception of a brief portion of one episode, which we will come to later—he does not present conversation directly to us, or even transmit it through indirect speech. His description style typically works in such a way that we do not get to find out any of the actual content of the *logoi* (utterances) of Socrates that Alcibiades repeatedly asserts to be so unusual.

The *Symposium*'s elaborate compositional form must serve some purpose, and there are varied ways of making this out. Positing so many people devoting so much effort to memorizing a representation of the occasion indicates their yearning for contact with Socrates (Halperin 1992 thematized the phrase "erotics of narrativity"). Also Plato, who will be going well beyond what he takes the historical Socrates to have been doing, may use the distancing effect of the chain of third-person narrators to emphasize our lack of reliable access to history.

He also, more subtly, exploits his resources to make the instruction Socrates receives from Diotima stand out. The report of this is the only lengthy passage in the *Symposium* in which we find the philosophically involving mode of conversation (as opposed to long-form speech) presented in the style of the *Charmides*: free from telltale infinitives of indirect discourse and so free of intrusive mediation. Thus we have the sophisticated result that this (tied-for) most embedded conversation is the one presented the most directly to our attention. While the rest of the reported exchanges are presented to us in a way that distances us from them, those Socrates relates in his transparent fiction are presented to us with all the directness of a novel.

Why should Plato go to so much trouble to contrive this? I suggest that the intrusively mediated reports of what went on with the original party-guests are there to provide background for the Socrates/Diotima exchange. This is the one we experience as most directly presented because it is the one that Plato has designed to draw us into philosophical activity.[4] In the next few sections, we will read the portions of the *Symposium* that present the speakers through Socrates in accordance with this idea. We will then conclude by going on to the intervention of Alcibiades to see what it adds. Bottom line: the Socrates/Diotima story does have privileged status, but we cannot content ourselves with receiving it passively.

The speakers before Socrates

The namesake event of the *Symposium* takes place at the home of the tragic poet Agathon to celebrate his maiden victory (theatrical productions were public competitions). The guests are among others our friend the enthusiast of speeches Phaedrus, Agathon's lover Pausanias, a physician named Eryximachus, the comic poet Aristophanes, and Socrates. They agree to follow a suggestion attributed to Phaedrus that one should respond to a lack of speeches in praise of the deity Erōs by producing some. The turns of the other invited guests build to the high point of that of Socrates. This takes off from a preliminary elenctic exchange with Agathon that leads into Socrates' recounting of his supposed instruction from Diotima. (This otherwise unheard-of woman from Mantinea is widely regarded as fictional.) The speeches that precede that of Socrates represent existing associations with erōs in the surrounding culture and how they can be developed. Some prepare ideas that will be incorporated later; some take positions that will be corrected.

Phaedrus and Pausanias both emphasize a connection between pederasty and honorable exploits, Pausanias adding a distinction between a higher and lower erōs and associating the good kind of erōs with what the secondary literature has come to call "educative pederasty." The cultural situation we have reviewed explains the defensive justification of these characters of the practice they are committed to. The physician Eryximachus then claims that far from being limited to human interactions, Erōs governs all harmonious and good situations throughout the cosmos.

Next come the turns of Aristophanes and Agathon. Given the role of poetry in Greek life in general and sympotic culture in particular, the offerings of these two men were bound to be of special interest. And the speech of Aristophanes is indeed a masterpiece. It is truly funny. And the idea it contains is so striking as to have been received in some quarters as Plato's own view of love. Its conceit is that human beings as we are now have resulted from a punishment of bisection that was imposed (in the mythic past) on originally spherical creatures. Each of us naturally seeks to be reunited with someone who is literally our other half. The descriptions of these creatures and what Zeus and Apollo did to them are comic. But much of the appeal of the story comes from its playing at explaining important parts of the phenomenology of falling in love: the "You complete me" idea, together with the sense that there is someone out there who is uniquely "the one" for each of us.

This speech, though not in verse, has many traits of an outstanding poetic production. It appeals powerfully to our feelings, and initially strikes us as saying something deep about the human condition. But it has its limits if, taking it perhaps more seriously than it was intended, we press it. As with Aesop's fables and with just-so stories, it asks us to suppose that "a one-time event in the past (such as a young elephant's encounter with a crocodile) has universal consequences in the present (all elephants have long trunks)" (Hunter 2004: 65).

Moreover, important problems come in connection with the psychology of the creatures it envisages. And it does credit them with a psychology; they—ourselves after all—are described as having desires, emotions, and realizations. First of all, while I can fairly easily reinterpret my body as the severed half of an original spheroid creature, it is not at all clear that I can conceive of my mental and emotional life as really that of a proper part of some original organism unless that creature just happened to have two loci of consciousness—but why should that have been? Second, even granting some reinterpretation, the desirability of the reintegration scenario may be different with respect to the physical and psychological aspects. Thinking of our bodies, the reintegration of severed limbs or even the restoration of ones that have been missing since birth is clearly desirable. But when I am fused with my complement so as to be one rather than two in Hades (i.e. as souls; 192e), the implied fusing of my mind and emotions with those of someone who has been living a separate life, especially if it has been since our births, raises questions. Is it really plausible that this will restore lost wholeness in such a way as to be clearly desirable from the point of view of the "half" that I presently am? I might think that the transformation in question would bring it about that the person I now am will no longer exist. And I might not desire that! So there is a variety of kinds of consideration that can go to support such an assessment as that the performance of the Platonic Aristophanes is "inventive, witty, appealing, naggingly suggestive, but at heart utterly empty" (Hunter 2004: 70).

The questions just articulated concern the particular need that Aristophanes makes erōs address. The more general idea that erōs addresses a lack that is part of our human condition will also figure in the speech of Socrates. But the need he identifies will be different, as will be the way erōs impels us to address it. The speech of

Aristophanes has fun with the idea that in sex we are trying to form a single creature with our partner, but mentions the possibility that children can result merely in passing. In Socrates' speech, the power of *erōs* will be precisely its generative capacity: it is responsible not just for biological reproduction but for all our creative activity. But before going on to this, we must consider the speech of Agathon.

This is, in a different way, a *chef-d'oeuvre* of presentation. Its most notable virtue is, ironically, responsible for its not registering strongly in translation: the speech is remarkable for the aesthetic properties of its verbal expression in the original Greek. Plato has written for Agathon a speech full of the tropes of the rhetorician Gorgias. The peroration of this prose composition is made up almost entirely of clauses set in the metrical patterns of lyric poetry. Thus Agathon is smooth, dainty, and beautiful not just in the way he looks, but also in the way he sounds. In his speech, the tragic poet depicts Love as dainty and delicate, young and lovely, the personification of the beloved. As both the role and the characteristics are Agathon's, he has cast Love in his own image. He even makes *Erōs* a creative artist like himself.

Socrates starts his turn with an examination of the poet, in which he will focus not on his host's beautiful presentation but on his understanding of *erōs*. In content this exchange is a fairly typical Socratic *elenchos*, though transmitted to us with the intrusively distancing infinitives of mediation. The poet agrees to these steps:

1   Love is the love of something (199d–200a).
2   Love desires not what he/it has, but what he/it does not have and needs (200a; cf. 200e where this is treated as equivalent to a claim in terms of "a man or anyone else who has a desire").[5]
3   There is love of beautiful things and no love of ugly ones (201a).
4   So Love is of beauty (201a).
5   So Love needs and does not have beauty (201b; treated as equivalent to not having beautiful things at 201c).
6   So Love cannot be beautiful (201b).

If you are wondering what exactly is the force of the result that Love cannot be beautiful, you should be! Some candidates: (a) That a lover as such is not beautiful. (b) That a beloved as such is not beautiful. (c) That the relationship, Love, is not beautiful. (d) That the divinity, Love, is not beautiful. Yet Agathon does not ask. Nor does he try to work out whether any of them really follows from (1) - (3). Rather, he simply accepts that he has now come to a position in tension with his original idea that Love is beautiful: "It turns out, Socrates, I didn't know what I was talking about in that speech" (201b).

Socrates invites Agathon to "take it a little further" as follows:

7   Good things are beautiful (201c).
8   So Love in lacking what is beautiful also lacks what is good (201c).

Again, what Socrates is driving at here is not completely clear. The minimum claim needed as a premise here is (7), understood as: if a thing is good it is beautiful. Are we supposed to accept this on its own? Or should we supply as well that whatever is beautiful is good? Or ground these in an even stronger claim, that beauty and goodness are identical? Many scholars assume that the identity of beauty and goodness is what lies behind the claim that good things are beautiful. But nothing requires us to build that in (so I would not). The whole issue of the relation between the beautiful and the good[6] engages almost everyone who reads this passage. But not Agathon. He merely reacts as if this seals his defeat, and wants only to give up (201c). For him this seems to be a final result.

The inadequacy of Agathon's understanding could be the main point of this stretch of text. However, this little passage—perhaps because it is one of the few in the dialogue that lends itself to formalization—has also attracted to itself a considerable amount of attention as a putative demonstration of its conclusions. Let's consider whether it works well if we take it that way.

(1), (2), and (3) make sense if we think one loves a beautiful object one is deprived of and needs. But somehow once (4) and (5) lead to (6) the issue must be lacking the property, beauty. How does that come in? Not all pairs are like Beauty and the Beast (and even the Beast does not completely lack the property beauty)! We could *consider* building in that when one loves someone beautiful, the real object of love is beauty (rather than the particular person who is a beauty[7]). But this would be importantly disanalogous to the cases Socrates gave when he derived the wanting-what-we-don't-have principle at 200a–e using such examples as that we want health only when we don't have it. When I don't have health and desire it, what I desire is that I acquire health: that I *be healthy*. But the way in which *erōs* is oriented to beauty is not that I desire that I *be beautiful*.

The line of thinking on offer in this passage just does not seem to work. If we are to regard it as meant to prove to us that Love is not beautiful, then all the points on which we saw above that Agathon failed to press for clarification become worrying. The two possible courses of imagining that seeing the difficulties is beyond Plato or trying to figure out how to make it work after all are both unattractive. But the difficulties here are no defect if we go back to the reading that took its cue from Agathon, according to which the main agenda item is testing him. Then his failing to pursue these issues is part of his characterization. As we are about to see, there is a significant contrast between the pairing of Agathon with Socrates and that of Socrates with Diotima. Agathon confines himself to the most passive role possible. Socrates in Agathon's place will be more active, and Diotima will present way more in her role of teacher than was possible in this early exchange. We can regard the further developments in the exchange of Socrates with Diotima plus our own thought on these points as meant to supersede anything problematic to which Agathon in his passivity may not have objected.

As always, elenctic examination of a leading contemporary serves an important role in relating the inquiry under way to the present understanding of the community. And even if the argument Agathon swallows is less than perfect in its entirety, the discussion does bring out that erotic longing is conditioned on a lack. This idea had already been intimated in the speech of Aristophanes; the view Socrates attributes to Diotima will offer a different way of developing the thought. We can go back later and ask whether there is not some respectable way to reach the conclusion about *erōs* not being beautiful. A longing for what we lack may well imply imperfection in the needy. We have also registered how this passage highlights that love is oriented to beauty, as well as containing the tip of the iceberg of the role of the good. If we are more active than Agathon we should be on the lookout for further clarification of these points.

Characteristics of Socrates' lessons from Diotima

Now let's read on into the main part of Socrates' turn. He effects the transition and softens the blow of Agathon's defeat by claiming that he himself had formerly thought the same as his host, and had been shown the error of his ways by the wise Diotima, in lessons which he then recounts.[8] Socrates picks up the narration without giving the details of the exchange corresponding to his discussion with Agathon, to which he alludes in summary. Then he embarks on narrating the positive part of his lessons. From 201e to 212a is the exchange which we saw is privileged by feeling most directly presented. We will now begin our study of this important passage by collecting global observations about Socrates and Diotima. This will then prepare us to reanimate the thinking the lessons are designed to provoke, which we will do in the balance of the chapter.

With Socrates' recounting of his first utterance, "So I said, 'What do you mean, Diotima? Is Love ugly, then, and bad?'" we can already see the difference between him and Agathon. While the poet had been content to register defeat, for Socrates seeing his confusion is the occasion for further inquiry. His query prompts Diotima to exposition of the point next in order, that what is not beautiful need not be ugly but may be in between. Then she responds to a further question from Socrates by giving a story according to which Love is the offspring of Poverty and Resource, and so while not replete with goods, is always aiming to get some. Her description here of Erōs obviously applies also to Socrates himself ("tough … shoeless … sleeping at people's doorsteps and in roadsides under the sky … resourceful in his pursuit of intelligence, a lover of wisdom;" 203c–d). This story of the parentage of Erōs fills a standard encomium slot—though normally one praises the glorious lineage of one's subject and here the genealogy is rather shabbier. The circumstance that this is a standard encomium topic though is a hint that Socrates is fabricating at the party. Diotima's account of parentage takes advantage of the traditional encomium topic to prefigure the connection between *erōs* and philosophy that will take on increasing importance in the discussion to come. Socrates then launches the philosophical core of Diotima's teaching with his question about what the use of *erōs* is for human beings (204c).

The difference between Socrates and Agathon shows itself in the scope of the former's commitment. In confessing that he does not know the answer to one of Diotima's questions, Socrates says, "... if I had known, I would not have been so amazed at your wisdom, nor would I have come so regularly for instruction at your hands" (206b, tr. Jowett 1892). This translation brings out a feature of the representation of Socrates that has generally received insufficient attention: he portrays himself as actually *frequenting* Diotima for purposes of this tutelage—that is, their exchanges form a series. Despite the fact that Socrates does not do very well early on, he keeps coming back.

Some scholars see a *double entendre* in the word "frequenting" which can be used of visits to a prostitute. But the uncontroversial core force of the word, the idea of repeated action, seems to have been lost sight of. And similarly it gets little attention that while Diotima's teaching as recounted up to 207a is presented as if it were given in a single continuous conversation, at 207a Socrates says, "All this she taught me at various times⁹ when she spoke of love" (tr. Jowett 1892). Yet there is an important intellectual consequence of their lessons' forming a series: Diotima has scope to employ pedagogic techniques not available in the one-off elenctic encounters we have been used to.

If we imagine individual occasions that formed part of the series spread over "various times," it seems likely that she sometimes developed sub-portions of her view separately. A natural sub-topic may have been our fundamental goal (204e–206a); another how the impulse to generate and protect offspring is aimed at satisfying the wish for immortality that the fundamental goal turns out to contain (a lesson Diotima gives twice, even as Socrates recounts it: 206c–207a and 207a–208b). I think it quite plausible to suppose that ideally one should devote at least one lesson to each such sub-topic. Once the lessons have been separately mastered, students (Socrates or ourselves) can try to put the parts together.

Seeing this text as derived from a series of lessons makes sense of certain important features it has. Often a discussion will slip in something additional to its primary focus—a marker, unexplained in its own context, for what will later be developed at length. A simple illustration of this is what we just saw about the association of *erōs* and philosophy. Another one: at 206b, Diotima says cryptically that the job of love is birth in beauty, whether according to body or soul; at 206c she says equally cryptically that humans are pregnant in body and soul. Then for pages we get the discussion of animal reproduction and how it represents an extension of the parent into the future. But during these pages the only birthing we can imagine is the bodily sort. It is only at 209a that the question of what the soul bears and brings to birth comes up explicitly.

More importantly, it makes sense to see certain sequences whose members otherwise stand in a puzzling relationship to each other as the natural result of a pedagogic technique still familiar today. Teachers often work from early statements that are approximations of some claim they will develop in future with greater complexity. The more correct and more complex formulations may be too much to take on board and understand at first. An obvious case of this is the sequence:

- Love is of beauties (formulation Diotima attributes to Socrates at 204d).
- Someone who loves desires to possess beauties (joint formulation at 204d).
- The job of love is to give birth in beauty (as Diotima finally articulates it in 206b).

To see such variations in this way is to see early versions, if later superseded by others that are justified by the content of the actual philosophical discussions, as first approximations that are employed because they work for students at that stage, even if not exactly correct. Far from being permanent official parts of Diotima's theory, such early versions should be regarded as anticipations of or elliptical for what we should really come to hold.

Or consider these transitions in 206a:

- People desire the good.

- People desire to possess the good.
- People desire to possess the good forever.

In this case, Plato has left "homework" for us readers. In general, we have to *reconstruct for ourselves* the analysis of *erōs* Diotima offers. In her leisurely pedagogy, Diotima introduces sub-topics without immediately showing how they connect up with others, and also sometimes goes over the same ground more than once, with altered emphasis. This presentational style is designed precisely to challenge us to activate ourselves in working through these indications. The circumstance that the character Socrates does not immediately see what to make of all this is also an encouragement to us: it is acceptable, normal, even happened to Socrates (who we are predisposed by the attitudes of the men in the frame and at the party to regard as a person of outstanding talent) not to take in everything immediately; we'll be "good students" if we follow his example by staying with the process. What follows in the next few sections is a start on the sort of activity the text is designed to promote in us.

Depth analysis of *erōs*

We have seen that the common understanding of the culture in which Plato lived was that *erōs* is a response to a beautiful object. One is struck by someone's beauty, falls in love, and longs for sexual engagement. To think of *erōs* in this way is to confine ourselves to the most obvious of the feelings we experience when falling in love. And these will have a place in the ultimate account. But Diotima both gives depth to the account and broadens it. We will come to appreciate the former in this section, and the latter in the next.

Here's how Diotima gives depth to her analysis. She drafts off of the notion that the sexual yearning that even the common understanding attributes to lovers has as its natural goal reproduction. So possession of the love object whose beauty excites us is *not* the ultimate purpose of erotic activity. As she puts it, love desires to give birth in beauty (206e). This is evident not just in our own case, but in that of all living creatures: all creatures show a tremendous natural impulse towards mating, and then towards protecting and rearing their young. What lies behind this universal biological imperative? Diotima says, quite plausibly, that this is the way we, as mortal creatures, extend ourselves into the future and achieve a kind of immortality (stated quickly at 206c and 207a; longer development through 208b).

Earlier in Diotima's presentation at 204e–205b, she had attributed to all humans a desire that now turns out to contain within itself the desire to extend ourselves into the future.[10] The lesson started from the skeleton of a way of thinking of motivation that is shared by the whole Socratic/Platonic/Aristotelian tradition and which, indeed, is presented by Aristotle in the *Rhetoric* as a matter of common sentiment. We all want to flourish: we want to achieve *eudaimonia* or, in the traditional translation, happiness. (Here as always in Greek philosophy "happiness" does not name a mood or affective state, but is the objective condition of living a well-favored or successful life, of doing well.) We want goods (that is, good things) because having them constitutes flourishing. After the initial phases of discussion, our text will tend to speak of desire for "the good" (206a and later) which I take to be shorthand for the appropriate combination of individual goods that together constitute happiness for us.[11]

So everyone desires to possess the good. But Diotima and Socrates agreed further at 206a that everyone wants to possess the good forever.[12] While this step is not justified in the text, here is one way of arriving at it: Everyone wants to possess the good (i.e. to be happy). Do we want this happiness to come to an end? Of course not! We must then want to possess the good forever. As always, readers are invited—indeed, on my reading, have already been invited by Plato's text—to critique/improve on this argument.

If I am to possess the good indefinitely, I must myself go on indefinitely. As 206e–207a shows, the fundamental desire to possess the good forever contains a further desire within itself: we might say that it is pregnant with the desire for immortality! Yet my very status as a mortal creature would seem bound to frustrate this desire. *Erōs* however enables us to transcend mortality through creativity.

Now we see how the bits that have been introduced so far connect up. The very earliest discussion based on the common view that Love desires beauties had broken off because Socrates was not then able to say what is gained when this desire is satisfied (204d). Diotima then switched to the new topic of our desire for goods, and we weren't sure how if at all these would be related (204e). But now we can integrate all our elements, as follows. One falls in love with a beautiful love object. In this way, the account respects the well-known importance of beauty in matters of love. But this is no end in itself. Erotic engagement with the beautiful love object leads to the birth of one's offspring, love's real task. The production and preservation of offspring is the focus of our greatest efforts because leaving behind an offshoot like ourselves is how we extend ourselves into the future. As mortal creatures, this is our only hope for immortality; only in this way do we have the possibility of possessing the good forever (our fundamental motivation).[13]

One sign of both the importance and perhaps the difficulty of the treatment of reproduction is that it is actually repeated in our text. Thus the first exposition (206c–207a) of love's task as birth in beauty waxes on about beauty and then connects reproduction with immortality, in turn necessary for possessing the good forever. At 207a6–c1 Diotima in effect gives Socrates a pop quiz. She draws his attention to the tremendous efforts animals put into their offspring—itself additional support for her view, which was initially most naturally understood in terms of human beings—in gearing up to ask Socrates if he can explain this. To answer the question he would only need to have mastered what she has already said, which can easily be applied to the whole animal kingdom. But Socrates is not able immediately to put all this together, and Diotima goes on to explain again, this second time with much more about how the mortal creature's only way to extend itself into the future and achieve a kind of immortality is by leaving behind something new like itself (207c8–208b6).

So we have seen what I meant by saying that Diotima gives depth to her account of *erōs*. She goes beyond the surface phenomenology of what we are aware of desiring when we fall in love to offer an explanation of the larger purpose that all this is in service of. Part of the power of the account is that it covers not just an isolated human phenomenon, but also goes equally for all other creatures. It is a fact that incredible efforts throughout the animal kingdom go to the progeny project. And there is a highly plausible explanation of this: that humans consciously and animals unconsciously seek to extend themselves into the future through their posterity.

Variants of this thought have by now become commonplace for way more than some circle of committed Platonists. Aristotle expresses a variant of it when he says, "for any living thing that has reached its normal development and which is unmutilated ... the most natural act is the production of another like itself ... in order that, as far as its nature allows, it may partake in the eternal and divine" (*On the Soul* 415a). Another version of the thought, in the form of the idea that the primary mission of living things is to reproduce and protect their young so that they may reproduce in turn and so on, is alive today as a standard part of modern biology.

It is beside the point to complain that Plato has not proved that in having children one survives *strictly speaking* as the subject of future goods. The whole context of this discussion is the admission that we are mortal creatures and so can't survive in *that* sense. What is doing the work here is not some supposed proof of this type of survival, but the observation of how widespread is the phenomenon in which creatures devote very great efforts to offspring, efforts which we naturally take as a way of extending themselves. The larger strategy is to use what we have discussed so far as the basis for the view still under construction. Let's now see how Diotima develops this further when she goes on to offer the idea that, given that we mortal creatures do in fact seek personal immortality so far as possible by extending ourselves through progeny, there are far better ways than the biological one of doing that.

Broader understanding of *erōs*

Are biological offspring our only way to extend ourselves into the future? Some special individuals have an even better option. As we saw in Chapter Three, it was a commonplace of Greek culture that the mighty heroes of the past had aimed to achieve a kind of immortality in their drive to "lay up glory immortal forever" (as the unattributed quotation at 208c puts it).[14] Homer had Sarpedon addressing his comrade:

> Glaukos, why is it you and I are honoured before others
> ... and all men look on us as if we were immortals ...? ...
> Man, supposing you and I, escaping this battle,

would be able to live on forever, ageless, immortal,
so neither would I myself go on fighting in the foremost
nor would I urge you into the fighting where men win glory.
But now, seeing that the spirits of death stand close about us
in their thousands, no man can turn aside nor escape them,
let us go on and win glory for ourselves, or yield it to others.
                    (*Iliad* 12.310–28, tr. Lattimore 1951)

These lines resonate all the more considering that the special characteristic of Sarpedon is the poignancy of his mortality. He is the son of Zeus, but even the most powerful of the gods cannot protect him from death.

Diotima makes many references that direct our attention to this tradition to help us understand what she will go on to say. She speaks of the love of honor among men, gives the example of Achilles—the greatest of the Homeric heroes—and uses a hexameter quotation (dactylic hexameter was the "heroic" meter of epic). While not all this is at first fully worked up in terms of her scheme, it functions by helping readers find an intuition that is friendly to the view under construction. Diotima also immediately assimilates the motivation to have biological children (her previous topic) to that which is explicit in this new idea by saying that through biological children we hope to be remembered (208e). The idea that the dead live on in our memory of them is a commonplace still. Diotima encourages us to think that living on in the memories of one's family is a sort of private version of the Homeric route.

The culturally familiar example of the route the Homeric hero takes to immortal glory thus would have helped Plato's original readers join his line of thought. In fact, this example is described a little differently each time it comes up, in accordance with its bridge function. First is the quotation and the formulation I have been using that the heroes were seeking immortal glory (208c); next we are told they sought immortal memory of their virtue (208d); and finally that what they wanted was immortal virtue and the glorious fame that follows (208d). This sequence travels from the popular conception to a deeper way of understanding the situation still consistent with the original spirit but also appropriate for the ongoing theory.

Diotima at 209a makes explicit that what we are talking about is in fact the generation of a special kind of progeny, the heretofore-mysterious offspring of the soul. She introduces a whole range of talented people who leave behind them offspring of this kind, which in general are identified as *phronēsis* (wisdom/thought) and the rest of virtue. People fecund in this way include poets, craftsmen who are innovators (*heuretikoi*) and lawgivers. Notice that now we have added to the survival of Achilles that of Homer: not only the one who did the deeds, but the one who composed the deathless song about them receives attention. We should regard it as a strength and not a weakness of the passage that it can accommodate a variety of ways in which people create legacies that live on after them.

The example of "the greatest and most beautiful part of wisdom"—that concerned with justice and *sōphrosunē*—gets detailed analysis. Here we learn that the lover ready to give birth seeks out a beloved beautiful in soul as well as body, and pours out to him discourses (*logoi*) about virtue and the qualities and activities a man should have. This production of discourses about virtue seems to be the manifestation in this case of the general giving birth to virtue that the passage concerns.

We can follow up the hint by supposing that the forms of the soul's creativity in view in our passage are typically verbal or propositional in some way. (This is explicit in the ascent passage at 210a ff until—at the very top, "no discourse is generated;" Ferrari 1992: 255–9.) This helps to make sense of the claim that the whole range of creative types mentioned in the passage all give birth to virtue. The poets and warriors of epic produced verses that manifest heroic virtue. Wait—do warriors really produce verses? Consider that "to exist fully in the eyes of the hero who longs to perform them," Achilles' great deeds "must be reflected and preserved in a song that exalts their fame. As a heroic character, Achilles exists to himself only in the mirror of the song that reflects his own image" (Vernant 1991: 59). As Odysseus is repeatedly compared to a singer, "perhaps there is also the meaning that action and the song of action are in a way one—he who does the deeds is creating the song and hearing its resonance" (Griffin 1987: 54).

More straightforwardly, lawgivers hand down codes that spell out and constitute their sort of virtue. And the discoveries of inventors constitute the wisdom of their arts. Notice that Diotima is not discussing here the manufacture by journeymen of individual objects according to an existing prototype. It is an *innovation* like that of riddling Champagne that is in view. (This is the widowed Mme. Clicquot's technique of incrementally twisting bottles so that they are finally upside down with the sediment concentrated next to the cork, allowing the "plug" to be removed and the bottle recorked; the house we know today as Veuve Clicquot was renamed in her honor.)

The glory of the heroes of whom Homer sang, traditionally conceptualized as immortal, has the capacity to last forever, in a way biological offspring do not. Astyanax perished as an infant when he was thrown from the walls of Troy, but even if he had escaped that fate he would by now be long dead, while the fame of his father Hector is more widespread than ever. The problem with biological offspring is ultimately due to their being the same in genus with the original mortal: mortal themselves, they can extend a parent's legacy into only a very limited future. Of course they may in turn have children, but it is all too easy to see that the line may become extinct. By contrast, in Plato's time, the *Iliad* was the common possession of everyone; notice that it had also become independent of direct transmission from one human being to another. Works can be neglected for a time and then rediscovered, as happened with Greek literature in the Renaissance. So, in a sense, these works have a being of their own.[15]

Even while one's biological line continues, its members may not be sufficiently identified with oneself or have sufficiently good lives to satisfy one's original motivation to go on possessing goods. Everyone can come up with an example along the lines of the following from the David Lean movie of *Doctor Zhivago*. The eponymous poet and his beloved Lara live on far more satisfactorily in his "Lara poems" than in the long-orphaned factory drudge in the kerchief who is their biological child. Here too, the soul's creations are more beautiful and more representative of their creator than any ordinary children, as well as being longer-lived.

The superiority both in beauty and in immortality of the soul's offspring (209c) allows us to make sense of the observation that people devote even more zeal to these projects than to children of the body—and the more so the better they are (208c–e).[16] It may also explain the unusual choice of Plato himself, who was doing something considered unpatriotic by not marrying to produce children. Part of the significance of the presentation of a theory of love in a strongly homosexual context must be to provide the countervailing idea that relationships one might have supposed barren actually favor the most wonderful fecundity.

The ascent and the mysteries

We come now to the transition between the passage we have been studying and the culminating passage in which Diotima describes what scholars today tag as "the ascent of love."

> Even you, Socrates, could probably come to be initiated into these rites of love [i.e. those modeled by Homer, Solon, etc.] But as for the full rites and final revelation—the goals [*hōn heneka*] of these [previous] rites when they are done correctly—I don't know if you are capable. I myself will tell you ... and you must try to follow, if you can.
>
> (209e–210a; my translation, based on Griffith 1986 and Nehamas and Woodruff in Cooper, ed., 1997)

Language from the Eleusinian Mysteries is prominent in the passage. While much about these rites is necessarily obscure to us—since it was forbidden to make them public—what we do know is useful.[17] The theme of conception/fertility and the principal purpose of securing better prospects for initiates after death of course make the metaphor thematically appropriate to Diotima's speech.

Most important of all is the structuring role of the metaphor of the Eleusinian Mysteries. The real mysteries involved a sequence: first came purification and initiation in the lesser mysteries; after an interval, initiates could go in for the greater mysteries. Initiates ideally progressed in the course of time from one to the other, and it was wrong to seek admission to the higher rites without having been initiated in the lower. It seems natural to describe this relation by saying that the purpose of the lesser mysteries was to lead on to the greater.

The quotation above shows Diotima invoking this relation between the lesser and greater mysteries. Which portions of her speech describe (the analogues of) which rites, and what is the difference between them? A family of readings that has recently become prominent is based on supposing that Diotima's lesser mysteries are the province of a population of honor-lovers who have been discussed in 208c1–209e4, before the text just quoted; then everything after the quote (i.e. the whole ascent of love) concerns the greater mysteries, enjoyed by a completely disjoint population of philosophically minded people (G. Lear 2006: 107–11; Sheffield 2006; a fore-runner is Ferrari 1992: 255–8).

This interpretation is natural on the assumption that the text always proceeds linearly, so that once the greater mysteries have been mentioned in 210a1 we never go back to hearing about the lesser ones. To identify love of honor as thematic for the earlier passage offers a way to distinguish Diotima's lesser from her greater mysteries. However, one may wonder if this distinction is motivated, perhaps improperly, by scholars' knowledge of the tripartite psychology of the *Republic* and *Phaedrus* (whose composition was probably still in the future when the *Symposium* was written). Much more importantly, if we take lovers of honor as a personality type, then we invite the following problem: the lesser mysteries can't function as a prerequisite for going on to the greater ones if the populations each is aimed at are permanently disjoint. Making the philosophically-minded people concerned with the higher rites a different population from the honor-lovers whose province is the lesser ones makes nonsense of Diotima's claim that the lower rites are for the sake of the higher ones (210a).

We have seen that Diotima's speech in general does not proceed with linear forward progress. To recognize this is to recognize the possibility that we are now dealing with another example of her leisurely pedagogy: the overlapping expository style with which we have become familiar. Thus the initial discussion of the lesser mysteries at 208c1–209e4 (the passage locating the intuition about heroes aiming for undying glory in the surrounding culture) could be a warm-up for the ascent passage, whose content will partially overlap with it. Diotima at the lower stages of the ascent will be revisiting, with some added detail, the lesser mysteries. There are obvious repetitions that establish correspondences between the two passages.

On this reading, we will come to the greater mysteries only at
210e ff. In fact this is introduced with language reminiscent of that
with which Diotima first made the distinction:

> When a man has reached this point in his education in love,
> studying the different types of beauty in correct order, he will
> come to the end [telos] of this education. Then suddenly he will
> see a beauty of a breathtaking nature, Socrates, which is the goal
> [hou heneken] of all his efforts so far ...
>
>   (210e; my translation, largely following Griffith 1986)

Diotima continues to describe this epiphany of Beauty, largely in
terms of how this wondrous object is not like ordinary beauties
(210e6 ff). Even then there is some looping back (211b–d) to
recapitulate the lower and lesser levels before returning to the
heights at the end of the passage. On this reading, the key distinction
between the lesser and greater mysteries is a matter of the beauties
the lover engages with: a safe but limited formulation is to say the
difference derives from whether or not a lover's engagement
(sunousia) is with the Form.

With this large-scale map of the passage in hand, let's look in
more detail at the ascent itself. Its lowest stage concerns a lover
("Platonic" in the proper sense) who is different from what we are
ordinarily used to. For while he at first seems familiar because he is
attracted to beautiful bodies and starts by falling in love with one
person, he begets discourses (logoi). Thus his offspring are of exactly
the sort we have been conditioned to expect by the warm-up
passage—he is producing love poetry or something of the sort.
Since the discourses he produces are praise of the beauty of his
beloved, and since the praise must involve general terms, the lover
is led to an apprehension of beauty of form in general. He sees that
the beauty of all bodies is one and the same (Price 1989: 41, citing
Robin and Moravscik). He now loves a series of people with
beautiful bodies—in this not departing from the ancient pattern
(Blondell 2006).

Next our lover "must" think beauty of soul more valuable than
that of the body, fall in love with someone beautiful in soul if that
person has some bodily bloom, and give birth to such discourses

"as will make young men better." While it is no doubt correct and familiar to the ancient Greek reader that the lover is here educating the beloved, we have learned from the warm-up passage also to describe this process as one whereby the lover has given birth to some sort of virtue. It perhaps best respects the over-all scheme to suppose that the offspring are these propositional items the lover produces. Then he gets the advantage of having produced something deathless.[18] We are now told that he moves on[19] to beautiful practices and laws, and then to the beauty of various kinds of knowledge, giving birth to many beautiful discourses (*logoi*) and thoughts (*dianoēmata*).

The new love object at each stage can be seen to be in some way the source of the beauty that attracted us at the previous stage (Patterson 1991). Hence the increasing value of the series of love objects. This is hardest to see for the early step from bodies to souls. The idea could perhaps be that one comes to think that what one previously thought of as "beautiful eyes" are so as expressing, for example, sympathy of spirit; what one thought of as a striking jaw is so as reflecting courage; and so on (cf. Price 1989: 47 n. 54). Increasing value of the love objects may also come from the increasing value of the offspring we have with them.

In connection with the intellectual creations of lovers, there is a puzzle that will be interesting to consider: "if the lover's understanding is genuine, then the account he grasps will not differ from the account of anyone else who genuinely understands. But in that case, how will his articulation of the account bring about the quasi-immortality of him rather than of anyone else who understands?" (G. Lear 2006: 111 n. 20) The idea seems to be that someone's articulation of a mathematical theorem say—whose truth many others can grasp—is not distinctively his. But let's reflect further on this case. Both in our notion of mathematical discovery and in Plato's picture of mathematics, one sees the truth of a theorem by providing a proof for it. What kind of proof one can come up with and how one presents it in fact do show the character of one's own mind; different people can develop brute-force and elegant proofs of the same result; surprising or systematic presentations, etc.[20] The *logoi* (discourses/accounts/arguments) and *dianoēmata* (thoughts) the lover is said to produce can easily be expansive enough to include a lover's proof together with his theorem, in which case his offspring will be just as much produced by and reflective of himself as love poetry and such lower-level progeny evidently are.

As we saw in our initial discussion of the lower mysteries, Diotima presented the great heroes of the past as having lived and died in service of the wish more recently expressed in popular culture by the theme song from *Fame* ("I'm gonna live forever!") The superiority of this strategy to that of animal reproduction was due to the dual circumstances that the offspring is better than an ordinary child and also not subject to the fragility and dilution attendant on the chains by which a biological line is propagated. Our present, fuller passage's direct treatment of scientific and mathematical offspring has just been the occasion for us to see that something analogous to what we said about Achilles will still be true: our Platonic lover will give birth to discourses distinctive of himself, with a much more robust being than a physical baby could be expected to have, and typically associated with his name (consider such tags as "the Turing test" or "Gödel's incompleteness theorem").

After the description of this stage comes the renewed fanfare I have already mentioned (210e); then Diotima describes the climax of the ascent (211a–212a). In the real Mysteries the ultimate level is some sort of special vision. Diotima's description uses the metaphor of a vision, while also keeping the elements that have constituted her theory of *erōs* very much in play. The lover gazes now on Beauty itself (*auto to kalon*) and is with it, so we still have a beautiful love object and erotic engagement. *Sunousia*, literally "being with," is commonly used in sexual contexts but is characteristically coopted by Plato to denote philosophical interaction—whether with conversation partners or, as here, with a Form.

The lover will give birth this time not to images (this status of the progeny at lower levels was not explicit before) but to true virtue. Following the suggestion that we regard all generated offspring of the soul as propositional, this would mean that the epiphany of Beauty enables the lover now for the first time to produce discourses/accounts and thoughts that are fully adequate. The reason for this must be because he now knows what Beautiful is (*ho esti kalon*; 211c–d). If we think of the lover's conception here as concerned *solely* with understanding Beauty, it is trivially true that only now (having seen that) can he do this fully adequately. If we think the lover is also discoursing on all of virtue and/or *acting* in a way that essentially involves understanding Beauty, then the idea would be that the epiphany of the Beautiful somehow completes his preliminary understanding, in the way the *Republic* will posit in the case of the Good.

Until now, we have been discussing the production of offspring that live on for indefinite durations in the world of change. But we must now consider something unique to the highest level. The lover at our passage's climax experiences rapture with a love object that is not in space and time, and not subject to any change or qualification (G. Lear 2006: 116–20). Beauty itself does not so much exist at all times, but in Plato's view has some mode of being which is outside time (Owen 1966 traces the development of the issues involved). If we can see the experience of the lover at the top of the ascent as taking on—from the inside—the timeless character of its eternal object, this would make the episode of contemplation timeless from within. Of course when viewed so to speak "from the ground" it would occupy only a finite stretch of time, but within the experience, the lover would take on the mode of being of Beauty itself. This would account for Diotima's indication that such a lover transcends the mortal (212a).

The progress of an initiate in the mysteries must have seemed a perfect parallel as soon as Plato thought of representing our highest achievement by the metaphor of gazing on a divine object, which experience is not available to any chance person but requires special preparation and then in some way cannot be communicated. This will be a favorite trope especially notable in the *Republic* and *Phaedrus* as well. The special experience that an initiate at the highest level undergoes was a culturally familiar analogue to the engagement with rarefied intellectual objects whose extraordinary status Plato now stresses—quite possibly for the first time—in the case of Beauty.

Is it fanciful to suppose that within the experience of gazing on the Beautiful itself our lover would take on the Form's mode of being? As confirmation for the way I have suggested we understand the highest level of Diotima's ascent, let us end with a quote from

Proclus, a later head of the Academy who was acquainted with the daughter of the Eleusinian hierophant. In his commentary on Plato's *Republic*, he remarks about the real Mysteries:

> They cause sympathy of the souls with the ritual in a way that is unintelligible to us, and divine, so that some of the initiands are stricken with panic, being filled with divine awe; *others assimilate themselves to the holy symbols, leave their own identity, become at home with the gods, and experience divine possession.*
>
> (Burkert 1987: 114; emphasis mine)[21]

Alcibiades

With this climax our chapter might end—but Plato's *Symposium* does not stop here. Alcibiades now bursts onto the scene: sudden, attractive, and dangerous. In real life, this famous and controversial figure failed notoriously to realize the promise of his brilliant talents and privileged background. A ward of Pericles who through his genius and glamour became a leading figure at Athens before flaming out, he has elicited opposite reactions from antiquity until today. Thus Aristophanes *Frogs* 1425 has it that "the city longs for him, it hates him, it wants to have him" (tr. Hunter 2004: 104). Embroiled in scandal and recalled from the Sicilian Expedition in order to stand trial, he fled abroad and went over to the Spartans. Meanwhile the expedition was left to the leadership of the incompetent Nicias and the ensuing disaster was a key event in Athens' comprehensive defeat in the Peloponnesian War. Of course these events are still in the future at the fictional date of the party— but in the past at the time of composition, so that Plato would have expected readers to see Alcibiades here in light of the well-known sequelae.

Where our symposiasts had waived heavy drinking, Alcibiades arrives already drunk. Where the others had agreed democratically on their procedure, he seizes control and appoints himself leader of the revels. Where Socrates has been discoursing on the relationship of humans to the good (*to agathon*), Alcibiades has been looking for Agathon ("Mr Good"). Where the others had discussed *erōs* in general, he narrates his own erotic encounter with Socrates.

Alcibiades' encomium of Socrates has special significance in light of the fact that the philosopher's reputation in some quarters as a corrupter of the youth was fueled by the belief that he was responsible for the career of Alcibiades. The speech of that famous figure here thus turns out to be among other things one more in the series of Plato's defences of Socrates. Praise of the philosopher as the best influence in the young man's life—despite which he was turned away from good courses by his own ambition—comes in the form of direct testimony from Alcibiades himself.

While this fascinating figure claims that he will tell the truth about Socrates (214e and throughout), his speech ends up revealing at least as much about himself. Instead of relying primarily on direct quotation so as to appear as a mere conduit for original speech, he proceeds primarily in what I called "description style;" he is explicitly giving us his interpretation and summary of the episodes he relates. Alcibiades ends up showing us his own philosophical passivity and how it has led to his being tragicomically at cross purposes with Socrates.

The figure of Alcibiades in the *Symposium* introduces a plethora of reversals—and not only along the dimensions I have mentioned. Central is the reversal at the core of the encounter between Alcibiades and Socrates (216d–219e). The glamour boy tells us that, confident in his attractiveness, he expected the notoriously susceptible Socrates to educate him in return for sexual favors. Descending from stratagems for seduction to outright propositioning of the older man, the beautiful Alcibiades offered his body to the philosopher—and was spurned. Thus the pursued had become the pursuer, and not sexual penetration but the withholding of sex was experienced as insult. The one passage of conversation Alcibiades presents through direct quotes is when Socrates commits the outrage of rejecting him (218c–219b). It is this rather than any of the extended philosophical discussions they have had that he takes the trouble to impress directly on us. Thus he unwittingly shows us his real priorities.

Alcibiades has made all the running in courtship but still expects to take the passive role in intercourse, and is disappointed when nothing happens. Similarly when it comes to his supposed interest in his own improvement, his activity is confined to stratagems to seduce Socrates; he assumes that he will then get to hear all Socrates' knowledge (217a). Alcibiades thinks that he can acquire knowledge by transfer (cf. Agathon at the party, 175c–d). The social stigma associated with sexual passivity finds a Platonic parallel in intellectual passivity: the problem with Alcibiades is that he expects Socrates in each case to "give it to him." In fact, as we saw in Chapter Two, this attitude is completely unphilosophical. And Diotima's speech in this very dialogue (recounted of course before Alcibiades' arrival on the scene) has just shown the very extensive program of activity a lover must embark on if he is going to attain virtue and truth (Hunter 2004: 98–112). Alcibiades, like Agathon, trivializes knowledge by the ease with which he expects it can be acquired.

From the perspective of Alcibiades, the Platonic ascent of love is incomprehensible. He reminds us of a familiar constellation of feelings that can be associated with *erōs* when it is fixated on the unique—and maddening—character of an individual person: adulation, possessiveness, jealousy, etc. Putting this intervention after the recounted wisdom of Diotima prevents us from being too complacent in having received "the authoritative account;" we must consider Diotima's lessons in juxtaposition with this outburst. Moreover, Alcibiades' complexity is such that we may well alternate unstably between admiration of his glamour and condemnation of his unreliability. Plato has set it up so that our competing reactions to Alcibiades will generate competing assessments of his response to Socrates. In effect, Plato both helps us crystallize incipient rejection of the program he has just suggested, and provides an impetus for us to have second thoughts about any such hasty rejection. If the intellectual passivity of Alcibiades is indeed the reason for his failing to make the progress he had hoped would result from his association with Socrates, Plato is doing what he can to set us up to exert ourselves and not assume we can gain knowledge simply from any such short-cut as sitting next to Socrates, sleeping with him— or reading about him.

Further reading

The *Phaedrus* also contains a significant treatment of *erōs*.

Secondary literature

See Bibliography for full details of the works listed below.

G. Ferrari (1992) "Platonic Love."

R Hunter (2004) *Plato's "Symposium."* Very good on the literary elements.

L. Kosman (1974) "Platonic Love."

J. Lear (1998) "Eros and Unknowing." Psychoanalytic significance of Alcibiades.

J. Lesher, D. Nails, and F. Sheffield (eds) (2006) *Plato's "Symposium."* A collection of "new millennium" articles.

M. Nussbaum (1986) "The Speech of Alcibiades."

R. Patterson (1991) "The Ascent in Plato's *Symposium*."

A. Price (1989) *Love and Friendship in Plato and Aristotle.* Has a chapter on the *Symposium*.

G. Santas (1988) *Plato and Freud.*

F. Sheffield (2006) *Plato's "Symposium."*

G. Vlastos (1973b) "The Individual as Object of Love in Plato." Enormously influential though the problem he set has now been solved by realizing the topic of the *Symposium* is *erōs* as opposed to *all* types of love.

Notes

1 Thus *erōs* is a fundamental force that lies behind all non-biological creativity as well as all biological fecundity. The anticipation of Freud which strikes modern readers is confirmed by Freud's own remarks See J. Lear (2005: 19, 83–4, 87).

2 In the *Symposium*, the shortcomings of the speeches of Aristophanes and Agathon are relevant. The *Protagoras* and *Republic* (the former by example and the latter both by example and by direct discussion) also indicate problems with relying on great poetry as a guide.

3 Using ellipses to take out parts of the formulation special to the *Republic*, which Ferrari was describing.

4 Plato will use a similar technique in the triply framed *Parmenides* (McCabe 1996; Meinwald 2005).

5 Remember that Love can be construed as the personification of a force manifested in human life. A parallel explanation: these are what Peterson (1973) called "Pauline predications" (named after the star example: "Charity suffereth long," etc.).

6 The frequency with which Agathon is shown bearing the designation "beautiful" together with the fact that by his name he bears the designation "good"

(eliciting a pun from Socrates in the action before the party) gestures towards this issue.

7 I use this phrasing because calling people "beauties" is more normal English than calling them "beautifuls."

8 One possibility for why Plato made Diotima a woman is to show that, despite the presentation in a group made up of men only, the doctrine itself is not connected with hatred of women. Not seeing women as essentially erotic objects for men may actually free Plato to see that both sexes have the fundamental human capacities in common. There were two women students in Plato's Academy. Paula Gottlieb (personal communication) has offered the brilliant suggestion that "Diotima of Mantinea" refers to them—one was named Axiothea (i.e. a name with parallel meaning to Diotima's), and the other hailed from Mantinea.

9 This translation makes explicit that Jowett takes *edidaske* as the imperfect of iterated or customary action.

10 Since the fundamental goal is to have the good forever, extensions of our lives in frustration or torment are not in view.

11 By speaking schematically of the fundamental motivation as being possession of "the good" or "goods" because this constitutes happiness our text avoids having to go into the details of what things actually are good, and of how particular goods are arrayed in making up happiness.

12 Our text says only that we want "the good" forever (and never that each particular good is such that we desire to go on enjoying it forever). Thus Diotima is not subject to Santas's objection of the ice cream cone: he desires the ice cream, but not that he go on eating that cone forever (1988: 53–4 with fn 35). True enough; that particular cone has only a momentary contribution to make to the good, which is what we desire to have forever.

13 I regard as a red herring the widespread view that a distinction between "generic" *erōs* (desire for any good) and "specific" *erōs* (which gives birth in beauty) is thematic for our passage. It is hard to cash out the genus-species relationship, and there is a problem reconciling the implication of 205a-d that special *erōs* is the regular sexual kind with the fact that 206b (which proponents of this view take to introduce special *erōs*) is about pregnancy in body *and* soul. Forcing everything into this model prevents Santas (1988: ch. 2) from carrying out his early insight (ibid.: 31, 52 fn 31) that we can usefully distinguish the love object from the aim of *erōs* in Diotima as in Freud.

14 Consider the useful remarks of Vernant (1991: 57): "Archaic Greek culture is one in which everyone lives ... under the eyes and in the esteem of others ... real existence—for the living or the dead—comes from being recognized, valued, and honored ... [the hero] continues, beyond the reach of death, to be present in the community of the living. Converted into legend and linked with others like it, his personality forms the skein of a tradition that each generation must learn and make its own in order to enter fully into social and cultural existence ..."

15 To compensate for its loss of cultural centrality, Homer's work now is encoded

in so many places that its loss is almost inconceivable without the destruction of the planet.

16 Consider this from Alexandra Styron: "if each creation is, in effect, an artist's offspring, I think Daddy put his nonfiction in the category with his four living, breathing, children ... But the Novel owned his heart" (Wood 2013: 72).

17 Sattler (2013) provides a comprehensive review of pre-Platonic evidence which is useful though insufficient to determine a single correct interpretation of the ascent of love.

18 Not the case with "educative pederasty," which makes the success of the lover depend on a chain no less fragile than that we earlier found characteristic of biological parents: the beloved *may* in turn educate another, who may educate another, and so on—or not. Sheffield (2006) rejects "educative pederasty" as providing the essential products of the lover.

19 While lovers who ascend are able to put their earlier love objects "in their place" and see them as less significant than higher objects, this need not imply that they have no further dealings with them. Apprehension of Beauty itself must after all lead to better appreciation of individual beauties.

20 Netz (2009) gives a wealth of detail in connection with Greek mathematics, and offers the intriguing thesis that different styles of proving theorems are also cultural, so that there is, for example, a mathematical analogue to Alexandrian poetry.

21 Burkert (1987) says that the varied descriptions show that Proclus is giving actual observations and not "speculation based on postulates."

Five

Psychē I

From pre-Platonic sources to the *Phaedo*

Introduction

The Greek *psychē* (pl. *psychai*) conventionally appears in English as the "soul." This entity is central in Plato's discussions of human beings, and its existence is challenged by none among his varied cast of characters. Yet in today's world, most uses of the word "soul" are not even meant literally. (Consider "his playing lacks soul" or "give me some more of that soul food.") Serious talk of the soul is reserved for specialized religious and theological contexts. The relevant communities typically accept a raft of commitments which many in our secular society would prefer not to make. Atheists regard tenets about the soul as misguided; biology and cosmology proceed without reference to this entity. Most philosophers dispense completely with considering the soul. And if it has to be a subject of philosophical discussion, it seems that the main question should be whether we even *have* a soul: whether there is any such entity at all.

The difference between the present dialectical situation with regard to the soul and that concerning the *psychē* in Greek antiquity is not due to the advance of science so much as to the way in which our usage of the word "soul" differs from that of the Greek *psychē*. While "soul" for us if meant literally carries with it the religious idea of the immaterial and immortal subject of sin or redemption, the core notion of the *psychē* was simply that of whatever makes the difference between things that are alive and things that are not. Thus the existence of *psychē* was no more controversial than the distinction between the animate and the inanimate.[1] Yet specifying the *psychē* by its functional role left it completely open what in fact plays that role. So while the question whether we have a *psychē* did not seem pressing, questions concerning its nature and character were very much in order. As far as the core notion goes, our *psychē* might—but need not—be identified with something physical. It might—but need not—be a "fitting together" of physical elements or a functional organization. It might—but need not—be separately viable. It might—but need not—be taken to be our real self. It might—but need not—be thought to have what we today consider "psychological" capacities of feeling, intellect, and action. And it might—but need not—be thought to be immortal.

Ēthikē—by word-formation the study of character—is for Plato the study of the character of our *psychē*, which he takes to be the real subject of our moral, emotional, and intellectual life (and hence as we might put it our real self). This "moral psychology" has been in vogue among philosophers in recent decades because of contemporary interests. Yet Plato also takes our *psychē* to be a non-physical entity that is joined with a body in forming a living creature, and he repeatedly discusses its immortality. He clearly has taken on elements from the Orphic and Pythagorean religious tradition, just as he in turn would influence developments among the Neoplatonists and in Christianity.

Why did Plato put all these elements together? If we start our study of the *psychē* with the Phaedo, Plato appears to be a wishful thinker who decided for some bizarre reason to identify the factor that makes the difference between a live human being and a corpse as reason, and then declared this soul to be immaterial and immortal. What he is doing becomes more interesting if we appreciate the intellectual context for Plato's work. Thus our starting point will be this background. We will see that in our earliest source, Homer, the *psychē* is a "shade" which goes to the house of Hades on the death of a human being. On Homer's primary picture, the *psychē* has none of the psychological capacities. However, by Plato's time, a series of influences—none accompanied by adequate argument—had led to ordinary speakers' attributing the whole range of capacities we now consider "psychological" to the *psychē*. Concerning whether or not it was material and whether or not it was immortal, opinion was divided. Our review of this background will make us aware of the particular questions that needed attention, questions that we will see addressed in Plato's work.

After the section on background, we will go on in this chapter to read the *Phaedo* with a view to its contribution to this program. (Chapter Six will take up the story with continuing developments in the *Republic*.) The inner dialogue in the *Phaedo* represents Socrates' conversation with his friends in prison right before and as his death sentence is carried out. Thus the question of his attitude to death naturally arises: he is jokingly accused of not being sorry enough to leave his friends. The defense Socrates gives to this charge introduces the main philosophical agenda of the dialogue (63b ff). This defense is that our best chance of enjoying wisdom, the goal of a philosopher's life, is after death when the soul will be freed from the distractions and distortions forced on its thinking by embodiment. For Socrates' defense to work, we must identify ourselves with our soul, which survives our present life, and has wisdom. Thus the dialogue is to take up some of the leading points we will have identified as needing philosophical attention in the historical context.

In the major portion of this chapter, we will read each of the *Phaedo*'s arguments in turn to see how they contribute to the dialogue's main agenda. First will be the "cyclical argument." This offers support for a cyclical pattern of the soul's career as in the ancient story mentioned in 70c. Plato introduces for this purpose the prototype of the Aristotelian model of change. Despite this philosophical innovation, its application in the cyclical argument is open to a variety of objections. Moreover, the argument does not begin to address whether the *psychē* has any interesting capacities or why we should identify ourselves with it.

Thus when we come to the immediate sequel, the "recollection argument," we will have been prepared to appreciate the importance of its contributing—alone in the dialogue—an argument for considering our soul to be the real possessor of intelligence/knowledge/wisdom, and for identifying ourselves with it. On the other hand, we will note that, when it comes to the extent of the soul's career, the recollection argument does not attempt to show more than that the soul pre-exists our present life. Socrates himself says that for survival of our present life, we must join this to the preceding cyclical argument (or, presumably, one of the immortality arguments still to come.)

We will then trace out how the "affinity argument" takes off from a two-tiered world-view already in use in Presocratic science. That argument's achievement concerning the soul's career is limited in a different way: the affinity of the soul with eternal beings only establishes that it is likely to be immortal or *nearly so*. The discussion provides further information on the eternal, fundamental objects to which the soul is akin: what Plato considers "real" and "true." This affords a translation into Platonic of traditional Pythagorean talk of purification, and of the optimal state of the soul.

So at that point in our reading, we will have a fairly good understanding of the claims in the text about the soul being our real self which is happiest when able to enjoy wisdom free from the concerns of embodiment. Thus we will see how Socrates' defense and equanimity in the face of death would be complete—if only survival was better established than by the cyclical and affinity arguments. We will thus appreciate the role of the "final argument" and the "intellectual autobiography" that leads into it. Plato in those passages gives a sketch of a philosophical program for giving explanatory accounts and also saying "more sophisticated" (or "more fancy": Denyer 2007b) things. While all this is tremendously general, in the context of the dialogue the point is a single application. I will offer a reconstruction of Socrates' argument for the conclusion that the soul is invulnerable to death.

In the final section of this chapter, we will note a protreptic dimension to Plato's compositional strategy in the two most important arguments. He actually includes explicit statements at the ends of both the recollection argument and the final argument that make this clear. Socrates tells his friends that in order fully to understand these, one must grasp more adequately their starting-points. Thus the interest all of us naturally have in our own prospects and those of our friends after death is transferred to the claims the arguments have employed about fundamental reality: the Platonic Forms.

Our overall objective in this chapter is to understand how the historical development of the notion of the *psychē* left important issues needing philosophical work, and how Plato undertook some of the most important parts of that in the *Phaedo*. The story will continue with the *Republic*, which we will take up in Chapter Six.

Background and context

Our earliest source (from around 700 BC) for the *psychē* is Homer. While *psychē* in the *Iliad* and *Odyssey* is sometimes rendered by "soul" as with later Greek, alternatives include "shade," "ghost," and "phantom"—or even "breath of life." We can readily see why "soul" can seem out of place: Homer speaks of the *psychē* only when people are dead (or knocked out), and even then, on his official conception, it lacks any significant capacities. Far from considering the *psychē* to be our true self, Homer seems rather to identify the body with the person. Indeed, the Homeric *psychē* is no more than an insubstantial likeness of the body. In light of this, I will stick to the transliteration *psychē* for this archaic context. Let's consider the situation now in some detail.[2]

The signature activity of the Homeric *psychē* is this: at the death of a human being, it goes to Hades. From among myriad texts, we can take the opening of the *Iliad*, where we learn that the theme is "the wrath" of "Peleus' son, Achilles, that baneful wrath which brought countless woes upon the Achaeans, and sent forth to Hades many valiant souls [*psychai*] of warriors" (*Iliad* 1.2–4, tr. Murray 1924–5).

Existence in the underworld is not to be desired. As Achilles puts it, thinking of the death of his comrade Patroclus: "Alas, there survives in the Halls of Hades / A soul [*psychē*], a mere phantasm [*eidōlon*], with its wits completely gone" (*Iliad* 23.103–4 as quoted in *Republic* 386d). Perhaps the most famous judgment on existence in Hades is rendered by the shade of Achilles when its wits are temporarily restored, at *Odyssey* 11.489–91.

Psychai of those who have died are repeatedly called *eidōla* (phantasms; in addition to the passage just quoted, see *Iliad* 23.72; *Odyssey* 11.83, 476, 602; 24.14. In this paragraph I draw on Vernant 1991: 186–8 and Heubeck and Hoekstra 1989: esp. 69, 90.) They are apparitions in the literal sense that they give the appearance of the living, while no longer possessed of the substance of corporeality. Thus Homer tells of "the ghost [*psychē*] of unhappy Patroklos / all in his likeness for stature, and the lovely eyes, and voice" (*Iliad* 23.65–7, tr. Lattimore 1951).

Psychai are called or likened to smoke, shadows, and dreams, presumably because we are familiar with the way these can take on the shapes of things without their reality (*Odyssey* 10.495; 11.207, 222; *Iliad* 23.100). A *psychē* cannot be embraced (*Iliad* 23.100–101; *Odyssey* 11.205–7) and, bodiless, must be generally incapable of physical action (the occupants of Hades are called "strengthless heads of the perished dead" at *Odyssey* 11.49, tr. Lattimore 1967). As is natural given their status in the same category as smoke and shadows, Homeric *psychai* are normally without wits or mind (*Iliad* 23.103–4; *Odyssey* 10.491–5; 11.475).

Homer generally does not identify these phantasms with the original heroes. Thus our opening quotation famously continues: "that baneful wrath which ... sent forth to Hades many valiant souls [*psychai*] of warriors, and made themselves to be a spoil for dogs and all manner of birds" (*Iliad* 1.1–5, tr. Murray 1924–5; emphasis added). That is, "themselves" refers to the dead bodies by contrast with the *psychai* that have gone to Hades.

Odysseus' narration of the advice Circe gave him about his consultation of the *psychē* of the prophet Teiresias (*Odyssey* Book 10) and also of the consequent necromancy episode (Book 11) is composed to maintain consistency on the points we have been considering (in this paragraph and the next, following Heubeck and Hoekstra 1989 on the passages in question). Circe informs Odysseus that he must:

> reach the house of Hades and of revered Persephone,
> there to consult with the soul [*psychē*] of Teiresias the Theban,
> the blind prophet, whose senses[3] [*phrenes*] stay unshaken within
> him,
> to whom alone Persephone has granted intelligence
> even after death, but the rest of them are flittering shadows.
> (10.491–5, tr. Lattimore 1967)

This reaffirms that, without special dispensation, the *psychai* in Hades lack *phrenes* (wits) and *noos* (often translated as "mind" or "intellect"—but not "mind" in the broadest usage: the characteristic activity of Homeric *noos* is recognizing the true nature of a situation: Lesher 1981). Book 10 and the first part of Book 11 stress the need for the drinking of sacrificial blood if the witless wraiths are temporarily to recover the original person's memories (e.g. at 11.144–9, 153). Without this infusion, what Odysseus takes to be his own mother—really her *eidōlon* (image/phantom)—cannot recognize him.

But after a point, the blood is no longer mentioned. Book 11 goes on to include meetings with *psychai* who are able to recognize and converse with Odysseus without sanguinary aid, and to show Odysseus observing the punishment of famous sinners. And in Book 24, the occupants of Hades are shown in full possession of their memories. They make judgments and recognize the *psychai* of the suitors to Odysseus' wife Penelope when these arrive in the underworld.

From the point of view of our present inquiry, these passages are confusing. We cannot help asking: Wait, are these occupants of Hades really the original guys? And do they have their wits after all?

In terms of what the poet wants to give his audience, it is desirable to include such episodes as the cameo appearances by favorite characters from the *Iliad* (most of whom were dead by the time of the events related in the *Odyssey*), the set-piece of the punishment of the legendary sinners, and the climactic meeting with Hercules (whose own greatest exploit had been the descent to Hades to fetch Cerberus). We may suppose generally that this type of consideration counts for more with Homer than any tensions between the way these must be presented and his official treatment of the *psychē*. After all, his purpose is to compose a song for the entertainment of an audience, not to write a metaphysical treatise. (On how the purposes of the poet can outweigh concern for consistency of the poem as a whole on this among other points see Griffin 1987: 26–32, 87–90; on glimpses in Homer of popular conceptions of Hades inconsistent with his official view see Heubeck and Hoekstra 1989: 77, 112, 114.)

To return now from the underworld, we should consider how our epics describe those capacities of living persons that we ourselves have come to consider psychological. We find pervasive mention variously of the heart (*kradiē* and related words) and the spirit (*thumos*), as well as of *noos* and *phrēn* (pl. *phrenes*), in connection with the full range of psychological and mental activities that would later be absorbed by the *psychē*. So while Homer is, of course, able to treat human beings in all their richness and complexity, he nowhere says that the activities of our heart, spirit,[4] *phrēn*, and *noos* belong to the *psychē* and as we saw, he denies *phrēn* and *noos* to the *psychē* in Hades. It goes beyond his brief as a poet to discuss explicitly whether there is any level other than that of the human being at which one thing is the subject of all this.

To sum up, Homer clearly associates the *psychē* with the difference between life and death. The Homeric *psychē* goes, on the death of the human being, to the house of Hades. On Homer's official conception, the *psychē* is a mere shade, no more than a phantasm, but sometimes we get traces in his text of other conceptions, according to which *psychai* pick up socially where the living characters left off, and receive punishment for misdeeds in this life.

What would a bodiless *psychē* have to be to qualify credibly as a subject of experience after death, and for these vicissitudes to be rewards or tortures for us? An extreme answer to this question is due to the philosopher and mystic Pythagoras (sixth century BC). Pythagoras was an important influence on Plato because of his interest in the mathematical proportions that underlie music—he pioneered the idea that these were literally of cosmic significance, explaining the harmony of the spheres and everything else that is ordered well. But our present concern is not his mathematical investigations but his florid doctrine of metempsychosis (for texts, translations, and discussion see Kirk, Raven, and Schofield 1983: ch. 7). According to this, our *psychē* is temporarily housed in a body. After departing from our present body it can come back to be reincarnated, and so on, again and again. If it has purified itself through the cultivation of virtue, it may be released from the cycle and live on in discarnate form. Since the idea is meant to be that this whole career is ours, the *psychē* must not just go on after our death but be plausibly identified with ourselves.

So for Pythagoras, the post-mortem career of a person's *psychē* was to be seen as the continuation of the same person. An insubstantial simulacrum of the body was not suited to that role, so the *psychē* had to be bulked up with at least some of the capacities and attributes of the living self (Furley 1956; Barnes 1982: ch. 6). An interesting question arises here about whether the soul should for this purpose have all our traits and capacities or, if a subset will do, what that should be.

Pythagoras seems to have gone to an extreme. In a famous story, he begs someone to stop beating a puppy because it is "a friend, a human soul" which he recognized when he "heard him yelp" (Diogenes Laertius *Lives of Eminent Philosophers* 8.36, tr. Hicks 1925). So not only does the Pythagorean soul maintain its identity in extremely different incarnations, but its expression is still recognizable! On the Pythagorean picture, our present life is an opportunity for purification which may be rewarded by the soul's being freed from further incarnation. So while some of the Pythagorean soul's activities are done during this life, in its most pure form it is unsullied by embodiment. Unlike the Homeric shade, the Pythagorean soul is in a happy and blessed state when it manages to escape from the body.

By contrast, many Presocratic philosophers identified some physical thing as psychē. For remember that the basic notion of the psychē was what makes the difference between something living and something dead; this did not dictate whether or not the entity in question is physical. One candidate, which may pick up on the notion reflected in the idiom "he breathed his last," was air (the choice of Anaximenes and of the eclectic Diogenes of Apollonia). The choice of fire (Heraclitus) may draft on the association represented in the phrase "cold as the grave." Yet this physicalism about the psychē need not mean denying it mental capacities: Heraclitus is actually the earliest surviving author (fifth century BC) to give the psychē a crucial intellectual role in addition to other functions. And Diogenes would hold that psychē was responsible for intelligence as well as life. By his time the culture had already come to give intelligence to the psychē; Diogenes seems to have made explicit some support deriving from the correlation of our loss of breathing, loss of life, and loss of intelligence (fragment 4).

Even before the Pythagorean speculations we have been considering, the lyric poets had invoked the psychē in connection with emotion. But by the fifth century BC usage broadens dramatically: we find an extremely wide range of contexts concerning character and thought as well as emotion in which authors who are not developing a special theory of the *psychē* mention it. Some extracts will give us a feeling for the range of this usage.

In Euripides, Hippolytus has a "virgin *psychē*" because of his sexual innocence; the soul in the *Ion* is interested in food (translations in this paragraph from Furley 1956). In general not just desires, but love, grief, joy, and anger are the province of the *psychē*. In Pindar we have the earliest surviving use of *psychē* in connection with courage: "Surely it will remind him in what battles amid wars he once held his ground with steadfast *psychē*" (*Pythian* 1). This usage soon spreads from poetry to prose (cf. Herodotus 7.153; Thucydides 2.40.3). And the Hippocratic *Airs, Waters, Places* puts its theory of the impact of local conditions on people in terms of souls: we are informed that in the lowlands endurance is not naturally in souls, and that the natives enjoying a benevolent climate are weak in soul (chs 23 and 24). *Psychē* can also be straightforwardly invoked in connection with planning and decision-making. From Sophocles we have "A kindly *psychē* with just thoughts is a better inventor than any sophist" (fr. 101; cf. Euripides *Orestes* 1180). Antiphon in a law-court speech relies on both the what-is-lost-at-death and the deliberator roles when he says "take away from the accused the *psychē* that planned the crime" (4a7).

Thus, by the fifth century BC, it was standard to speak of the *psychē* not just as what we lose in death, but as the real subject of our actions and passions while we are alive—of our emotions, plans, moral characteristics, and thoughts. The *psychē* had taken on the whole range of states, activities, and receptivities that we today consider psychological.

On the subject of the soul's survival however, there was no general agreement within Plato's culture. Orphism and mystery religion presuppose it—otherwise punishment after death, or a better afterlife through initiation in mysteries make no sense. Yet clearly this was not universally supposed to have been established. Cephalus in the *Republic* reports that when we get old we become fearful lest tales about reward/punishment in Hades, which we had previously been confident enough to ignore, might be true after all. Cebes in the *Phaedo* gives us a window into everyday thinking when he says to Socrates:

men find it very hard to believe what you said about the soul. They think that after it has left the body it no longer exists anywhere, but that it is destroyed and dissolved on the day the man dies, as soon as it leaves the body; and that, on leaving it, it is dispersed like breath or smoke, has flown away and gone and is no longer anything anywhere.

(70a)

Cebes himself has studied with the Pythagorean Philolaus. So these touches indicate that, far from that sect having convinced everyone else of the soul's immortality, the influence on this point was the other way around: ordinary people's doubts undermined the confidence even of card-carrying Pythagoreans. In general, through the background of the characters of the *Phaedo*, Plato makes the point that the Pythagoreans have not established important theses of the soul's character and immortality adequately (Sedley 1995).

And perhaps the reference to smoke also takes a swipe at Homer: on his conception the *psychē* was like smoke, so what keeps it together? In fact, the Homeric notion that the body, not the *psychē*, is ourself still has some pull. In the *Phaedo*'s depiction of the deathbed of Socrates, Crito asks his childhood friend how they should bury him—earning a darkly humorous rebuke from the philosopher for having missed the whole point of the discussion, according to which our real self is our immortal soul, which goes on to better things leaving behind an unimportant corpse (115c–116a).

Putting all this together, the picture we get is that by Plato's time the tenet of the soul's immortality was in a similar position to that it occupies today: some people had religious doctrines about it, everyone was familiar with tales about rewards and punishments after death, but many did not believe definitely in immortality. It is of course open to individuals today simply to give up belief in the soul and to stop talking about it.

But the situation was other in Plato's time. One could hardly deny the existence of the *psychē* understood as what makes the difference between things that are alive and those that are not. And since the ordinary person spoke uncritically of the soul as having all our emotional, moral, and intellectual traits and capacities, there would be significant cost to giving up these enrichments of the notion. We have seen that Pythagoras had not provided adequate justification for his doctrines on the soul, which pioneered the expansion of the soul's capacities in connection with the doctrine of metempsychosis. Heraclitus—at least going by what survives of his gnomic writings—omitted to argue for or explain his attribution of intellect to the *psychē*. The notion of the soul as it came to be held by the ordinary person in the fifth and early fourth centuries certainly did not have sufficient justification from these two. And Diogenes' point about *correlation* of loss of breathing, of life and of intelligence—if it is even correct—is hardly conclusive.

In fact, by Plato's lights, nothing about the soul had been established satisfactorily. Here we have a situation in which ordinary thinking called for some philosophy. It was clearly of importance to investigate the identification of the *psychē* as our real self. To establish this, one would have to show that it has (at least some key) psychological capacities associated with the person. And it was obviously of considerable interest to see if philosophy can provide a rational foundation for belief in the immortality of the soul.

We will now be able to see as highly artful an aspect of the way the *Phaedo* is composed that we don't see at all when we just raid the dialogue for immortality proofs that we then study for validity and soundness. Both the notion of what death is and the portrait of the soul become progressively richer as the dialogue proceeds. This goes some way to explain why there are so many different proofs—otherwise why not just give the best one and be done with it?

The cyclical argument

The *Phaedo*'s first immortality argument (70d–72d) starts by analyzing change. Cebes agrees that things "that have an opposite must necessarily come to be from their opposite" in the sense that what becomes larger must formerly have been smaller and vice versa; what goes to sleep must formerly have been awake and vice versa. He also agrees that in such cases there are pairs of processes that link the pairs of opposites, as for example growing and diminishing in the first case and falling asleep and waking up in the second. The interlocutor is brought to apply the general schema to being alive and being dead, and to link them by a pair of processes.

Accordingly, what is dead becomes so from having been alive and vice versa; and coming to life must always follow dying, unless life on earth is to be exhausted. (The argument is open to criticism concerning both whether there are *in all cases* processes in both directions, and whether we have a right to the premise that life on earth cannot be exhausted.)

This argument is independently interesting as offering the prototype of Aristotle's famous analysis of change: Aristotle also holds that any change involves two opposites (or something and its privation). Aristotle, however, draws explicit attention to the circumstance that there are three terms involved (*Physics* Book 1): in addition to the two opposites there must be *an underlying thing*. This last had no special designation in the *Phaedo* and appeared only in formulations such as "when something comes to be" larger etc. Aristotle's scheme makes explicit that change is not just from smaller to larger, but for the fullest description we should say that, for example, *a shrub* goes from smaller to larger.

For the cyclical argument to be at all to the purpose, we must take the thing that oscillates between its two states to be a soul. But the passage does not, when anatomizing the process, identify the soul explicitly as the underlying thing: it sticks to the formulations that speak of something living/something dead. The familiarity of the idea that at death the soul goes to the underworld means that everyone in fact will supply the soul as the thing which must exist elsewhere in order to come back. However, not discussing in explicit detail the soul's role as the underlying subject allows Plato to avoid a formulation that would be problematic. It's not that the change in question is *from a living to a dead soul*—the death of the soul is what the immortality thesis denies!

We might see Plato's reticence here as motivated by where in our study of death and the soul he takes us to be. At this early stage, we operate only with the notion that death [of a human being] is the separation of soul and body (first made explicit at 64c). Thus strictly speaking the notion of the death of the soul is undefined. The natural way to make sense of the idea is that death for the soul would be going out of existence in a way that would be the *analogue* of the going out of existence that a living creature suffers at its death. This is what Cebes in his initial challenge to Socrates was speaking of when he said that what people believe about the soul is that when it "has left the body it no longer exists anywhere, but that it is destroyed and dissolved on the day the man dies ... and ... has flown away and gone and is no longer anything anywhere" (70a). But it is only in his long speech at 87a–88c that he introduces the idea that this being destroyed and no longer being in existence anywhere would be *the death of the soul*. The pattern in view in the cyclical argument would more accurately be described as one in which the deathless soul goes from being incarnated to its discarnate form, on to a new incarnation, etc.

Finally, we should note that the mere continuing existence of some *psychē* after life here is not necessarily our survival. Nor is it necessarily a happy outcome: the persistence of the Homeric *psychai* satisfied no one, least of all themselves. For these reasons, the Pythagoreans had added capacities to the basic Homeric shade. Plato starts the analogous thing in his philosophical recapitulation of that process when he follows the cyclical argument with the recollection argument.

The recollection argument

Phaedo 73c–77a has received tremendous attention in the secondary literature in connection with its primary topic, and tremendous attention as well in connection with disputes over how we should understand Plato's Forms. In this section, our focus will be on the former. A striking fact about the passage as a whole is that it is rather confusingly disorganized. Is this because Plato is not clear about the argument? A more satisfactory explanation is that he is embedding its elements in a natural conversational form, with "some assembly required." Given the topic of the *Phaedo*, there is considerable danger that Plato's characters and his readers as well will want so much to believe the conclusion as to be over-inclined to take on authority what is offered. This passage (like that giving the final argument) forces us into activity if we are to make anything of it; even to choose among different ways of specifying the argument, we have to do a fair amount of work to identify and evaluate the potential viability of the different options.

For present purposes, I will focus on 74d4–76e. (Ti de in 74d4 marks that we are moving on to a new point, as Patterson 1985: 98

pointed out.) This offers an analysis of our ability, present at birth, to use our senses; its claims are restated repeatedly and interlinked with each other in various ways. It may be useful to lay them out separately, and then proceed to some discussion.

1   When we perceive equal objects[5] such as sticks and stones, we must "refer" them to Equality; this involves realizing that they want/strive/desire to be "such as" the Form but are inferior; they don't seem equal in the same way as "what Equal *is*."[6] Analogous things hold in the cases of sensibles that are greater, smaller, beautiful, good, just, pious, etc.

2   The activity described above requires our being able to operate with the notions of Equality, Beauty, and the rest; we must have prior knowledge of them.

3   Since we can see, hear, etc., as soon as we are born, our knowledge of Equality, Beauty, etc. must not be acquired in this life; we/our souls must have acquired it before.

4   So our souls must have existed before, and already had intelligence/wisdom.

5   Since we don't have conscious awareness of knowledge that lets us give full accounts of all fundamental realities from birth, it must be that at birth our knowledge was forgotten. What we call learning in this life is the recollection of our latent wisdom (making relevant the preceding discussion of recollection).

The claim I've put as (1) requires considerable interpretation. Let's start from a fairly extended quotation that includes its main components:

> Our sense perceptions [of sticks etc.] must surely make us realize that all their objects are striving to reach what Equal *is*, but fall short of it ... before we began to see or hear or otherwise perceive, we must have possessed knowledge of the Equal itself, what it is, if we were about to refer the equal objects of sense to that and realize that all of them were eager to be such as it, but were inferior.
>
> (75a11–b8, my translation, based on Grube in
> Cooper, ed., 1997[7])

Here's a rather minimalist way to interpret the idea of referring the equal sensibles to the Equal itself, what it is. Sense perception of equal sticks involves having Equality in mind: to see sticks as equal one must put them mentally into a relation to Equality. Not just any relation, but it is difficult initially to specify it. Saying that the sticks are striving to reach what Equal *is* could be a non-literal way of getting at that—and talking of the sticks' desire and striving requires a non-literal reading in any case. Indeed, we ourselves could perhaps say that the account of Equality (which tells what it is) specifies what equal sticks and stones are "trying to live up to." What about the falling-short aspect? It is also important that when we refer the sticks in sense perception to Equality, we aren't taking this to be a matter of identity: we are not taking the sticks to *be* Equality (cf. Bostock 1986: 88–90). This minimalist understanding of the claims in play gives plausibility to Socrates' saying that we must (75a11–b2) have the realizations in question. To see sticks as equal, we do have to bring Equality to bear, but not as being identical with them.

So we can read (1) in a way that makes it reasonable. Let's go on to (2) and (3). We may feel inclined to object: why can't we construct our notion of Equality from our experience in this life? We may want to propose that we can derive our understanding of Equality from our experience by a process of abstraction. All we need to do is line up a bunch of examples (even if some are rough or approximate), see what they have in common, and voilà, Equality! Yet (1) requires us to ask how we know which things to line up, and which aspects of them to focus on. The point is that before we can do any of this, we must have some command of Equality. To put this thought in the way that indicates its vaguely "Kantian" flavor: some knowledge of Forms is necessary if we are to *have* sense-experience.

Note in connection with (5) that recollection need not be all-or-nothing: it is perfectly open to us to suppose that it can initially be partial. This is very familiar when recollecting a tune or some poetry. A prompt may give someone the feeling of having something just on the tip of her tongue or of almost having something that she cannot quite bring to consciousness, or only very imperfectly. Then later it may rush back much more clearly. Or consider e.g. someone who sees a portrait of Simmias: he first may think only that the figure in the portrait "looks *so*"—and then that, he recalls, is what Simmias looks like (adapted from Dancy 2004: 259).

An analogous though more complicated process would then explain why most of us have not recollected most Forms enough to pass the Socratic test by giving accounts of them. We might come across some sticks and find they look "so" (in fact, equal). We grope to recover what "so" amounts to, and may eventually—perhaps after much experience and thought—recover the account of what Equality is. Note that even then we need not necessarily have a theory about the *status of what is so defined*; we certainly need not swear fealty to a determinate theory of proprietary, transcendent Platonic Forms.

Returning to our present topic of the soul, we can now notice—and solve—what is a real puzzle about this argument if read ahistorically. For the interlocutors point out (77a–c) that the argument only establishes that the soul pre-exists our life, not that it survives it, and Socrates replies imperturbably (at 77c), "It has been proved even now ... if you are ready to combine this argument with the one we agreed on before [i.e. the cyclical argument]." Here's the puzzle: if we have to appeal to the cyclical argument for the recollection argument to reach its goal, why offer the recollection argument at all?

Clearly, if the only agenda were to prove the soul's immortality, the recollection argument would not advance us at all. But in the context of the concerns we have been considering, we can see it as adding something very much to the point. The cyclical argument was framed to do no more than establish the death-and-return pattern of what might be merely a Homeric shade or for that matter, some physical "engine" of living creatures. The recollection argument starts the project of adding capacities to the soul—capacities that are needed if it is to live up to the assumptions that it is the subject of our intellectual and moral activity, and indeed that we can pretty much identify ourselves with it. (Our identity with our soul was assumed at 62b, 63b–c, 66e, 67a, 67b.)

For after all what the recollection argument urges us to accept is not just the existence of the soul prior to our present life, but also the attribution to the preexisting soul of knowledge of fundamental realities. Indeed, most of the stretch from 73c–77a is spent discussing what recollection is, what kind of knowledge we have and how and when we could have gotten it. That is, the passage discusses our cognitive vicissitudes, and the corresponding activities of our soul. Socrates' conclusion (4) expressed at 76c—"So then … our souls also existed apart from the body before they took on human form, *and they had intelligence*" (my emphasis; *phronēsis* is also translatable as "wisdom")—is importantly related to the challenge at the start of the whole immortality discussion, that he show "that the soul still exists after a man has died and *that it still possesses some capability and intelligence*" (70b; my emphasis).

In this stretch of conversation Socrates legitimates the assumption of our identity with our soul, through the connection step (3) makes between *our* acquisition of knowledge and an achievement that can only belong to the soul. To see this, note that for most of the passage, Socrates speaks for pages in terms of what "we" do and cannot do (with plural masculine and first person forms). So after the point (75b) that as soon as we're born, we start to see and hear and use our other senses, Socrates says (75c) that *we* must have acquired knowledge of the Equal before this; again at 75e he says (with my emphasis):

> But, I think, if *we* acquired this knowledge before birth, then lost it at birth, and then later by the use of our senses in connection with those objects we mentioned, we recovered the knowledge *we* had before, would not what we call learning be the recovery of our own knowledge, and we are right to call this recollection?

How, one may wonder, could *we* do anything before our birth? Only if we can identify ourselves with something that existed before then. And note in fact that at 76c, Socrates speaks in terms of our souls (*psychai*, feminine plural), saying, "When did our souls acquire the knowledge of [the things we were mentioning just now]?" And then draws the conclusion about their prenatal existence and wisdom. Once the soul has emerged as the real possessor of knowledge we must recollect and use in this life, it is plausibly identified with ourselves.

The affinity argument

78b–80b contains an argument to the conclusion that the soul is immortal "or nearly so;" this leads into a reintroduction of some traditional Homeric and Pythagorean notions and a specifically Platonic interpretation of them. Let us take each of these in turn.

The argument takes its cue from the worry that at death the soul might be dispersed: it considers what kind of thing is liable to dispersal, and actually makes use of a scheme that Plato inherits from ancient natural science. We will go into the inherited scheme in more detail in Chapter Eight. For now we need only note that an important development in Presocratic cosmology was the idea to explain the ordinary world of birth and death, variety and change we see around us in terms of fundamental entities that are immune to generation and destruction. So a derived item like a tulip is really a composite. For Leucippus and Democritus, it is a temporary combination of atoms, which perhaps undergoes various substitutions over time until the complex is ultimately dispersed and ordinary people register the tulip as dead. In such Presocratic theories (atomism was only one), the derived items are *made up out of* the fundamental entities or portions thereof, the fundamental entities being ungenerated and indestructible, and eternally what they are.

In this type of theory, the derived items are the ordinary things we see, scent, and handle, while the fundamental entities do not appear to perception, but are things we have access to with the mind—we posit them in the course of *understanding* the derived items. Different theories result from different choices of the fundamental entities. But without going into the details of the different theories now, we can already appreciate that this general scientific schema for making sense of our world provides the two clusters of properties from which the affinity argument will work. One cluster, the properties of things not subject to destruction by dispersal, is: invisible, incomposite, always the same. These properties typically belong in a two-tiered theory to the things the theory takes to be fundamental (which in Plato's version of the program will be the Forms). The second cluster, the properties of things that are subject to destruction via dispersal is: visible, composite, changeable. These properties are attributed by two-tiered theories to the derived things, the objects of the world around us.

Now there are three zippy considerations each of which shows an affinity of the soul with the fundamental realities characterized by the first cluster, and of the body with the derived items characterized by the second.

- The soul is invisible, the body visible.
- The soul's optimal investigation is not done through the senses; it concerns the non-visible realm of stable and eternal reality.
- The soul rules, a role that is more divine; the body serves, a role that is mortal.

So the soul has more affinity with or is more akin to the fundamental entities. Socrates offers the conclusion that it is immortal or nearly so, drawing attention to the fact that, like the recollection argument, this does not get us all the way to full-strength immortality.

But it does lead in to development of notions thematized in the dialogue. Courtesy of the word *aïdē* (invisible) which has figured prominently in the first cluster, Plato now gives a new interpretation to the traditional language of "Hades" (80d). As always Hades is where the *psychē* goes without the body, no longer to be seen by the living. But instead of this realm of the unseen being populated by miserable shades that are insubstantial likenesses of bodies, the occupants of the true Hades are now the fundamental realities accessible to thought, and the souls that are akin to them. The old underworld is replaced by the domain of Beauty, Equality, Justice and so on: the traditional dank house of Hades has been transformed into Platonic Heaven!

Consonant with this is Plato's interpretation of the Pythagorean recommendation to purification from the bodily as a precondition for bliss. All the language (of purification versus pollution by the bodily, of mysteries, wisdom, happiness, and freedom from bondage) that Socrates used at the beginning of the discussion in his defense passage returns. We hear again that the soul, if it manages to get free from the body, will return at death to its own natural realm, where it will exercise its capacities on appropriate objects, and so be happy (81a); on the other hand, if it is polluted with the body this agenda will be frustrated. But we now have two ways of understanding this.

First we have, perhaps as a joke, the literal interpretation that association with the body and adoption of its tastes physically weighs down the soul so that it hangs around graveyards as people say—hence the sighting of phantasms there (and notice that these are described with the language of *eidōla* and *phantasmata*, i.e. the terminology belonging to Homeric *psychai*.) These misguided souls eventually get their wish and are reincarnated. Depending on their detailed tastes and values, this might be as donkeys (those overfond of food, drink, and sex), or wolves or hawks (aggressive types). Those who are social and civic but without philosophy might come back as bees or wasps or ants—or moderate humans.

But lest we be put off by the idea of the soul as being physically weighed down, this is immediately followed by the discussion of what lovers of learning say to themselves, a more sophisticated interpretation of the same notions, or so to speak a way of translating the traditional language into Platonic. We now learn clearly that the detrimental effect of the soul's excessive trafficking with the physical is not that it is literally weighed down; rather the drawback turns out to be cognitive. There is the obvious circumstance that the needs of the body for food, rest, recovery from illness and so on prevent us from seeking wisdom all the time—and much more so if we become involved in the quest for possessions and honor beyond what is necessary and so are led into wars etc.

But more insidiously and fundamentally even than this, what really binds the soul most to the body and militates against its purification is that:

> the soul of every man, when it feels violent pleasure or pain in connection with some object, inevitably believes at the same time that the thing in connection with which it experiences such feelings must be very clear and very true, which it is not.
> (83c, my translation, based on Grube in Cooper, ed., 1997[8])

The disastrous consequence of this is that the soul "believes that truth is what the body says it is" (83d); in other words, it is thinking *like the body* that imprisons the soul. We too use expressions along the lines of "thinking with your ...." Socrates is warning here against letting the soul make such thoughts and values its own.

Now let us draw together and interpret the pervasive remarks that, for purposes of attaining wisdom and truth, focusing on the objects of the senses is disastrous. First we should articulate, in order to bracket it, a reading of this claim that is natural for us yet inappropriate to our text. Plato is not claiming that we can never be correct when we taste that something is sweet or see that it is equal or beautiful. Rather *to alēthes* or *alētheia*, "truth," like *to on* or *ousia* ("what is," "being," "the real") is used in an elevated or honorific way: these all designate what is fundamental. We fail to reach wisdom and truth when we make sensible objects our primary focus because they are not fundamental entities.

The affinity argument just showed us that, at the schematic level, Plato supposes that what is real and true is accessed by reason. As we ourselves probably think and Anaxagoras did before Plato, you can gaze on golden objects, but when it comes to identifying *what gold is*, you have to use your mind. Similarly, it is plausible to assert that we can handle cylindrical baked goods, but we consider *what it is to be a cylinder* with our minds. Our dialogue develops a special use of the words *logizesthai* and *logismos* (65c, 78d–79a) for this type of basic theorizing: it is not any old "reckoning" or "doing accounts" but what the soul is capable of when it is coming to grips in its own proprietary way with Plato's true realities. In each case of F sensible things, the true being is what is common to and explanatory of them. It is the real F for exactly the reason that made us gloss the *Doctor Who* quote "The soufflé isn't the soufflé; the soufflé is the recipe" by saying that the recipe is the real soufflé (see Introduction).

Now that we have a "translation into Platonic" of the claim that the philosopher purifies the soul from the bodily so far as possible in order to reach wisdom, we can understand how the claim that the philosopher will be truly virtuous is connected with it: simply because his value system is so transformed that he won't care about the pleasures that motivate vice (82e–84b). With the understanding of the soul and its capacities the dialogue has offered so far, we can also see how the tranquility Socrates will show as he faces the separation of his soul from his body is supposed to be grounded—except for the niggling fact that the immortality which would make him secure of his soul's continuing in better circumstances is still not well-established. Only the cyclical argument was presented as having that conclusion. As we have seen, the recollection argument at most showed that the soul preexists this life, and the affinity argument that it is akin to things that are indestructible. With everything else in the development of the defense themes in place if only immortality is shored up, we can appreciate the role of the coping-stone of the dialogue, conventionally called the "final argument."

The final argument

Socrates prepares for this by saying that he must treat in general of the causes of being and becoming. He gives what one might call an "intellectual autobiography" telling how his youthful enthusiasm for natural philosophy led to puzzlement. Then his hopes to learn teleological accounts from Anaxagoras were disappointed. When Anaxagoras wrote that Mind arranged all things, Socrates expected everything would be explained by showing the good that Mind was aiming at in each case. But Anaxagoras "failed to use his M/mind" (to translate to bring out the word-play) and gave only material explanations.[9]

Socrates was thus thrown back on his *deuteros plous*. The idiom, literally a "second voyage" gets at some sort of Plan B: falling back on the oars when the wind fails. He announces a method of hypothesis. This involves positing what seems strongest, examining what is *concordant* with it, and if more justification of the hypothesis itself is needed, ascending to something higher with which it is in turn concordant.[10] Accordingly, he hypothesizes a Beautiful (*kalon*) itself, a Good, a Large and the rest: the entities he says the interlocutors are used to hearing him invoke (and so are we!)

He says that accepting these will lead to an immortality proof, but he talks a lot before he gets to the core of the proof. Further complicating matters, our passage has suffered some corruption and in addition contains many sentences that admit multiple and importantly different construals. Thus every translation has to build in extremely non-trivial interpretative choices on the part of the translator. The passage is also the subject of an extensive secondary literature in connection with the theory of Forms, in which scholars typically go well beyond the formulations in the text.

I will concentrate, on this first pass, on the immortality argument. I will use phrases that parallel formulations in the text, arranged so as to make a fairly idiomatic and plausible progression of thought. (Formulations based on Sedley 2006, purging metaphysical glosses as in Denyer 2007b but even more). My purpose in this is to mimic for ourselves the impact of this passage on its original audience: they did not have access to the mammoth collection of journal articles and books that deal with "Plato's theory of Forms," nor were they, presumably, reading the passage initially with a view to gleaning information about that theory.

First we learn that, having given up the old attempts, Socrates now contents himself simple-mindedly with a safe kind of explanation (100b–e).[11] This is that things are, for example, beautiful because they have a share of/participate in [alternate renderings in English of *metechei*] the Beautiful; he goes out of his way to disclaim any exact notion of what this participation amounts to. Our narrator also introduces the vocabulary of eponymy (having a derivative name): beautiful things are *called after* the Beautiful itself (102b). But the final argument does not trade directly on the simple, safe kind of statement—the only type which it presents as causal or explanatory (as an *aitia*). In fact, Plato does not use *aitia* and its cognates, or the associated language of *making* F things F or being that *by which* F things are F for the fancier replies we are about to consider (Denyer 2007b: 93–4).

Socrates works up by stages to a kind of answer one can give that he calls *kompsoteran* (fancier/more sophisticated) at 105c2. The idea that an opposite itself cannot be opposed to itself is foundational (102d, put most clearly in the recapitulation at 103b–c). This claim concerns Forms of the usual order like Largeness, Smallness, Wetness, and Dryness; our passage sometimes refers to these as the opposites "in nature." In addition Socrates speaks of some items special to this text: opposites "in us," that is, in sensible particulars. No one of the opposites in us can "admit" its opposite; on the approach of its opposite it must either flee or perish (102d–103a). So, to make up an example modeled on 102e and 103d, the wetness in my risotto can never accept dryness i.e. become dry. This does not mean the dish cannot be dried out. For that to happen though, the wetness in it must either go elsewhere or perish. (It is hard to determine exactly what these items are and what the passage is saying about them; some points may be problematic.) This level of opposites "in us" forms a bridge to yet another group which will include the main target of the final argument.

Let's move on to this group. These are things which, while not identical with any opposite nevertheless—while they exist—always *have* one of a pair of opposites, and never the other (104b). These things too, on the approach of the antagonist opposite to the one they always have, must either flee or perish. We can see that snow has this special relation to cold: snow is always cold; it cannot "admit" heat (i.e. become hot). In the characteristic mark of this class, snow brings both its own character and that of coldness to other things: anything in which it is present is both snowy and cold. "Snow" here names the usual stuff. In fact, for the present passage what really seems in question is particular portions of snow that may be in snowy country or snow-cones or snowmen.

The traditional notion of the soul makes it natural to suppose that this case fits our bringer-on-of-an-opposite scheme. Accordingly the soul, the bringer-on of life, cannot admit death. At this point Socrates points out something special about this case. In the more usual case of snow, the pattern has it that, as the bringer-on of cold, snow can never accept heat. This still leaves open two possibilities. At the approach of heat, a particular portion of snow (let us say, the snow in some rustic dessert) may either withdraw or perish (go into the freezer, or else melt). We might start out thinking that there are the corresponding two possibilities in the case of the soul. Since, as the bringer-on of life, it cannot undergo death, we start off with the two possibilities that at the approach of death, the soul in one of us may either withdraw or perish. But in this special case, on reflection, the second option makes no sense: for something alive to perish would be to admit death, which is the very thing that was ruled out for the soul by the basic application of the pattern relating to opposites (D. Frede 1978). So when death approaches the living creature, the deathless and indestructible soul must withdraw safe; or to put it in the traditional terms, it must depart for Hades and exist there.

The basic moves of the argument as I have presented it are:

1 No one of the opposites in us can "admit" its opposite; on the approach of its opposite, it must either flee or perish.

2 There are additional items in us each of which, while not identical with any opposite, nevertheless always *has* one of a pair of opposites, and never the other. These vehicles bring both their own character and that of an opposite to anything in which they are present, as anything in which some snow is present is both snowy and cold. These vehicles too, on the approach of the antagonist opposite to the one they always have, must either flee or perish.

3 The traditional idea of the soul makes it fit this vehicle-of-an-opposite scheme. So the soul cannot admit life's opposite, death; on the approach of death the soul must either flee or perish.

4 But for a living thing to perish is to admit death, so we can rule out the second disjunct in (3). Therefore, on the approach of death the soul must flee safe to Hades.

The role and presentation of Forms in the arguments of the *Phaedo*

Now of course, once we have got the sweep of our dialogue's immortality arguments, we should also realize that the exact interpretation of some of their initially plausible-sounding starting-points requires further work. The very great variation in what professional scholars produce when they try to precisify and formalize them may well result from the fact that the text underdetermines any official theory of Forms. In particular, it is not committed on the crucial question of whether they are along the lines of the "Platonic ideal of the banana split"—perfect, flawless, exemplars.

So the final point I'd like to make about our dialogue concerns its protreptic nature of preparing our interest for some of Plato's special concerns. The *Phaedo* overall of course takes up issues everyone may be supposed to have a stake in: both the immortality of the soul and its having capacities that make it our real self are issues that affect everyone. Note how Socrates highlights the relation of the whole class of Forms to the recollection argument when he says:

> for our present argument is no more about the Equal than about the Beautiful itself, the Good itself, the Just, the Pious, and, as I say, about all those things on which we set the seal "what it is," both when we are putting [Socratic what-is-it] questions and answering them... we must have acquired knowledge of them all before we were born.
>
> (75c–d, my translation, based on Grube in Cooper, ed., 1997)

In particular, the argument claims that everyone, once born, is in a position to refer equals (for example) to what Equal is: to realize that they strive for it while falling short. As Socrates puts it in his summing-up:

> If the things which are our constant refrain really exist, I mean a Beautiful and a Good and all that sort of being, and if we refer to this being everything derived from our senses, rediscovering our ownership of what belonged to us before, and compare them to it, then just as these things exist, so too must our soul also exist even before we are born. But if they don't exist, then wouldn't this argument turn out to have been propounded to no effect?
>
> (76d–e, tr. Sedley and Long 2011)

Simmias is ready with full endorsement (76e–77a). Yet he has not been an ideally active interlocutor, and we readers may well feel that our grasp on the claims in question is insufficient.

Must we be aware of sensible equals as falling short of Equality itself, and what is this falling short supposed to consist in? For the overall argument, we used only the most basic idea of falling short as non-identity of sensibles with the Form. Yet a feeling persists among many that Plato commits himself to more in the preceding discussion. That discussion started: "We say, don't we, that there is an Equal—I don't mean a stick to a stick or a stone to a stone, or anything else of that sort, but some different thing beyond all those, the Equal itself" (74a; Sedley 2007 argues for this translation). Soon after, the interlocutor agrees to a question put with a very compressed formulation (74b). We can parallel what he agrees to as the following claim:"Equal stones and sticks sometimes, the very same ones, appear equal to one and unequal to another."

The Greek rendered here as "appear" does not necessarily carry the suggestion of *merely* appearing (i.e. misleadingly or falsely); it can just as well be construed as: "are plainly," "turn out to be," or "show themselves to be." Nor does the Greek determine whether "to one" and "to another" pick out different observers or different objects our sticks and stones appear equal and unequal to. Moreover, there's another manuscript reading that would yield "… appear equal at one time and unequal at another." Given all this, myriad interpretations are possible! But on all of them the point very broadly put is that things like sticks are in some way compromised in their display of equality.

This can seem to indicate that the contrasting case of the Forms must be a matter of their making a superior display: Equality must be a thing that is purely, perfectly, unqualifiedly and so non-relationally equal. It must be a thing that is "just equal, never mind to what" (Penner 1987: 48–9 reporting the interpretation of Owen 1957). Note that the core of the recollection argument we discussed above did not require commitment concerning this vexed issue. In Chapters Nine and Ten we will consider another way to understand the contrast in question.

There is an analogous phenomenon with respect to the final argument. It ultimately depends on the positing of Forms as causes, and in particular its claims about Forms of opposites are foundational as we saw. But note that the detailed bits of the argument as I reconstructed it are not at that level. Plato has carefully distinguished the claims Socrates clung to simplemindedly from claims about vehicles like soul and snow. For he calls the former a kind of *aitia*, that is, a kind of causal account that gives a special kind of reason or explanation. But he does not say a vehicle like snow is *what makes* things cold or *that by which* they are cold; he does not give it in an *aitia* of things' being cold; he does not say it is the cause. Indeed, by his lights it could not be, assuming that snow does not account for all cases of being cold. The point is even more clear with other examples in play in the passage like three-odd or fever-sick.

So there is considerable daylight between what this passage says about on the one hand such vehicles as snow and soul and on the other Platonic Forms. There is no reason to suppose that Forms must work in the same way as vehicles. Forms are Platonic causes, even if they aren't "causes" as we think of them. Vehicles may be causes as we think of them, but they are not Platonic causes. The passage does not license us to assimilate the two. Certainly, the core argument I presented does not require us to suppose that Forms must in the same way as vehicles "bring along" and for this reason must exhibit the very property that they are. Also note that the reconstruction I gave held back from giving *any particular interpretation* of the foundational claim that an opposite itself "in nature" cannot be opposed to itself.

Do things said in the passage that don't figure in the core argument nevertheless require this self-exemplifier view of forms? Some feel that Plato's view on the role of Forms as causes requires this; we will take that up in Chapters Nine and Ten. Others are led to the same impression by their apportioning of which statements in the discussion of the final argument are about Forms "in nature" and which are about forms "in us," or the way they take claims about one group to parallel those of the other. Because of the complexities caused by both corruption in the text and the considerable scope for varying translation and interpretation, the relevant issues cannot usefully be discussed in the present book. I'd just like to sum up with three claims. (a) The passage, like that on recollection, contains language that *can be read* as taking Forms to be perfect exemplifiers of themselves. (b) It may be possible to read the passage as *not* committed in this way. (c) The commitment in question is not actually necessary for the core argument as I presented it, though of course it will be of interest to anyone who wants fully to understand all the entities in play in the passage.

So it is quite apt that Socrates says after the final argument: "our first hypotheses require clearer examination, even though we find them convincing. And if you analyze them adequately, you will, I think, follow the argument as far as a man can" (107b).

A certain indefiniteness in his "theory" serves Plato's compositional purpose. Our awareness of the controversial and underdetermined nature of the claims about Forms, together with the oft-stressed connection between those claims and the results about the soul, should motivate us to develop our understanding of Form theory further. The *Symposium*, *Phaedo*, and *Republic* indicate the outlines and importance of a theory that we will be helped to develop more fully in later works, notably the difficult *Parmenides*, *Sophist*, and *Philebus*.

Closing thoughts

The *Phaedo*'s immortality arguments, psychological investigation, and sketches of views in metaphysics and epistemology make up a work well suited to the historical context. We have seen that Plato found in daily use a notion of the soul that had developed higgledy-piggledy and without sufficient justification. The soul's capacities, identity with ourselves, and immortality (or lack thereof) all needed work. Thus he quite naturally turned to exploring how the notion of the *psychē* could be supported or reconstructed philosophically.

As we have read the *Phaedo*, it has become evident how much valuable philosophical equipment Plato develops in this work—whether or not he succeeds in proving the soul's immortality. I have tried to reorient perceptions so that we need not continue to regard the immortality proofs as misguided attempts to make a philosophical silk purse out of a sow's ear. Rather, finding that his contemporary society had an insecurely stitched pigskin wallet in daily use, Plato experimented rather interestingly with various ways in which philosophy might help to reinforce some of its seams.

Further reading

Recollection also figures in Plato's *Meno* and *Phaedrus*. In the *Meno* it is introduced (81a–86c) to answer the puzzle famous as "Meno's problem" (80d–e): how can you inquire into anything? If you already know it, you won't be searching, and if you don't, you won't be in a position to recognize it when found (see Fine 2014). In the *Phaedrus* it is part of the "palinode" Socrates tells as Stesichorus from Himera to Phaedrus in terms of the soul as composed of a charioteer driving a white and a black horse (244a–257b; see Ferrari 1987). Different strands from the recollection argument come apart later on in Plato's work. He treats the topic of the role of the *psychē* in perception and thought in the much more technical *Theaetetus* and *Sophist* (each of which needs to be read with great care in Greek and/or with the help of serious scholarship.) A brief proof (along different lines) for the soul's immortality appears in the *Phaedrus* (245c–e). It has been suggested that Plato "never found a satisfactory argument for it, and later in his life it became for him more a matter of faith" (Mason 2010: 109).

Secondary literature

See Bibliography for full details of the works listed below.

D. Bostock (1986) *Plato's "Phaedo."* Detailed analysis and discussion of each argument, considering many possible interpretations of each formulation.

N. Denyer (2007b) "The *Phaedo's* Final Argument." A bracing anti-dote to usual readings of what is involved in giving an explanation along the lines of "it is by the Beautiful that all beautiful things are beautiful."

D. Furley (1956) "The Early History of the Concept of Soul." Compact survey of the tradition before Plato, with myriad references. The essay is "based on a number of papers read to a seminar in University College London and in the Institute of Classical Studies," the contributors being E. G. Turner, E. W. Handley, T. B. L. Webster, as well as Furley himself.

D. Scott (1999) "Platonic Recollection."

D. Sedley (2009) "Three Kinds of Platonic Immortality." Survey concentrating on the *Phaedo* but with discussion too of the *Timaeus*, *Symposium*, and *Republic*. The *Phaedo* section discusses the famous criticism of the final argument originated by Strato.

Notes

1   Originally *psychē* is spoken of only in connection with human beings; over time *empsychon*—ensouled—came to mean "alive" quite generally; animals and plants accordingly had their own *psychai*. It is possible to hold that different kinds of things have different kinds of *psychai* (as Aristotle does in *On the Soul*), so that while a plant has a principle of life, it does not have what we today consider "psychological" states.

2 Discussion in this entire section on the whole pre-Platonic tradition draws both broadly and in many particulars on Furley (1956) and Lorenz (2009).

3 "Senses" here has the force that it has in such phrases as "being in/out of one's senses," and is not a special reference to sense-perception.

4 There is overlap in contexts in which Homer speaks of *psyche* and *thumos*. Many deaths are narrated in terms of *thumos*: "breathing out his *thumos*" and "the *thumos* left his bones" (Furley 1956). Does this mean *thumos* is part of or identical with *psyche*? Homer does nothing to answer this.

5 Phrases along the lines of "perceiving sticks as equal" never seem to occur in our passage—because of which scholarship seems to avoid them, as I have in this précis. Yet it seems we have to take the formulations we do get (translated along the lines of "seeing equal sticks") in this way for the argument to get off the ground: I could see equal sticks under conditions in which I don't see them as equal, and then there would surely be no need to "refer" anything to Equality.

6 Reading *to ho estin ison* in 74d6 as in the text of Duke et al. 1995; for the choice "what Equal is" in this passage generally see Sedley (2007; cf. Kahn 1981). Alternatively, with Burnet's 1900 text: they don't seem equal in the same way as "the what-it-is itself."

7 There is an important error, possibly typographic in origin, in 75b as rendered by Grube in Cooper, ed., 1997 ("Then before we began to see …, we must have possessed knowledge of the Equal itself if we were about to refer our sense perceptions of equal objects to it, and *realized* that all of them were eager to be like it, but were inferior," emphasis added.) This makes it sound as if the realization was contemporary with our being *about to refer* and so predated the act of perception in question. It should be "if we were about to refer … and realize …".

8 We shouldn't translate "what causes such feelings," since this case won't live up to being a Platonic cause according to the discussion later in the *Phaedo*. No problem for Plato, because *aition* and its cognates don't appear in the Greek in 83c.

9 In the *Philebus*, Plato will do what Anaxagoras omitted.

10 Bailey's brilliant "Logic and Music in Plato's *Phaedo*" (2005) must be right to use the sense of concordance from harmonic theory. His preferred formulation of his interpretation of concordant claims as those that form an explanatory unity in which each explains the other may be cast infelicitously—if Bailey relies on calling explanations what Plato would not.

11 Safe, that is, if one grants the entities in question. Note this can apply individually as well as globally. It is not just that one must grant things *on the order of* the Beautiful, the Just, and the Good (i.e. Platonic Forms). See Denyer (2007b) for the hilarious (and historically real) case of the od force versus electromagnetism.

Six

Psychē II

The divided soul in the *Republic*

Introduction

The previous chapter has brought us partway into Plato's work on the soul. We have examined thought about the *psychē* before and up to Plato's time, and located the project of the *Phaedo* in relation to this historical context. We saw that Homer, our earliest source, had given the *psychē* no psychological capacities at all, instead invoking such items as *noos*, *phrenes*, *thumos*, and heart. And we saw that by Plato's time the ordinary person had become accustomed to speak of the soul as the subject of the full range of our emotions, desires, plans, and thoughts. Yet we also saw that there had been no good justification for this expansion. Moreover, opinion was divided on the question of the soul's immortality. Thus we can locate Plato's progress along the bridge from the archaic conception to that of his contemporaries by saying that in the *Phaedo* he provided arguments for the *psychē* as immortal and the true possessor of wisdom. Now in the *Republic* he will continue by developing a picture of our souls (in this life) as having the full range of psychological capacities.

The *Phaedo* had featured a pervasive contrast between, on the one hand, the soul's interest in achieving, enjoying, and acting in light of wisdom and, on the other, interruptions or misguided thinking that came about through being embodied. The dialogue actually contains passages that go further to make explicit the attribution of various beliefs, pleasures, desires, and fears to the body (83d, 94b and 94d). Thus the *Phaedo* position seems oddly in between the two basic types that are most familiar in philosophy today. That is, if we are inclined to think that all we are is our bodies (construed as including our brains), that naturally goes with attributing *all* our beliefs and desires to our body. Oppositely, if we are inclined to mind–body dualism, that goes with thinking the body has *no* beliefs or desires. Either way, it seems oddly mixed-up to assign some beliefs and desires to the body and others to the soul. Moreover, this parceling out makes puzzling the way we experience the beliefs and desires in question. To assign some to the body and others to the soul seems to go against our felt unity of consciousness.

In this chapter we will see how the *Republic* will conceive of the full range of interests of the person as belonging to the soul. The dialogue will develop the idea that the soul of the embodied person is a complex of parts, each with its own characteristic form of motivation and cognition. One of the parts is rational in the lofty Platonic sense familiar from the *Phaedo*; here too reason is our immortal component (611b–612a). But Plato now introduces into his theorizing two further parts of the soul, corresponding to forms of motivation and cognition that can come apart from the rational.

Homer had already made everyone familiar with a usage in which thumos is invoked in connection with desires to excel in war or maintain status through competitive activity. So, at the funeral games for Patroclus:

> the drivers
> stood in the chariots with the spirit [thumos] beating in each man
> with the strain to win, and each was calling aloud upon his own
> horses, and the horses flew through the dust of the flat land.
> (*Iliad* 23.369–72, tr. Lattimore 1951)

But of course to speak of thumos (spirit) is not yet to settle its relation to the *psyche*. If we want to develop a position on the matter, a variety are available: in the abstract one can map out the choices that thumos and *psyche* could be identical, they could be wholly separate, or one could be a part of the other. Plato will reconcile the assumption of his contemporaries that the type of desire in question belongs to the soul with familiar Homeric usage by having the thumos be a part of the soul. But this does not yet round out a full psychology. The most common sort of desire will belong to another non-rational part: appetite (the *epithumētikon*). (The question of why we should stop at exactly three parts already arose in antiquity. Indeed, within our text itself, 443d indicates that there could be additional parts. Oppositely, for the purposes of Book 10, Plato uses only the fundamental rational/non-rational distinction, not needing further subdivision of the non-rational part.)

A strategic caveat: the *Republic's* division differs in a significant respect from a familiar modern one, present in Hume and due perhaps to Hobbes. On that modern conception, cognition and desiring are as it were different departments. Passion/desire motivates us; reason by contrast determines facts but is devoid of motivations. Thus beliefs and desires are separate elements in us that work together to produce action. The vocabulary of Plato's scheme could seem to suggest this.

However, that is not right. In Plato's conception of reason and appetite and spirit too, *each* is motivating, and each has some cognitive capacity. The distinction between them is a more subtle one: Plato distinguishes the *kinds* of desires characteristic of each part, and the *sort* of cognition of which it is capable. We will see in this chapter that reason with its characteristic desire for truth (again in the lofty Platonic sense) and concern for the good of the whole soul desires in accordance with its understanding of Goodness; spirit is sensitive to what it takes to be honorable and loves competitive success; and appetite desires what strikes it as pleasant.

Positing desires of a rational part of the soul allows us to recognize—as the *Phaedo* conception of the soul already did—not only that there is something in us interested in getting clear about reality, but that we form some of our desires accordingly. Our potential for cultivating this part and making it the leading element in our lives is, to a certain way of thinking, precisely what distinguishes adult humans from children and other animals. But that is not all there is to us. The *Republic* accommodates this insight as well by positing in addition non-rational parts of the soul with their own cognitive and conative responses.

Since our non-rational components are not interested in or capable of working out whether the things they want are *really* desirable, we can see what is misguided about a person who urges us to eat something we don't care for because, as they insist, "It's so

delicious!" Non-rational desire is what is recognized by the traditional tag *de gustibus non disputandum est.* The *Republic* scheme allows Plato
to take account of the experience that there is something in us that,
when it has a desire, just wants what it wants. For, in this scheme,
we have non-rational parts whose conative and cognitive activity is
largely insulated from our rational reflections. This is a picture on
which a human being can have responses to the world that are
robust even in the face of competing views on the part of that same
person's reason.

Yet the responses of each part of a person's soul are not
completely fixed at birth. The *Republic* holds that how each part of the
soul develops is affected by influences on and eventual self-maintenance of the individual. This text gives culture and upbringing a big
role as a (though not the sole) determinant of a person's psychological constitution. This is the reason for Plato's concern (registered
in Chapter Two) with the total cultural environment in the broad
sense that by now would take in stories, TV, movies, stuff online,
ads, music, art, architecture, furniture, housewares, textiles, and so
on. A person's attainments in mathematics and dialectic are essential
as well. Because there is a variety of ways in which each part of the
soul can develop, there is a huge variety of personality types.

We can already anticipate a broad distinction between people in
whom all the parts of the *psychē* concur and those who suffer
internal disagreement. People of the latter sort are stuck with a
certain degree of frustration and ambivalence since a real part of
themselves cannot be satisfied. As we will see in this chapter, the
existence of this possibility allows Plato to give a very satisfying
explanation of a phenomenon known as *akrasia*. This had been a
subject of philosophical interest since the time of the historical
Socrates, and has remained so to the present day. It is something
many of us seem to experience frequently, roughly characterized as
when we knowingly do something other than what we understand
to be best for ourselves—typically because we cannot resist the
appeal of pleasure. Yet the historical Socrates is famously thought to
have taken the position that this is impossible, so originating a
lasting debate. (For the distinction between works of Plato that are
meant to represent the historical Socrates and those that are not, see
Chapter Three.)

So, to characterize the theory Plato develops in the *Republic* at the most general level: it makes fundamental the thesis that the *psychē* is divided into rational and non-rational parts. (He even makes some of our psychological operations inaccessible to waking introspection.[1]) Whether or not the considerations in Plato's argument for the soul's division by themselves *force* the conclusion that the soul is divided, the thesis can claim to be a good explanation of a treasury of facts accessible to introspection and straight-forward observation. In fact, Plato with his divided soul anticipates students of the mind and brain contemporary with us who emphasize the modularity of several autonomous sub-systems. He is the forerunner of many philosophers and experimental scientists in holding that an important class of our mental states are automatic (at the time of occurrence), capable of originating and working through non-rational operations, and capable of persisting in conflict with others that have resulted from explicit inquiry and reasoning.[2]

In this chapter, we will see how different parts of the dialogue contribute to Plato's study of the parts of the soul, ongoing throughout the whole work. The inquiry is originally put with this question:

> Do we learn with one part, get angry with another, and with some third part desire the pleasures of food, drink, sex, and the others that are closely akin to them? Or, when we set out after something, do we act with the whole of our soul, in each case?
> (436a–b)

Then, in what we can now recognize as Plato's standard operating procedure, subsequent discussion in the dialogue operates both to deepen the significance of the terms of the original thesis and to refine it in other ways. Our starting-point will be the basic argument establishing the parts of the soul: we will map how it works and note what it tells us about the parts. Then we will trace how the portrait of the parts is enriched in the course of the dialogue. Once we have the *Republic's* account in hand, we will compare it with the picture of the agent associated with the historical Socrates. Finally we will consider the role of an individual's history in shaping their psychology. We will see that Plato's basic ideas on this are perfectly reasonable in light of recent empirical results on the formation of tastes and preferences of all kinds.

The *Phaedo* with its governing Pythagorean metaphors of the soul's purification and escape from imprisonment in the body had colored very negatively its portrayal of all interests except that in wisdom. The *Republic* however, with its thematic metaphors of psychic health and harmony, is a study of the appropriate development and relation to each other of all of our psychological parts. After all, harmony is not a matter of a single voice drowning out or silencing the others! With the head start the present chapter will give us on the dialogue's basic understanding of the soul, we will be prepped to go on in Chapter Seven to Plato's investigation of the good life.

The argument for the soul's division

The argument used to establish parts of the soul introduces explicitly as a hypothesis a proto-logical principle, which it will apply to cases we accept pre-theoretically. We will be invited to see that the reason these cases do not violate the principle is that the soul has parts. This section will explore Plato's use of this strategy in Book 4.

What commentators call the "principle of opposites" is stated with some verbal variation (the second version here being perhaps a little more specific because adapted to the psychological case):

> The same thing will not be willing to [i.e. cannot] do or undergo opposites in the same respect, in relation to the same thing, simultaneously.
>
> (436b, translating literally)

> For the same thing can't, we say, do opposites with the same part of itself about the same thing, simultaneously.
>
> (439b, translating literally)

Plato first shows how the principle applies to a physical case, which features a single person, opposites, and the same time. He specifies a person who someone might say is standing still and in motion simultaneously (436b–d). Let's imagine an umpire at a sporting event and say that, while fixed in place, she is signaling vigorously.

More fully specified descriptions show why this case does not violate the principle, by making use of the fact that the body has parts. We can say that the umpire's feet are still while her hands are moving. We can say that she is still with respect to her feet and moving with respect to her hands. We can say that she is still with some parts and moving with others (following Brown 2012).

Now Plato turns to psychological cases. The strategy of the argument for the soul's division is to produce examples in each of which a human being desires and pulls away from the same thing simultaneously. Like that of our stationary and moving umpire, these cases feature a single person, opposites, and the same time; in addition, the object of desire/repulsion will now be accommodated by the mention in the principle of opposites "about the same thing." We will be invited to see that each of these cases of opposition shows that the soul has parts, each one of which is immediately the subject of only one of the opposed tendencies. The soul in each case will be desiring the object with one part of itself and pulling away from the same object with another part. Or to put it the other way: with respect to one of its parts, the soul will be desiring the object; with respect to another of its parts it will be pulling away from it.

Notice that not all cases in which one simply has desires that cannot be jointly satisfied will be suitable for use in this argument. For example, a desire to have my dinner tonight in a pizzeria and a desire to have it in a Peking duck restaurant cannot be jointly satisfied. Yet assuming I desire each menu with no pulling away from the prospect of the other, the principle of opposites does not apply. We must have cases in which a person experiences both a desire for and an actual pulling away from the same thing for the argument to get off the ground.

With this idea of the argument schema in mind, let's turn to some cases. We can start with Plato's underspecified example (439c–d) of a thirsty person who desires to drink yet refuses to. The attraction and rejection here are simultaneous, and both have the same object. We are invited to recognize that, in this example, two parts of the soul are pulling against each other: one bids the person drink, the other forbids it. Socrates says that the part that forbids here is motivated "as a result of rational calculation [*logismos*]." A bit later we are told that the job of the rational part includes taking thought for the good of the whole soul (441e). So putting these hints together, our thirsty person's rational part could be making a calculation that includes the thought that, for some reason, to drink now is unhealthy and so not good. By contrast, what in this kind of case "drives and drags" us to drink is associated with symptoms and diseases (*pathēmatōn te kai nosēmatōn*; 439c–d). Socrates also describes the contrast as being between *that by which the soul* calculates, and *that by which* it lusts etc.

But our text does not stop with these two parts. As our Homeric background made clear, the ancients were very aware of a type of spirited desire, which the *Republic* will assign to a third part of the soul. In this initial presentation, it is described primarily as the part that gets angry without calculation (441c); there are indications that spirit's reaction is affected by whether we believe we have done or suffered a wrong (440c). Later passages in the dialogue will make official a fuller characterization of this part which will build in explicitly more of the elements familiar from Homer. But first, if we are to accept a third part of the soul, we must be convinced that it is distinct from each of the initial two. This can be done by continuing to use the original strategy, looking both for cases in which spirit opposes appetite, and also for those in which it opposes reason.

Plato starts off with the lurid example of Leontius (439e–440a). The exact nature of the appetitive desire this person feels to gaze on corpses has eluded definite identification. But something in him, soon identified as spirit, is clearly pulling back from what his appetite desires. When appetite wins out, Leontius (who had been at a distance from the spectacle, covering his eyes) runs over, wide-eyed, and expresses his frustration with the famous phrase: "Wretches, take your fill of the fair sight!" (tr. Jowett 1892). To take a more definite example: perhaps a conflicted woman secretly enjoys pleasing a certain kind of man by wearing stockings with garters, but hates herself for this.

Maybe it's just the rational part that is pulling against appetite in such cases? If we are to count spirit as a third part of the soul, we must also establish that the part responsible for the reactions in question is distinct from reason. Glaucon suggests that it must be, since young children seem to have spirit, while "as far as rational calculation is concerned, some never seem to get a share of it, while the majority do so quite late" (441a–b). That is, he seems to use the consideration that since a child can have spirit without reason, they are distinct. One might be worried that this observation could be explained without positing the distinctness of reason from spirit, if in children spirit/reason is simply imperfectly developed. Socrates in his follow-up however establishes the distinction between spirit and reason as he had established the others, employing the now-familiar strategy. Homer provides the case in which Odysseus—finally returned incognito from the Trojan War to his home on Ithaca—sees his wanton maid-servants carousing with his wife's suitors. The outraged king longs to spring up and take revenge, but also knows that he should wait for a more strategically viable opportunity. We are invited to see that "Homer clearly represents the part that has calculated about better and worse as different from the part that is angry without calculation" (441b–c); Plato here starts us off with a bit from *Odyssey* 20.17–18 that he had quoted earlier:

> He struck his chest and spoke to his heart:
> "Endure, my heart, you've suffered more shameful things than
>   this."
>
> > (*Republic* 390d)

Overall it develops that spirit is more noble than appetite, though on its own just as non-rational; spirit is naturally suited to be the ally of reason in opposing appetite (440a–441a).

Three categories of value

The basic picture of the divided soul has now emerged. But we have only begun to understand the text's full characterization of each of its parts. In this section we will start to see how Plato elaborates our understanding of these in the course of the dialogue.

While spirit's initial characterization was in terms of that by which we get angry, that turns out to be connected with a richer complex of ideas. Indeed this had been prepared for by Homeric usage—and we just saw how Plato actually quoted from the *Odyssey* in establishing this part of the soul. His fuller discussion calls spirit the "honor-loving" and "victory-loving" part, and we are told that "it is wholly dedicated to the pursuit of control, victory, and high repute" (581a). We can see how the various ideas invoked in connection with spirit go together. A rough start on articulation is the following. Competitive activity aims at securing honor and status. Anger is a natural response to perceived wrongs whoever commits them; shame is also appropriate if they are committed by oneself. Perceived wrongs involving oneself (whether as wrong-doer or as victim) are violations of honor and threats to status.

Now let's see why appetite should not be understood simply as all and only interest in food and sex. In fact, the lowest part of the soul (the *epithumētikon*) was characterized in the opening question as that by which we desire "the *pleasures* of food drink, etc." (436a; emphasis added). How does the mention of pleasure relate to the mention of food etc.? One mainstream answer is that appetite characteristically desires things because they are pleasant—a type of response that is most typically manifested in the common approach to things like food and sex. There is some diversity of opinion concerning how widely this type of desire can range. Plato writes in Book 8 of the "democratic" man:

> he spends as much money, effort, and time on unnecessary pleasures as on necessary ones ... he ... declares that all pleasures are equal and must be valued equally ... he lives on, yielding day by day to the desire [*epithumia*] at hand. Sometimes he drinks heavily while listening to the flute; at other times, he drinks only water and is on a diet; sometimes he goes in for physical training; at other times, he's idle and neglects everything; and sometimes he even occupies himself with what he takes to be philosophy... There's neither order nor necessity in his life, but he calls it pleasant, free, and blessedly happy.
>
> (561a–d)

Here we have a description of the various appetites of the democratic man. If we take these to be appetites in Plato's technical sense, then this passage shows that maximally various things can catch the attention of the *epithumētikon*. The appetites of the democratic man are aroused not only in connection with drink etc., but even by "what he takes to be philosophy." What this passage stresses is how this person's fancy flits from one pleasure to another, treating all equally. So if these desires are all appetites, it is clearly in virtue of the fact that they are all oriented to what the person at that moment happens to get pleasure from (Cooper 1984; Burnyeat 1999: 225).

We should also note that a later passage points out that since appetitive desires for "food, drink, sex, and all the things associated with them … are most easily satisfied by means of money," the appetitive part can also be called "money-loving" (580e–581a). Whether appetite learns to find money and gain themselves pleasant, or whether the moniker comes solely from money's role in securing the pleasures appetite is after is unclear.

From what is clear so far, we are already in a position to realize that the Republic psychology goes together with the positing of different categories of value. We knew all along that the job of the rational part includes taking thought for the good of the whole soul (441e; cf. 442c). Now we've seen that in addition to that part's orientation to calculations concerning goodness, a second part pursues honor, and a third wants pleasures. We have here the ancestor of Aristotle's treatment of human motivation, in which the three categories of value are the good, the *kalon* (see Glossary) and the pleasant (*Nicomachean Ethics* 1104b; Aristotle's middle category of the *kalon* is different from though not wholly unrelated to what spirit in Plato seeks.) Plato already develops the view that the satisfaction of *each* of these three forms of motivation is attended by its own pleasures, so that what distinguishes the lowest kind is not that the things it desires are pleasant, but that it is attracted to them exactly *because* it sees them as pleasant. In fact, Plato and Aristotle will both hold that those who can pursue all three categories of value in a harmonious way actually have more pleasant lives than those who give themselves over wholly to the pursuit of the lowest type of desire.

This section has put us in a position to see clearly why it's not the object (specified simply as, say, food) that determines which form of motivation is in play. As we previewed in Chapter Two, it is possible for reason to desire some food that it has in view—perhaps a bowl of leek and potato soup—because it is healthy and so good. The same person's appetite could want the same food because it is delicious, and her spirit's interest in status could be attracted by the ingredients' being sustainably sourced etc. (As before, readers can and should customize examples: if you don't care for the one I gave, then perhaps a frittata, or the Persian parallel kuku sabzi, or a heartwarming bowl of homemade pelmeni or wonton.) In a case like this, a single object is desired by each of the three parts of the soul—each part wants that object to satisfy its proprietary interest.[3]

The signature activity of the rational part of the soul

Now we will start to deepen our understanding of the rational part of the soul (the *logistikon*). Let's first remind ourselves of the formulae Book 4 used in this connection. Socrates' initial question introduced the rational part as that by which we learn. Then in the associated discussion, we saw that this part's motivation comes about from calculation (439c–d) and that its job is to rule in the soul as being wise and taking thought for the good of the whole soul (441e; cf. 442c). We will now see how, in the course of the dialogue, the vocabulary of "learning," "calculation" and "wisdom" takes on much greater depth than we might have originally realized. All this vocabulary gets invested with special reference to deep engagement with fundamental reality.

We can start by considering the characterization of reason as desiring in accordance with calculation/reasoning (*logismos*): how should we understand *logismos*? If indeed children don't have rational calculation and some people never develop it, it must have a somewhat special sense. In the *Phaedo*, Plato developed a special use of *logismos/logizesthai* to pick out the activity by which the soul, freed from the concerns of the body, engaged with basic reality: the Forms (65a–66a and 79a). The middle books of the *Republic* sketch views in metaphysics and epistemology very consonant with that. The key point is that our vocabulary has a narrow use in Plato to indicate the special giving of philosophical accounts. Thus, what is proprietary to the rational part is not "reasoning" such as the means-end calculation of a gold-digger, the cost-benefit analysis of a business school assignment, the explanation of talking heads on a political TV show, or the accounts one gives on one's income tax return.

We will return in later chapters to consider the *Republic*'s presentation of its sketch of metaphysics and epistemology, and that will be the time to consider how definite a theory we should find in it. Relevant texts occur throughout Books 5–7, so rather than quite arbitrarily quoting bits now I will summarize a minimum core of claims that are agreed to be there. The middle books put over both in "plain text" passages and in the extended figures of the Sun, the Divided Line, and the Cave the idea that real love of learning, real desire for knowledge and for truth require way more than just being correct in ordinary observations or even in everyday calculations. Rather, to achieve knowledge and truth, we must get into touch with what is real through a decades-long program that includes fundamental work in mathematical harmonics as a prelude to achieving an ultimate understanding of Goodness in general and all other subjects of genuine understanding.

Central in all this is Plato's claim that there are such things as what Justice, Beauty (*to kalon*), and the Good really are, in exactly the same sense that there are such things as the real natures of the Double and the Equal—the sense in which we may well agree that there are such things as the real natures of Water and Gold (which this text does not discuss individually). Remember that we saw in the Introduction that there is a natural sense in which I might claim that the recipe is the *real* soufflé. According to this thought, the recipe—or at any rate, whatever it is that the soufflés we can eat all have in common and which accounts for them—has a better claim to be the real soufflé than any eatable particular I might bake and serve. So for Plato, each Form, the F, is the real F. As we will see in more detail in Chapter Eight, these basic entities are not immediately accessible to the senses or to be read off from ordinary experience or taken in from the ambient culture. In Plato's view, one must become oriented to basic research to achieve understanding of them.

The dialogue's final comparison of lives confirms that this is the correct understanding of the signature activity of the rational part and of its desire for truth (580d–588a). We learn here not only that reason has its own characteristic pleasures, but it is amply confirmed that neither means-end calculations nor risk/reward analysis is what the *Republic* has in mind as the signature activity of the part that desires knowledge and calculates the overall good of the soul. The phrase "the part with which we learn is always wholly straining to know where the truth lies" (581b) is filled out in a way that picks up on the middle-book passages. This activity is described in such a way that we can see it is clearly associated with wisdom and the philosopher's life, engaging with what is really real (581b, 582b, 585b–587b). Rational desires in Plato's picture are desires of the part of us that is naturally fit to understand—in a deep and fundamental sense—what Goodness is in general, as well as to grasp all other basic entities.

Poetry and non-rational cognition

In this section, we will deepen our understanding of the operation of the non-rational parts of the soul (generally following Lorenz 2006: ch. 5). Our texts will be taken from the return to the discussion of poetry in Book 10. This discussion raises the question which part of the soul traditional poetry appeals to, and somewhat surprisingly identifies that with the part of the soul that is subject to a certain kind of confusion in sense-perception. This passage then goes on to describe the part of the soul tragedy nurtures in terms that are familiar in connection with the non-rational parts. We need to understand why Plato makes these identifications.

At first, there can appear to be a real disconnect between the previous discussion and that in Book 10. Though Book 10 repeats the familiar strategy of using examples together with the principle of opposites to establish a division of the soul into parts, what these parts *are* looks different. Let's start with the preparatory work Socrates does. He draws Glaucon's attention to instability in how sensibles sometimes appear. The same magnitude doesn't appear equal when viewed from near and from far. A stick partially under water appears to be bent, though it looks straight when out. Socrates points out that we have another type of resource to bring to such situations. Measurement, weighing, and calculation—functions of the rational part of the soul—assist us so that we aren't ruled by what appears large or small, or more or less, etc. (602c–e). One need not worry that such engagement with sensible particulars can't belong to the *logistikon*. After all, to measure seriously, one must have reasons for employing the procedure one does. One's measuring must ultimately be based on understanding what it is one is aiming to measure, the design and materials of the measuring device, the right way to use it, etc. What material should a ruler to be used for a given purpose be made from? Why look at a graduated cylinder with one's eyes on a level with the "meniscus"? Thus serious measuring must rely on the high-grade kind of understanding that we have seen is the signature of the rational part.

Now we are ready to apply the basic argument schema:

> And to this [i.e. the rational part], when it has measured and signifies that some given objects are greater or less than or equal to some others, often opposite appearances [to some of the kind formed without measurement mentioned in 602d8] present themselves at the same time with regard to the same things.
>
> (602e, tr. based on Adam 1963[4])

This description fits most exactly a case like the Müller-Lyer illusion, in which we believe on the basis of measurement that two line segments (each with a different arrangement of arrow heads at its ends) are the same length, but one nevertheless continues to *appear* longer than the other.

The principle of opposites is recalled, now in the customized application that it is impossible (*adunaton*) for the same thing at the same time to *believe* opposites about the same things: presumably having opposite opinions about something is a case of "doing opposites" concerning it. Thus we may conclude that the part of the soul that believes according to the measurements is distinct from another whose belief is in conflict with them (602e–603a). Yet these parts can look different from the ones we have become familiar with. Now it's a matter of distinguishing a part that goes by measure versus a part that is subject to perceptual illusions; before Book 10 it was a matter of concern for the truth and the overall good of the soul versus concern for other categories of value.

Yet here's evidence that this is supposed to be the same division of the soul. Book 10 suggests the new division in telling us that the imitative poet makes images with which he gratifies the thoughtless part of the soul that "cannot distinguish the greater from the less, but calls the same thing now one, now the other" (605b–c, tr. Shorey 1930); by making this strong he destroys the rational part (605b) which is "willing to follow ... rational calculation" (604d). But we also get in Book 10 the characterization that the non-rational part that tragedy nurtures is the source of spirit, desires for sex and all the appetitive desires and pains and pleasures in the soul (606d): this harks back to the Book 4 distinction.

Let's now see what could motivate Plato in making these two divisions coincide. In each, the rational part of the soul with its signature passion for truth and signature activity of calculation contrasts with a non-rational part not capable of either. Before Book 10, we had already realized that the rational part's interest in learning means that it is not content to engage only with how objects appear to our senses. It seeks accounts that explain such matters, and forms its own subsequent beliefs and desires according-ly. We can now apply that to the Müller-Lyer illusion: in that case, the rational part is able to reach a determination based on science that comes apart from how the stick appears and indeed will continue to appear to our sight.

What does this have to do with poetry? As we saw in Chapter Two, central to Plato's critique of the poets is the claim that they typically show what is going to strike their ignorant audience as a brave action, a great love, and so on (as do the creators of TV shows, movies etc. today). In fact, in Plato's view, the artists themselves typi-cally do not know what real bravery and real love are. (We will explore this claim further in Chapter Eight.) This is what makes so pernicious their production of works whose characters will func-tion as role models. The imitative poet will "go on imitating, even though he doesn't know the good or bad qualities of anything, but what he'll imitate, it seems, is what appears fine or beautiful [*kalon*] to the majority of people who know nothing" (602b).

In fact, a wide range of appearances are appearances of value (Moss 2008: §3). In the theater and in life as well, the non-rational part of the soul responds to how things simply strike it ("Yumm-o!", "Very sexy ...", "I've been wronged!" or "Vengeance! Great!"). Reason, by contrast, has more resources as its disposal. Its having gone more deeply into fundamentals informs its operations with particular situations. The rational part's fundamental knowledge may affect which aspects of a situation it considers salient as well as its assessment concerning a given point. No doubt sometimes further reasoning of the ordinary sort—whether means–end, cost–benefit, strategic calculation, etc.—will ensue. But the central point is that an understanding of, for instance, the real nature of Justice will lead a person to very different responses than those of an Achilles, a suicide bomber, or a gang member.

It is ultimately its capacity for coming to grips with what is real that enables reason (if it is doing its job) to determine and in turn desire the good of the whole soul of which it is a part. Its knowing the Good in general lets it see the good in this case; depending on the situation, the rational part's understanding of other fundamental realities will typically also apply in its calculations. The lower parts, by contrast, do not have access to any such resources; they can only go with how things simply strike them.

Comparison with the Socratic agent

Should we accept Plato's divided soul? One way to assess it is to consider the alternative take on the agent that lies behind the famous denial of *akrasia* (often translated "moral weakness" or "weakness of will") associated with the historical Socrates. The phenomenon is, roughly, not doing what one regards as really best for oneself because one is overcome by pleasure.[5] Akratic behavior is so commonplace that examples of it tend to sound trite, but they are along these lines. On some occasions, when one sincerely believes that it will be better for oneself to study, one ends up watching TV. Or one has decided not to eat the chips that come with lunch, but can't resist. Or one thinks one should close one's bedtime novel "at the end of this chapter" but keeps turning the pages and reading on, wide-eyed. It is a broadly common experience that the historical Socrates (as Plato represents him) was speaking of when he claimed that it could not occur—or at least that it could not occur *as originally described*. As we will see, he will give a different explanation of what is really going on in cases whose usual description he problematized.

Protagoras 351b–358e gives the view that Aristotle and the Stoics attribute to the historical Socrates. The fundamental supposition of that text is that we have just one kind of motivation; there is just one kind of thing that a person is going for. Socrates works dialectically from the claim (granted by his interlocutor, the sophist Protagoras), that when people assess the goodness or badness (for themselves) of various things, they consider nothing other than (their own) pleasure and pain.[6] (Of course this assessment often takes account of more than a single moment: medicine, for example, can be good/pleasant *overall*, the bitterness of the moment being outweighed by its contribution to a pain-free stretch of the future.) Socrates suggests that the phenomenon of *akrasia* as people generally think of it is incoherent.

1   *Akrasia* is supposed to be choosing something one regards as bad for oneself because one is overcome by pleasure.
2   But if people assess good and bad in terms of pleasure and pain, the phenomenon in (1) would be equivalent to choosing something one regards as painful because one is overcome by pleasure. (It would be knowingly choosing the thing that provides more pain than pleasure overall because of the attraction of the pleasure of the moment.)
3   It is not credible that any agent, assessing options in terms of this single category of value, would knowingly take the option laid out in (2). Given what (2) reveals the phenomenon in (1) to amount to, it cannot really occur.

Of course, Socrates cannot stop there. He must do something to redescribe the cases we used to misreport as occurrences of *akrasia*, since otherwise most of the human race will testify against his claim! His brilliant suggestion is that what must be going on in the cases we thought were akratic is that the person *miscalculates* the overall pleasure to be got from two courses of action. Socrates makes this very plausible with an analogy from our estimates of spatial magnitudes when viewed at different distances. To take a specific example: when viewed from the air, the Hancock building (and, indeed, the whole of downtown Chicago) looks small, while the plane's wing looms large. So too, the suggestion is, the pleasures on offer from eating onion rings or watching TV *now* loom large while there is a tendency to underestimate the countervailing pains that will come with hardened arteries in several decades, or even with being unprepared for class tomorrow. On the Socratic view, when we act "akratically" we temporarily don't believe we are choosing the option that is less good/pleasant for ourselves. Rather, we are acting on a (temporary) false belief about what actually is most pleasant/best overall.

So according to the Socratic take on things, our "salvation in life" would be an "art of measurement" (356d–e). All we need is to be correct in our hedonic calculus, since there is no separate source of motivation in us that could pull us wrong. A victory for intellectualism indeed if true—and a picture that the Stoics will revive in Hellenistic times.

But the *Republic* develops a portrait of the human *psychē* as having distinct parts with different types of cognition, and oriented to different kinds of value. If my appetitive part is focused on unhealthy pleasures, then I can desire them *even* if my reason takes them to be bad for me. And if my personal history is such that this non-rational element has grown strong, then I will actually act on this desire even as reason tries to pull me back. While Socrates in the *Protagoras* had to ingeniously redescribe what we thought were akratic lapses and say that I pass up studying in favor of TV under the (temporary) false belief that this is good for me overall, Plato is able to accommodate the introspection that sometimes, *even as we click the remote, even as we reach out for that third portion of chips, even as we join our friends to go out the night before an important exam*, we are in fact thinking "I really shouldn't do this" and feeling terrible about it. We get that we are not making the better choice, but a part of us just does not care about that.

Influences on our development

What determines whether our psychological components are in conflict or in concord with each other, and whether each desires healthy or unhealthy objects? For Plato, a person's history has a great impact on each of the parts of their *psychē*. The reactions of the non-rational parts of the soul, however robust in the face of reason's disagreement they may be when they occur, are very susceptible to being shaped by our upbringing and later self-maintenance. Plato also takes what we are exposed to as children to have an effect on how our reason will develop when the time for that comes. (Burnyeat 1980 is a seminal discussion of Aristotle's recognition of these points and his indebtedness to Plato.) This theme is pervasive throughout the *Republic*, and accounts for Plato's concern with the culture (in the broadest sense) that surrounds us (Burnyeat 1999). The dialogue's interest in the utopian possibility of limiting to healthy ones the total set of surrounding influences, and its remarks on the self-maintenance of healthy adults, show how we may guard against even the formation of unjust implicit biases.[7]

While scholars have often voiced disagreement with Plato's supposedly naïve assumptions about our malleability, his position becomes less implausible if we consider that he appreciates the difference between us once we are "set in our ways" and our previous development. Empirical investigation now supports the idea that the food, music, fashion choices, etc. people find attractive are very largely set by what they develop a taste for in their formative years—the window of receptivity typically closes for 95 percent of the population between the ages of 20 and 35 depending on the area (see Sapolsky 1998 for an accessible account by a neuroscientist).

While tastes even among people with similar backgrounds are of course not uniform, and there are no doubt some things no humans enjoy eating, different childhood experiences do seem to be a big factor in why some groups (on the whole) love tofu, for example, and others do not. Cultural influences (at a variety of levels: our family, religious affiliation, peer group, etc.) also clearly have a significant role in our reactions concerning such matters as whether it is shameful to eat beef or pork or fish or honey. Indeed, the difficulty of finding an example that works on everyone of a meal that satisfies all three parts of the soul (and I have given up on this!) is itself a testament to how various our reactions on this sort of matter are: even the group of people who have been test-readers of my manuscript is heterogeneous enough that no one example works on all of them.

Someone for whom steamed asparagus was a treat in childhood typically continues to love it, later perhaps developing additional adult reasons for making the choice as appropriately sustainable and healthy. The appetitive desires of someone else whose childhood treat was fried onion rings will typically persist, and newspaper articles by nutritionists are unlikely to have much impact, though the possibility is not completely ruled out. This is the insight which has led to the efforts of Alice Waters, Jamie Oliver, and others to introduce food that is both healthy and delicious as school lunches, before the tastes of kids get disastrously fixed on junk foods.

If our appetitive desires for food, for which there is a physiological need, are shaped in upbringing, how much more so must this be true with the interests of the spirited part of the soul. Much of great children's literature would be relevant for this point. Fairy tales are full of sympathetic characters who function as models for readers; likewise the Harry Potter series; there are some even in *Game of Thrones*. Touches in the now less-known nineteenth-century *Treasure Seekers* series (by E. Nesbit of *Borrowers* fame) actually model how much interest our young narrator Oswald has in catching on in this domain: nothing has more motivational impact on him than the slightest comments of "Albert-next-door's uncle" when Oswald's behavior has fallen short of "gentlemanly."

Indeed, Plato holds not only that each part of the soul may get oriented to desiring healthy or unhealthy objects. We can also note that early upbringing and habit formation affect the role of different types of desire in our lives. One child becomes used to a regime of eating moderate meals that allow for successful competition in races during recess while another is indulged with double orders of favorite foods on demand; one child becomes accustomed to right wrongs by giving to the homeless while another accumulates an enormous hoard of toys and video games. These histories will manifest themselves all too clearly in the types of gratification of the eventual adult, even if the precise objects within the types change over time. In Plato's terms, this is because a person's history may nurture each part of the soul to just the healthy extent—or if we are unlucky, may as it were stunt one and inflame another.

There is another important way in which Plato thinks that what children are exposed to has broad effects. Let's revisit briefly the discussion between Socrates and Adeimantus of the primary education of the guardians of their ideal city. One of the extracts quoted in Chapter Two goes on:

anyone who has been properly educated in music and poetry will sense it acutely when something has been omitted from a thing and when it hasn't been finely [*kalōs*] crafted or finely made by nature. And since he has the right distastes, he'll praise fine things, be pleased by them, receive them into his soul ... he'll rightly object to what is shameful, hating it while he's still young and unable to grasp the reason, but, having been educated in this way, he will welcome the reason when it comes and recognize it easily because of its kinship with himself.

> (401e–402a; see Glossary on *kalōs* and related terms)

Both because of this and obviously because the development of the rational part is aided by good opportunities for advanced education, personal circumstances affect that part. Thus while the ideal course of development envisioned by Plato takes reason to the comprehensive understanding of everything real—using mathematical disciplines and grasping the fundamentals of ethics, aesthetics and all else—the ideal is not often attained.

Sadly, one may even oneself join in the corruption of one's own reason. Consider what Socrates says about the "oligarchic" personality:

> Don't you think that this person would establish his appetitive and money-making part on the throne, setting it up as a great king within himself ...? ... He makes the rational and spirited parts sit on the ground beneath appetite, one on either side, reducing them to slaves. He won't allow the first to reason about or examine anything except how a little money can be made into great wealth.

> (553c–d)

Only consider Scrooge from Dickens' *Christmas Carol* (before his reform) or, to skip centuries ahead, the more unsympathetic of the Wall Street characters in *Margin Call*, the movie about the 2007–8 financial crash. While cases involving money are perhaps the most obvious, reason could be depraved, disoriented, and dictated to by a lower part of the soul in a range of people—as usual, there is fun and profit in supplying one's own candidates. In such cases, the rational part of the soul is not doing its job properly. It is supposed to secure and apply an understanding of the real Good, not adopt an alien agenda as its own and devote itself to debased calculations about how to achieve that.

Let's close with a famous image whereby Socrates presents the soul as a composite of three animals joined together (and enclosed within a human form). He figures the appetitive part itself as "a single shape of a manifold and many-headed beast that has a ring of heads of tame and wild beasts and can change them and cause to spring forth from itself all such growths" (588c, tr. Shorey 1930); this is the largest of the three. Spirit is represented by a lion, and the rational part, the smallest, by a human being. Socrates offers a benignant model of their association when he asks whether someone who holds the position he himself endorses isn't saying:

> that the aim of speech and action should be to give the inner human complete control over a person, and get him to be like a farmer in the way he tends the many-headed creature, feeding and domesticating the gentle animals, and not allowing the fierce ones to grow? He should make the lion's nature his ally, have a common care for all and tend all, making lion and creature friends with one another and with himself.
>
> (589a–b, tr. Ferrari and Griffith 2000)

In this chapter, we have seen that each of Plato's three parts of the soul—reason, spirit, and appetite—has its own characteristic cognitions and motivations. This means that each of the three is very agent-like.[8] Thus a question now arises. What is the status of the overall individual that I am? Am I (or my soul) something beyond the three parts? Some one thing composed of the parts? Or not really one thing after all? Can the whole soul in some sense have all the responses of each of its parts (even though it is the parts that are *immediate* subjects of the responses)?[9]

Some regard these questions as problems for Plato's theory. But we might think, oppositely, that Plato's view or one like it correctly describes our condition. Then our psychological complexity is not so much a problem for the theory, but something that we as humans have to come to terms with—and can perhaps even benefit from—in living our lives.

We now have in hand an understanding of the *Republic's* analysis of the *psychē*. This gives us a head start on the topic of the next chapter. We will see there how the dialogue's discussion of which life we should choose for ourselves relies on this understanding of the soul.

Further reading

Phaedrus. The divided soul in the context of a dialogue featuring speeches on *erōs* and discussion of them (see Ferrari 1987).

Timaeus. The tripartite soul in context of dialogue featuring mathematical cosmology and activity of divine craftsman (see Lorenz 2006: pt 2).

Secondary literature

See Bibliography for full details of the works listed below.

R. Barney, T. Brennan, and C. Brittain (eds) (2012) *Plato and the Divided Self.*

M. Burnyeat (1999) "Culture and Society in Plato's *Republic.*"

J. Cooper (1984) "Plato on Human Motivation." Less textually detailed than some more recent work, but brings out much of the philosophical interest of Plato's view, and how Aristotle's develops from it.

G. Ferrari (2007a) "The Three-Part Soul."

T. Irwin (1977a) *Plato's Moral Theory* and (1995) *Plato's Ethics.* Each includes influential discussion of the associated psychology; the later book is an accessible version of the earlier monument of scholarship.

H. Lorenz (2006) *The Brute Within.* Parts 1–2 concern Plato.

J. Moline (1978) "Plato on the Complexity of the Psyche."

A. Price (1995) *Mental Conflict* and (2009) "Are Plato's Soul-Parts Psychological Subjects?"

Notes

1　We are subject to lawless desires some of which come out in dreams (571b–d). Cf. the work of Freud, though of course the identification of the parts is different (J. Lear 2005: ch. 6; Santas 1988).

2　Landmark contemporary work includes Fodor (1983), Gendler (2008a, 2008b, 2014), and Kahneman (2011).

3　On the maximal reading of appetite's range mentioned above, one can desire appetitively what one takes to be philosophy—quite possibly even philosophy itself. In parallel, if one desires philosophical activity because it provides a chance for competitive success, this would be a desire of spirit. Thus philosophical activity too could be desired by each of the three parts of the soul, each in its own distinctive way. In fact, it is possible to see the image of the Cave as designed precisely to induce the non-rational parts of the soul to desire philosophical progress (J. Lear 2008).

4　Thanks to Jan van Ophuijsen for suggesting this way of doing it. The important goal is to avoid the problematic suggestion that the opposites are both appearing to the *logistikon*. For a variety of ways of achieving this and discussion of the issues involved, see Adam (1963 vol. 2: 407–8, 466–7), Barney (1992: 286–7), Ferrari and Griffith (2000: 323 fn 10), and Lorenz (2006: 66–8).

5　Initially the *Protagoras* discussion is in terms of what one knows, but at 358b–d Socrates puts it in terms of what one *thinks*. Another complication: for Aristotle and later philosophers, whether akratic action can have motivation other than pleasure becomes controversial.

6　Notice that Socrates could run the same argument with any view according to which there is just a single category of value—there is a huge secondary literature about whether or not Socrates himself endorses the hedonism Protagoras grants on behalf of "the many."

7　Of the sort discussed in Gendler (2008a, 2014).

8　There is controversy—and room for philosophical work—in deciding what the force of there being parts of the soul is and how they relate to the whole. See Moline (1978), Irwin (1977a, 1995), Bobonich (2002), Lorenz (2006), and Brown (2012).

9　Brown (2012) shows how it may be possible to get beyond problems made famous by Bobonich (2002) and Lorenz (2006).

Seven

The good life
Ethics and political theory in the *Republic*

Introduction

How can we achieve the good life? This is the main issue of the *Republic*. While we have already pulled out some particular passages from this sprawling work, in this chapter we will address its main agenda. The work we have done in Chapter Six suggests that our psychological constitution will have a central role to play in this regard. Now, we will see in detail how Plato develops his answer. But first, in this section, we will get an understanding of how the theme question of the *Republic* arose in Plato's culture and what it means in our terms.

In antiquity it was assumed, and assumed to be unproblematic, that what each of us wants more than anything is to achieve *eudaimonia*: happiness, the good life. (Remember that happiness when it translates *eudaimonia* is not a matter of feeling cheerful, but is something that is won over the entirety of a well-favored life: human flourishing.) The theme question of ancient ethics was tantamount to "How can I be happy?" And the different philosophical schools thought they were making contributions of enormous practical importance when they undertook research on this topic. Their answers competed directly with others that were around in the culture such as the traditional notion that the good life is the life of the person with social position, or beauty, or health; or the rather more cynical beliefs that money or power are what it takes.

In fact at an abstract level there was an answer to the question "How can I be happy?" that was guaranteed to be correct. Human excellence or virtue (Greek *aretē*) in the fundamental meaning of the term must put us in a position to achieve the good life.[1] For the excellence or virtue of anything that has a characteristic work, function, or performance is what enables the performance to be done well (as both Book 1 of the *Republic* and Book 1 of Aristotle's *Nicomachean Ethics* spell out). We still follow the descendant of this usage when we speak in musical contexts of a virtuoso: a person who is able to perform well the characteristic repertoire of their instrument. So a person with Greek *aretē* would be so to speak a virtuoso of life.

While the conceptual link between happiness and virtue in the fundamental sense guarantees that virtue is key for happiness, simply knowing that is not informative. For if we do not know which life is the good life, we cannot know what virtue really amounts to. The conventional list of cardinal virtues including justice (*dikaiosunē*), piety, bravery, moderation (*sōphrosunē*), and wisdom was already familiar in Plato's day. But are these *really* the things that put us in a position to live the good life? That is, are they really virtues in our fundamental sense? That could of course be challenged.

Among the papyrus fragments discovered at the turn of the 20th century west of the Nile at Oxyrhynchus[2] are some from Antiphon the Sophist, making just such a challenge. Antiphon holds that what we are conventionally supposed to do is unrelated to what is good for us in nature. Indeed, in many cases they conflict. He writes:

> It is for all these reasons that we are making our investigation, because most of the things that are just, according to the law, are laid down in a manner hostile to nature.
>
> For it has been laid down legally what the eyes must see and not see, what the ears must hear and not hear, what the tongue must say and not say, what the hands must do and not do, where the feet must go and not go, what the mind must want and not want. Now, these are in no way more likeable to nature or more akin—what the law averts men from, or what it turns them to.
>
> On the other hand, to nature belong life and death; and life for men is from whatever is good for them, death from whatever is not good for them. But the things laid down as good for

you by the law are fetters on nature, whereas those laid down by nature are free.

(2.23–4.8, tr. Furley 1981)

Antiphon's idea here is to oppose the natural distinction between life and death to the legal one between what is required and what is forbidden. Associated with the primary value of life, he conceives goods as helpful things that contribute to life; similarly harmful things are those that tend to death. He claims that following the laws is, in many cases, going against one's own interests. It may make sense to do this when we are observed; our interest may be served by not getting in trouble. But flouting the laws can be advantageous to oneself in cases where no one will know:

So justice is to refrain from transgressing the laws and customs (nomima) of the city in which one is a citizen.

So a man would be treating justice in the way that is best for himself ... if in the presence of witnesses he held the laws in great respect, but when alone and without witnesses, the [claims] of nature; for the claims of the laws are imposed, whereas those of nature are necessary, and the claims of the laws are agreed, not natural growths, whereas the claims of nature are natural growths, not agreed.

So, one transgressing the laws and customs, if he escapes the notice of those who made the agreement, is rid of shame and penalty; if he does not escape notice, not. But if, contrary to what is possible, he attempts to force one of the things that grow naturally with nature, then the harm is no less if he escapes all men's notice, no greater if all see him. For he is damaged, not because of opinion, but because of truth.

(44 A, col. 1–2, tr. Furley 1981)

Antiphon's basic point is one that we can still appreciate today. For we still have a notion that justice is or centrally involves obeying the laws. We still have a notion that justice is or centrally involves refraining from the maximal pursuit of our own interest.

When Antiphon goes on at length sounding archaic about how it has been laid down what the eyes must see and not see etc., this is not just a laundry list of possible requirements. Rather, these connect with such ancient slogans as "Let each man look on his own." The association of justice with confining oneself to what is one's own paralleled an association between injustice and what the Greeks called *pleonexia*, a condition of wanting *more*. By word formation *pleonexia* is having/acquiring more, and the pleonectic agent is understood as one who is motivated to keep taking action in that direction. The etymology does not specify whether the problem is wanting more than others, or than one has at present, or than one's fair share, nor does it tell us more of *what* the pleonectic person wants. In fact, the type of motivation in question is still familiar. To see this, consider the scene in *Key Largo* in which Edward G. Robinson's band of criminals is occupying the hotel of Lauren Bacall's wheelchair-bound father-in-law. When the question is put, what he wants, the villain is at first speechless. But when Bogart's man of the world articulates the insight "He wants more," the classic Hollywood bad guy embraces the answer, snarling in his inimitable way, "Yeah! I want more!" Pleonectic motivation typically leads to violations of law and custom.

A young person of ability, starting out on life and wondering "Why should I be just?" would take away from Antiphon the idea that one should conform to justice when observed, and otherwise cleave to one's own interest. For there is no inherent connection between justice and what is good for us by nature. And only what we may suffer if we are caught flouting local laws and customs makes unjust behavior disadvantageous on certain occasions.

A popular understanding of Kant's philosophy renders ethics unable to engage in this debate. For on this understanding, the proprietary concern of ethics is with our duty or with some form of motivation that must be free from considerations of our own happiness or self-interest. Thus a discussion within ethics and one on the sort of issues Antiphon has in mind would have no point of contact. But as we have seen, ancient ethics was not set up in that way. In antiquity, ethics was the study of what sort of life really is good, and of the character a person needs to have in order to achieve that goal. The project of ancient ethics was not to try to get people to develop a higher concern than the one for their own interests. Rather it was to show us that our interests, rightly understood, are not served in the way Antiphon supposes.

Plato too will work with some of the apparatus in Antiphon: the contrast between what affects us when we are seen versus what by nature is good or harmful, between opinion versus truth. Plato will develop an account of the nature of justice that lets us see why it is inherently good for its possessor. He will vindicate the crucial importance in our lives of this virtue—once it has been properly understood. Justice in the individual turns out, in Plato's revisionist theory, to be the condition in which each of the parts of the soul properly does its own job. This means that the kind of person it is most in my interest to be is in fact one who is just. Correspondingly, injustice will turn out to be bad for me by nature, whether or not I am observed. The idea that our good is served by the untrammeled pursuit of wealth and power will turn out to be misguided. But can I really be better off having virtues that seem to involve sacrifice? We will see in this chapter that Plato's answer will be that a coward and cheat is a wretched specimen of humanity whose life could never be good.

We have already looked at some works that represent inquiry into human virtue. As we saw in Chapter Three, such inquiry was central to Plato's portrait of the historical Socrates. We saw that Socrates' program of inquiring into human questions by examining people who were plausibly thought to be experts had negative results concerning the interlocutors: each putative expert failed the test. Socrates and Plato took this as showing a need for revisionist thinking on these matters. While Socrates' exploration of new thinking may have been part and parcel of the very conversations that served as examinations of others, for Plato the elenctic and positive stages can be sequential. Notice that this does not at all involve regarding the elenctic stage as misguided or a waste of time. The elenctic stage is essential to show that research needs to be done. Thus the *Republic* itself begins with a series of exchanges showing that none of Socrates' interlocutors is able to defend an account of what justice is. After this ground-clearing operation the rest of the work will go on to innovate with a positive account of justice and its role in the good life.

Justice of course can be a feature of political entities (cities in Plato's context) as well as of individuals. Our text studies this virtue on both the civic and the personal scale. For while the originating question in the dialogue is: "Why should I be just?" Socrates suggests the construction of a city in thought as a heuristic device. The idea is that seeing justice "writ large" will help us identify and assess it as it appears on the smaller scale. In fact, the Republic is widely studied in the English-speaking world as a result of its place in the nineteenth-century Oxford Greats curriculum, which had been due to its supposed utility in training British civil servants. This led to a concentration on the Republic as a work in political philosophy, so departing from the ancient tradition which was more guided by the initial ethical set-up (Annas 1999). The choice of emphasis—on ethics or politics, the individual or the city—will turn out to matter, because the suggestions that are most antipathetic to us in their political form may not be problematic in their individual version.

Since this is the chapter on the main inquiry of the Republic, it is the place to take up study of how the literary elements and opening discussion of the work set that up. Having seen the strategy that prompts Socrates to found his city in thought, we will go on to trace his construction of that city. He will have to build it from scratch, and that will take a little time; we will gather the main points in its characterization from our dialogue as a whole. Then we will turn to the identification of the virtues of the city. After that, we will return to the small scale and take up the virtues of the individual. For this, we will have a head-start, since the all-important analysis of the divided psychē (introduced in the dialogue for this purpose) was our topic in Chapter Six. Putting that together with the contribution made to our present project by the identification of the virtues of the city, we will be able to understand Plato's identification of the cardinal virtues in the individual. Once we know what justice really is for Plato, we will be able to appreciate his basic argument that the just person has the best life. We will then deepen our understanding of it by considering some common objections. The chapter will close by noting the role of Forms in the dialogue. As with the Phaedo, a sketchy presentation of Form theory is foundational for all else in this work.

Setting, characters, and project

In this section, we will look at some of the literary elements and a naturalistic conversation arising out of social interaction so as to see how all this sets up the philosophical work of the dialogue concerning justice. Strictly speaking, the *Republic* is a one-man show starring the character Socrates, who narrates a marathon conversation that took place "yesterday." It is completely unspecified where and to whom he is narrating—so in a way he is speaking directly to us. The conversation he tells us about does have definite and significant setting and personnel. Between that and his recounting the conversation by quoting what was said in its original direct form, one tends to think of those he tells us about as being the characters of the *Republic*.

Socrates starts off, "I went down to the Piraeus yesterday with Glaucon, the son of Ariston." They went to see the first observance at Athens of the festival of Bendis, a goddess adopted from Thrace (historical facts in this paragraph are from Pappas 2003: ch. 1 and Ferrari and Griffith 2000: xi–xii). Having done this, they were accosted by Polemarchus, who prevailed on them to go home with him. The Piraeus, still a major port today, had been the creation of the first Greek civic planner; Socrates will be planning a sort of psychic layout of his utopia. Like other port districts, the Piraeus was not the home of high society. It was the base especially of non-citizen aliens like the family of Polemarchus, Lysias, and their father Cephalus who had come to Athens from the Greek colony of Syracuse. It was naturally home as well to the navy and to a certain criminal element. In the time of the Thirty (still in the future at the dramatic date of the dialogue, but in the past by the date of composition) the Piraeus was a center of opposition to the regime, so much so that "men of the Piraeus" became a way of referring to those who helped restore the democracy. Soon after the dramatic date of the dialogue, both Polemarchus and Niceratus the son of Nicias (327c) were killed and expropriated by the Thirty. Even the mention of the festival may hint at the political convulsions of Athens and those who were especially involved in them: the temple of Bendis was the location of the battle in which democratic forces overturned the Thirty in 403; Critias and Charmides were both killed in the battle. Our dialogue will contain a study of kinds of regime that will show what was wrong with the Thirty and with the Athenian democracy: each case exemplifies a different defective form.

Once he has arrived at the home of Polemarchus, Socrates is involved in a series of encounters, recounted in Book 1, like those we are familiar with from the Socratic dialogues. Because the division into books has to do with how much text could fit onto a single roll of papyrus, for much of the *Republic* that division doesn't have any particular significance. The first book, however, is a meaningful unit.

The conversation arises out of some remarks of Polemarchus' father Cephalus, who tells Socrates that now that he is past the gratifications of youth he enjoys philosophy, prompting his visitor to ask him for a scouting report concerning his time of life. Cephalus says that while many of his contemporaries complain about the indignities of old age, it isn't really age that makes these hard to bear, but a person's character. "For those who are civilised [*kosmioi*] and contented, then even old age is only a slight burden. Otherwise—for those who are not like this—both old age and youth prove hard to cope with" (329d, tr. Ferrari and Griffith 2000).

Socrates tells us that he admired this and wanted to hear more. To prompt Cephalus, he suggests that the many won't accept what he has said, but assume it is Cephalus' wealth and not his character that makes old age easy for him; "... the wealthy, they say, have many consolations" (329e). Yet the old man claims that the real value of his wealth is to have protected him from the fear of punishment in the afterlife. He has not been pressed by need to lie or to cheat anyone, so his wealth has enabled him to avoid wrongdoing/injustice (vocabulary related to *adikein*: 330d–331b). This leads Socrates to ask whether telling the truth and repaying deposits is what justice (*dikaiosunē*) really is. He immediately comes up with a famous counterexample (331c): what if a friend had deposited a weapon with you and demanded it back during a manic episode? In this exchange we see how broad the use of forms of *dikaios* and of its opposite can be: we say in ordinary English that it would not be *right* to return the weapon; I'm not sure about saying that doing so would not be *just*.

At this point in the discussion, the old man leaves. Let's take stock now of how the main theme of this massive work arises from this social conversation. Cephalus indicates that a person's character is of paramount importance: good character is better for you than bad throughout your life. And he dissociates the value of wealth from its power to provide comforts and pleasures of the obvious sort. Its chief value for a good man is its use in removing pressure to wrong anyone (330d–331b). That is, the real benefit of money is its use in preserving your good character. But what is good character? He employs conventional vocabulary speaking of those who are *kosmioi*—orderly/well-ordered/well-behaved—and of avoiding wrongdoing/injustice, yet is shown by Socrates not to have a developed understanding of these notions. It will take the balance of the dialogue for us to learn Socrates' views on what justice and injustice really are, and the sense in which people of good character have beautiful order not only in their external behavior but in their very souls, and why you are always better off being like that.

But first, let's complete our survey of the introductory skirmishes. Polemarchus, his father's heir and so "heir to the argument" enters the discussion and takes over the paternal position. He puts it under the aegis of a quotation from the poet Simonides that justice is to give to each what is owed (331e–336a). The heir to the argument represents a slightly higher level of cultivation than his father. He not only deploys the traditional education of the Greek gentleman but is interested enough in discussion to stay engaged. He shows eagerness to learn and a wish to cooperate with Socrates when each of his attempts to maintain his position fails (see esp. 334b, 334e, 335d, 335e). And fail they do. Having invoked lofty-sounding verses, he is unable to interpret them in such a way that a satisfactory position emerges—though it remains a possibility that a successful interpretation may still be found. Absent that, mere possession of the quotation cannot amount to wisdom. So conventional education has not equipped him with a proper understanding of justice. And the problem with this now becomes apparent, as we see from the onslaught of Thrasymachus (Annas 1981: ch. 2).

Thrasymachus of Chalcedon was a sophist famous for his ability to arouse and allay emotion in his audience (*Phaedrus* 267c–d). His name means "bold in battle" and indeed he strikes many readers as a man of anger. His approach is also shaped by his professional status. He expects to make a successful display that will win him future pupils and their fees, and can literally "not afford to admit defeat" (Blondell 2002: 183). The famous blush of Thrasymachus when he fails to maintain his position under questioning by Socrates is to be understood in this context.

Thrasymachus is the one in our dialogue who introduces the position that justice is another's good, the interest of whoever, being in power, is in a position to make the rules—which they do for their advantage, not mine. Making him the spokesman for this gives us a sympathetic angle on it if we take into account that his home city of Chalcedon had tried to revolt from Athens and failed in the attempt. We can see his cynical view that justice is what the stronger tell you to do for their good as a natural consequence of the *Realpolitik* of Athenian foreign relations. The experience of his city also explains why he regards another's good, the advantage of the stronger, and what the stronger lays down in law as equivalent. (Some have complained that these can diverge: if I am ruler then the advantage of the stronger is not another's good, but my own. Likewise, what benefits the ruler and what is in fact legal can come apart.) If we keep in mind that Thrasymachus' passion represents the experience of the oppressed, told what to do all dressed up in fancy terms but really determined by the pursuit of self-interest on the part of the oppressor who makes the rules, we can perhaps see why his position comes out as it does. Another's good seems equivalent to the advantage of the stronger if one is oneself stuck in the position of the dominated.

It also suits the casting of Thrasymachus as the interlocutor that while Cephalus and Polemarchus had been talking about how an individual treats other individuals, the discussion with him includes mention of how a city treats other cities (351b ff). Plato shows here that, despite the impressions of some readers, he is well aware that justice in a city has to do not only with the relations of its own citizens to each other but also with the external relations of the city to other cities.[3] As the *Republic* unfolds, readers will see that internal and external matters are actually connected.

Overall, Thrasymachus cannot maintain his position any more successfully than any other victim of Socratic *elenchos*. But generations of readers have felt that the discussion has not been sufficiently satisfying. Even though each of the little arguments Socrates lures him into leads to its contradiction, some of the sophist's individual claims have gut appeal. Maybe Socrates is naïve to think of a shepherd as exercising his craft for the sake of his flock, rather than for the sake of whatever the owner wants to get from the animals. Maybe Socrates is equally naïve to think a ruler's true objective is the good of the ruled (343a–c). And consider the argument Socrates introduces at the end: Living and ruling are the work of the soul. So the soul with virtue (which justice has supposedly been shown to be on the basis of its assimilation to the arts and sciences) must live well (353d–e). A few more simple steps yield the conclusion that injustice is never more profitable than justice (354a). But all this is way too schematic to be persuasive.

Far from Plato's not recognizing this, his compositional strategy trades on it. The unsatisfactory nature of the initial discussion is what motivates us to go on to the very lengthy balance of the text, in which the participants will undertake a much fuller discussion. Socrates proclaims himself unsatisfied by his discussion with Thrasymachus, and ends Book 1 with a diagnosis:

> So the result of our discussion is that I'm none the wiser. After all, if I don't know what justice is, I'm hardly going to know whether or not it is in fact some kind of excellence or virtue, or whether the person who possesses it is unhappy or happy.
> (354b–c, tr. Ferrari and Griffith 2000)

Now Plato will use the characters based on his own brothers, Glaucon and Adeimantus, as interlocutors: Glaucon restarts the inquiry, asking Socrates if he wants really to persuade them that "it is better in every way to be just than unjust" (357a–b). Since the brothers haven't been satisfied by the discussion of Book 1, they take the role of devil's advocates. They challenge Socrates to give an adequate defense of justice.

By substituting Glaucon and Adeimantus for Thrasymachus, Plato is acknowledging tacitly that he is not giving a proof on this topic that everyone can understand. One needs to have a certain endowment or receptivity in order to appreciate the points he will make—even though the truth is by no means a relative or subjective matter. Aristotle will make the parallel claim explicit when he says that in order to understand his lectures in ethics one must already have a taste for feeling joy and hatred *kalōs* (finely or nobly; *Nicomachean Ethics* 10.9, cf. 1.3, 1.4; *Eudemian Ethics* 6.8). Glaucon and Adeimantus show their fine nature by the very fact that, while able to sharpen up the challenge of Thrasymachus even more (and even more in the terms we saw in Antiphon), they still do not endorse the cynical view. Our last task in this section is to see how their challenge is put.

Glaucon brings in an early version of social contract theory (358e–359b). The origin of justice is that people have agreed neither to do nor to suffer wrong, in order to avoid the worst-case scenario, which is being helplessly wronged. For someone able to wrong others with impunity, though, that would be the best of all. He proposes a famous thought-experiment that is supposed to show that "what anyone's nature naturally pursues as good" is where they are led by "the desire to outdo others and get more and more" (*pleonexia*), while "nature is forced by law into the perversion of treating fairness with respect." (359b–c). He does this by telling a story in which the ancestor of Gyges the Lydian came across what seemed to be a giant corpse under awesome circumstances, and took a ring from the body; when he discovered that turning the ring made him invisible, the erstwhile shepherd used his new-found super-power to seduce the queen, kill the king, and mount the throne.[4] Glaucon says that if granted the same license, no one would stick to justice.

The thought-experiment works by severing unjust behavior from the usual social consequences punishing it, so if Glaucon's claim is correct, it shows that no one values justice for itself. Justice is only instrumentally good—and only under certain circumstances. Ordinary just behavior is motivated by the wish to avoid punishment and gain the good reputation that in turn allows one to form desirable marriage alliances, business partnerships, etc. And even those benefits not from what justice inherently is, but from our being *seen* to be just. Because of this, they can just as well go to a skillful *unjust* person who provides himself with a reputation for justice, and has as well the resources to correct any slips he may make.

Adeimantus reinforces his brother by showing at length that the traditional recommendations to justice by parents and poets are all along the lines of "crime doesn't pay." Such advice doesn't begin to suggest that justice is valuable for itself. Moreover, those very same authorities also indicate that we *can* get away with injustice: they tell us of how we may trick our fellow human beings, and propitiate the gods with sacrifices and rites.

Let's now sum up the position the brothers have taken. It looks as if just behavior is normally chosen (when it is) because of what will come to us as a result of being *seen* to be just. Yet the unjust, if they project a false appearance, can reap these rewards—in addition to all the other benefits that come from their unimpeded pursuit of their own advantage. Adeimantus imagines a young person of ability pondering his course in life and asking himself:

> Pindar's question, "Should I by justice or by crooked deceit scale this high wall and live my life guarded and secure?" And he'll answer: "The various sayings suggest that there is no advantage in my being just if I'm not also thought just, while the troubles and penalties of being just are apparent. But they tell me that an unjust person, who has secured for himself a reputation for justice, lives the life of a god. Since, then, 'opinion forcibly overcomes truth' and 'controls happiness,' as the wise men say, I must surely turn entirely to it. I should create a façade of illusory virtue around me to deceive those who come near, but keep behind it the greedy and crafty fox of the wise Archilochus."
>
> (365a–c)

Of course, all this has been in service of the challenge that Plato's brothers are making (358b–c, 360d–361d, 366d–367e). For despite their devil's advocacy, they tell Socrates that they themselves do not endorse the position they have been developing. They themselves actually reject the view that Glaucon had presented as "most peoples' opinion," namely "that justice ... is to be practiced for the sake of the rewards and popularity that come from a reputation for justice, but is to be avoided because of itself as something burdensome" (358a).

Rather, they agree with Socrates that justice is the sort of good that health is: desirable for its own sake as well as for its consequences.[5] Picking up on Socrates' own assessment at the end of

Book 1, the brothers call on their friend to show what justice and injustice each is. They want to hear what power each has by itself when it's in the soul—even if it remains hidden; they want to be shown that the most just (*dikaiotatos*) person without good reputation is better off than the skillful unjust person they have been imagining. In the very extended conversation to come, Socrates will lay himself out to show what justice really is and that it is inherently a great good for the possessor; he will also make the corresponding case that injustice is very bad for oneself whether or not it is detected. If we find we can agree with him in this, we will have a response to the challenge we saw in the historical Antiphon.

Founding Kallipolis

While justice in the individual person had been the main focus initially, Socrates will turn to the justice of a city in meeting the challenge. He uses a charming analogy (368d–369a) to explain why he proposes to found a city in thought. If we were faced with reading something written in tiny letters, and had reason to believe the same message was magnified hugely somewhere, it would make sense to look at the big letters first. Then we could go back to the miniature message and, with a definite possibility in mind, it would be easier to make out the letters, if they were indeed the same. Notice that he does not propose that we will just assume that we know the small message as soon as we have looked at the Jumbotron—just that having looked at the larger script will make it easier to read the smaller. So too, since a city and an individual may each be just, we will proceed by first looking at justice writ large, and then return to consideration of the case of the individual.[6]

We now start with Socrates' foundation in thought of his ideal city. The discussion develops naturally into a huge range of ramifying topics, many of which are of considerable independent interest. It will help to be aware from the start that, for our present purpose, the key result will be the structure of the city that emerges: there are three kinds of citizens with three kinds of roles in the life of the community. Socrates devotes considerable attention to the question of how the city may aid the development of citizens who are appropriate members of each of the constituent groups; the diverse ramifying topics typically arise in connection with discussion of aspects of that plan.

The starting point from which cities come into being is agreed in our text to be a circumstance of which people in antiquity were very aware, that a human being in isolation is not viable (369b–c). I need to be part of a community because I cannot on my own raise food, transport water, build a house, make shoes and clothing, forge tools, etc. This also makes it immediately apparent that within the city each person should not do each of these things for him- or herself. If that were possible there would have been no need for a city in the first place. Our text points out that, if we each specialize in a proprietary task for which we are naturally suited, we will be able to become skillful and hit opportune moments, and the jobs the group as a whole needs will be done optimally and with optimal efficiency (369e–370c).

Socrates at first describes a simple community of idealized rusticity. There are farmers, shoemakers, builders and so on, and even rudimentary businessmen to be dealers at home and importers from abroad, but these all provide basics and not anything elaborate or luxurious. People subsist on barley-cakes and wheat loaves, with olives, boiled vegetables, cheese, figs, and roasted acorns; they have wine of course for themselves after they make libations to the gods. Other aspects of their lives are correspondingly simple. While in a sense this regime is healthful, it shocks the aristocratic and urbane Glaucon, who calls it a "city for pigs" (372d). Glaucon's demand for feasting on couches alludes not only to the delights of the Sicilian banquet table but also to the cultural content of the Greek symposium at its best (Burnyeat 1999: lecture 1). Indeed, this first city lacks all intellectual endeavor and higher artistic attainment, though it does have hymns to the gods.[7]

Reflecting that after all we seek the origins of both justice and injustice, Socrates undertakes to create a luxurious city by allowing in all at once all manner of perfumers, pastry cooks, make-up artists, poets, musicians, pig-keepers, courtesans, doctors and indeed all those who supply and tend to us in our use of the whole variety of accoutrements of cultivated life. This will generate a fevered (372e) city—it is only after purifying and purging it in certain key respects that Socrates will have his ideal beauty of a city: Kallipolis. In the meantime, the natural resources of the original city are insufficient to supply all the wants of the consumer society, and the consequent shortfall of resources is revealed as the origin of war. The fevered city will need to grab stuff from its neighbor who, if also given over to unnecessary desires, will be on the warpath anyway (373d–e, cf. 586a–b). Now, by the principle of specialization, our city needs a special class of warriors—for surely combat demands at least as much natural endowment, training, and dedication to the task as the original trades like shoe-making did.

The military turns out to be not simply another trade but a different *type* of work to be carried out by a distinct class of people from among whom the best after decades of additional training and testing will be selected as the topmost class, the rulers (412b–414b, with much added in the extended discussion 473c–541b). It will turn out that the really significant application of the principle of specialization does not concern whether a member of the productive class should be a shoe-maker or a wood-worker: the important thing is the distinction between the three kinds of jobs and having the three classes each do the one naturally suited to itself (434a–c). Surely there is a kind of person who is good at growing or making things, but who might not be at all suited to going out and killing the enemy on behalf of the city at risk of their own lives. And, vice versa, we have the stereotype of the dashing RAF pilot or special-forces guy who can't settle down to civilian life. It may well take both an inborn disposition not everyone has and lots of training for anyone to be a good guardian of the city. And if the government leaders are to be the best of those—with considerable additional intellectual attainments, as we will find in due course that Plato envisages—they will be a select group indeed.

The next stretch of text takes the form of laying out the primary education and military phase of the life of the broad guardian class. (They have not yet been divided into guardians narrowly understood, i.e. rulers, and auxiliaries, i.e. the military.) As we read at 375e–376c, guardians should be like pedigree hounds—acute in senses, quick and strong, brave and spirited, but gentle to those they know, and so "philosophical" in nature (i.e. this is supposed to show the value they place on knowledge). We may well want to ask—wait, are dogs really philosophical? And asking that prepares us for what will later develop, after we refine our sense of what Plato takes a philosopher to be. We will see then that the broad guardian class is at least weakly related to philosophy: its members are all raised in accordance with the genuine philosophical understanding at the disposal of the leaders, and amenable to their direction. It is these leaders (the guardians narrowly understood) who must be philosophers in the fullest sense. The distinctive features of the political program of our dialogue are largely a matter of the arrangements concerning the broad guardian class. Since their job is to protect our city, we must ensure that they do not use their superior abilities and training to take advantage of their fellow citizens.

The primary education of these youths is aimed at exposing them to beauty/fineness and harmony in everything they are surrounded with, as well as to good examples in the stories on which we raise them. This is the purpose of the discussion of literature and the arts that we examined in Chapters Two and Six, whereby Socrates purges (399e) the fevered city he created at Glaucon's behest. Since cultural influence comes not just from literature and music but from architecture and all artifacts, these must all be salutary so that our youths, rather than grazing "as if in a meadow of bad grass," will instead "live in a healthy place" (400d–402c). As we have seen, the plan is that someone raised this way will have an affinity for beauty. But as we will see, this primary education is only that. "It educated the guardians through habits. Its harmonies gave them a certain harmoniousness, not knowledge ..." (522a). When we get to the discussion of higher education we will find there an amendment concerning this primary prep: our future rulers will have to learn some mathematics as children (536d–537a). But this will still not give them what the dialogue regards as understanding—mathematics is only potentially that; it needs to be completed by a great deal of further work.[8]

Our youths also have physical education, intended not so much for their bodies but to serve as a balance to the "music" we have discussed so that they will be psychologically neither too soft nor too aggressive (410b–d). The plan then is to select from among the young those who always identify their own interests with those of the city, and who thus always pursue what they take to be the good of the city (412c–413e).

To eliminate any possible temptation from conflict of interest, Socrates introduces the regulation that the broad guardian class is to have no private property (gold, land, or houses) of their own and no private families either (416a–417b, 457c–d, 462a–465c); as "the old proverb" has it: "Friends possess everything in common" (424a). Thus neither the prospect of grabbing wealth for themselves nor that of giving preferential treatment to their relatives will operate to corrupt them. Adeimantus initially reacts with disbelief, saying conventionally:

> How would you defend yourself ... if someone told you that you aren't making these men very happy and that it's their own fault? The city really belongs to them, yet they derive no good from it.
>
> (419a)

Socrates' reply contains the thought that the goal is to construct a happy city and not to maximize the happiness of any one group. He introduces a famous parallel:

> Suppose ... that someone came up to us while we were painting a statue and objected that, because we had painted the eyes (which are the most beautiful part) black rather than purple, we had not applied the most beautiful colors to the most beautiful parts of the statue. We'd think it reasonable to offer the following defense: "You mustn't expect us to paint the eyes so beautifully that they no longer appear to be eyes at all, and the same with the other parts. Rather you must look to see whether by dealing with each part appropriately, we are making the whole statue beautiful."
>
> (420c–d)

But this memorable analogy should not overshadow Socrates' prior remark at 420b, "it wouldn't be surprising if these people were happiest just as they are." He in fact returns (referring back to this earlier passage) to assert at 465d–466b that our guardians have a better life than Olympic victors.

Some of the arrangements governing the guardians are reminiscent of Sparta. Male citizens there devoted themselves to training as their main occupation, and messed together. So for a moment the Kallipolis looks like the sort of misguided proposal an aggrieved democrat might expect from an intimate of Spartan sympathizers. But in the further proposals the city being founded in thought will depart from any known historical model.

Against any precedent, Socrates will reveal that women will have equal opportunity with men to be selected and trained as guardians (451d–457b). In terms of the ongoing metaphorical identification of the guardians as "watchdogs" of the city, it makes sense that the females should keep watch and hunt along with the males, not being incapacitated for this work by the circumstance of giving birth. But this claim needs to be discussed directly and not just passed in metaphor. In thinking about this issue we will see in kernel some of what have come up today as basic issues in feminism.

The question for Socrates is whether this arrangement violates the city's foundational requirement that different natures have different jobs. After all, women and men have different natures (453b–c). Here Socrates makes the point that not every natural difference is relevant to job performance (454b–457c). In a way, bald and hairy people have different natures, but we don't assign them different work on that basis.[9] Socrates suggests that the difference between men and women is primarily a matter of different roles in reproduction, and so not anything affecting aptitude for jobs. Since the guardians have no private families and care of their offspring is done by specialized professionals, problems of child care do not arise. Plato's Kallipolis is more practical in this regard than a country like the US, even today!

Even on the assumption—problematic but made in our text— that women as a group are worse than men as a group at everything, extraordinary individuals will occur at the extreme high end of both groups. And it is extraordinary individuals the Kallipolis is interested in selecting. In part as a result of his reasoning from his armchair instead of building in heavily the beliefs of his surrounding society, Plato has the honorable position of being millennia ahead of his time in articulating a proto-feminism.[10] He prefigures the type of feminism which supposes women to have the same—human— potentialities as men, and rejects the other branch, which maintains that women have distinctive natures not just in reproductive function but in psychological and cognitive capacities.

What about the circumstance that women are generally not as strong physically as men? It is notable that the discussants don't consider this to rule out women guardians. The suggestion is simply that women should be given the physically less taxing of the duties (457a). Perhaps much of what needs to be done in defending one's city is not a matter of simple brute strength: to the extent that skill, right judgment, and values are key, the slightly weaker frames of women as a group would be no impediment. After all, the impressive performance of the foot-soldier Socrates in the retreat from Delium (described by Alcibiades in the *Symposium* at 220e–221c) was due to his character and not to physical strength. It was his characteristic comportment that intimidated the enemy: Alcibiades adapts Aristophanes' description (*Clouds* 362) of Socrates to tell us that he went about in both everyday life and battle "with swagg'ring gait and roving eye" (*Symposium* 221b). And remember in this connection that even the early physical education of the future guardians was not to maximize physical strength but to tune them up psychologically. What our text values in the city's guardians is the ability to stay on course in fearful situations but not become an overly aggressive threat to one's own society.

The suggestions that the guardians have no private property or families, and that women have equal opportunities with men for high office were of course unusual. However, the prescription for his ideal city that Socrates presents as at once the most crucial for making it possible and the most inviting of ridicule from the ignorant is that:

> Until philosophers rule as kings or those who are now called kings and leading men genuinely and adequately philosophize ... cities will have no rest from evils ... nor, I think, will the human race.
>
> (473c–d)

In a sense, this just gives a name to the rulers who have already been introduced. It had already seemed obvious that the rulers of our ideal city would have knowledge to apply on behalf of the city as a whole

(428c–d). But while we could then have supposed that practical men of experience, wise grandmotherly types, or some sort of tribal elders would satisfy this description, the middle books will now show us that the bar is set higher. There we find Plato's discussion of who has the wisdom in question, his sketch of metaphysics and epistemology, and his discussion of higher education (from 473c to end of Book 7). These passages make clear that our philosopher-kings and philosopher-queens will have real knowledge and wisdom only after a lifetime's devotion to the highest theoretical pursuits undertaken in addition to practical experience in civic administration and military service. The centrality of mathematical and philosophical activity thus completes the divergence of Kallipolis from any Spartan model. It was Athens that was associated with intellectual pursuits, both in her own self-conception and in the opinion of those who flocked there from before Plato's time to past Cicero's.

In fact, the people Socrates in this text means by "philosophers" are not who Glaucon and Adeimantus and many of us today at first suppose. Rather, the word is used as a success term for those who actually have the wisdom aimed at by "love of wisdom" (to render "philosophy" in accordance with word-formation). They have understanding of fundamental reality, and also have the traits of honesty, bravery, and justice that, it is argued, naturally go along with this (475e–487a; see Lane 2007 for discussion of the idea that the "natural philosopher" has the "natural virtues;" these proto-virtues are preconditions for attaining wisdom).

Plato develops the image of the ship of state and suggests that, in the hurly-burly of the struggle to gain control of the ship, hardly anyone realizes that there is an actual science of navigation (488a–489c). While those who compete for power achieve it by flattery, the few who could actually steer the ship properly are regarded as "useless star-gazers." Yet since there really is a science of navigation (recently developed with great success by Plato's time), we can see that we would be better off entrusting the helm to someone who had it. The stars in the ship of state figure stand for Forms that we can aspire to understand. Thus, as we saw repeatedly in Chapter Six, Plato relies crucially on the claim that there really are such fundamental realities. Given this, of course we should steer our course in life by them.

It will be a rare nature that even has this potential and in a passage that must refer to the disaster of Alcibiades we see how someone starting with the right gifts can be corrupted by his own connections (494a–495b). The image of the orphaned heiress who, with no appropriate suitors in sight, is prey for the pretentious, suggests the inadequacy of those who step up to consort with philosophy in these circumstances (495c–496a).

That our text rejects the usage in which "philosophers" properly designates everyone who might be called a philosopher today is generally recognized. Less frequently emphasized is that the educational plan advocated in our dialogue is incompatible with the assumption that the attainments of a philosopher are to be achieved through a lifetime in an ivory tower. The philosopher-kings and philosopher-queens of the *Republic* are far from being separated from the future auxiliaries in kindergarten as the nerdy ones and immediately sequestered to pursue their genius studies (519c, 537d, 539d–540c). Rather, the future rulers are the best and the brightest of the broad guardian class. They share not only the primary education, but also the physical and emotional training, and then the military service, of their fellows. Even after they start their advanced studies, these studies alternate with a long term of practical immersion, which is apparently relevant to their being able—as they complete their studies at the age of 50!—to achieve the final vision of the Good itself (539c–540a).

The virtues of the city

We've now surveyed the entire layout of Socrates' imaginary city. At the broadest level of description, it is made up of three groups of citizens: the rulers, the auxiliaries, and the producers. The producers possess ordinary goods and enjoy family life. They are protected by guardians who are statutorily debarred from exploiting their position, since they cannot have wealth or private families of their own. Instead the auxiliaries receive the gratification of a much finer life: they fulfill something very much like the highest aspirations of epic heroes. And the rulers of the city achieve what they value most, knowledge of the things that are most real, which they apply in the decisions of the city as a city.

We can now go back to Socrates' identification of the virtues our city has. It will immediately be apparent how important for this project are the classes that were identified in the city's founding. We start with wisdom. Here let's prepare a bit on our own by considering what matters when deciding whether to call a state wise or misguided. To take an example as close to uncontroversial as we can hope for, Nazi Germany as a country showed extreme lack of wisdom. There were no doubt wise individuals within the German population, but the problem was obviously the perverted understanding of those in power. Or consider that British policy of the era was wise under (at most) one of Chamberlain (appeasement) and Churchill (bulldog approach). Yet given the immediate succession, the population as a whole must have been much the same under both leaders. Thus if *Britain* was wise under one and unwise under the other, the wisdom of the government must be what matters. So Socrates and Glaucon are correct to agree that a city is wise in virtue of the knowledge of its rulers applied on behalf of the whole city to its conduct both towards itself and in foreign relations (428b–429a).

It also has plausibility that what makes the state as such brave is the power of the military to "preserve through everything the correct and law-inculcated belief about what is to be feared and what isn't" (430b). In battle the auxiliaries have to hold onto the correct beliefs transmitted to them about the value of defending the city that make it the case that what is really to be feared is failing in their military objective (to hold a certain line say). They must not lose their grip on these beliefs even when they are in circumstances that would make fear of getting hurt or killed overwhelmingly salient to an ordinary person. The bravery of a state is a matter of the relation of the military class to the values they get from the rulers.

Is every virtue of a state then the contribution of a proper subset of the population? *Sōphrosunē* (translatable as "moderation," "temperance," "soberness," and "self-discipline" among others) and justice each turns out to set conditions on the population as a whole. Moderation is "more like a kind of consonance [*sumphōnia*] and harmony [*harmonia*]" than the virtues that have already been identified (430e). While the overall strategy has been to find the virtues of the city first, in this case (430d–432a), Socrates starts by peeking at the case of the individual. There the virtue in question is traditionally thought of as self-control, but this immediately leads to the question how it makes sense for a thing to control *itself*. The solution is to see that there is an implicit notion that we have different components, so that the idea of self-control is that the *naturally better part* of the person is in control. When the virtues of the individual are discussed soon, the bare mention that moderation is "more like a kind of consonance and harmony" is unpacked by the specification of *agreement about the rational part's ruling* (430e–431b with 442c–d).

The analogous agreement of the parts of the city about who should rule and be ruled makes a clear contribution to the city's good condition. Obviously, if the non-ruling classes are dissatisfied with their lot and struggling to gain power, we would have party faction and civil strife. Equally, it is problematic if the natural rulers neglect their role. For this problem on the smaller scale of a family, consider how Lady Bertram's lazy disinclination to do anything about her children in *Mansfield Park*, coupled with the extended absence of her husband, gives inappropriate sway to her officious and mean-spirited sister Mrs Norris. This results in the fortune-hunting marriage of the eldest Miss Bertram as well as all the illicit passions given rein in the young peoples' enactment (which Plato would have warned against!) of the play *Lovers' Vows*.

The identification of wisdom, bravery, and moderation in the city has been comparatively straightforward. Justice is harder—Socrates makes great play in the text calling for Glaucon's help in hunting for it, and then realizing that it has been under their noses all along (432b–434c). For he identifies justice as closely related to the principle of specialization that has been foundational for the city:

> I mean that, though we've been talking and hearing about it for a long time … we didn't understand … that, in a way, we were talking about justice … Justice … is exactly what we said must be established throughout the city when we were founding it—either that or some form of it. We stated, and often repeated … that everyone must practice one of the occupations in the city for which he is naturally best suited … Moreover, we've heard many people say and have often said ourselves that justice is doing one's own work and not meddling with what isn't one's

own ... Then, it turns out that this doing one's own work—provided that it comes to be in a certain way—is justice.

(432e–433b)

Socrates proposes that justice in the city is the condition in which each of the three classes (rulers, auxiliaries, and producers) does its proper job in the city. That is clearly a virtue of a city. But is it justice? This is why he seeks to show a connection with an existing notion about the virtue. Socrates is claiming that his proposal about what justice is can be seen as a way—made possible by his analytical foundation of the polity—of capturing the truth in formulations about how justice is "doing one's own work" and "not meddling with what isn't one's own" (433a–b).

We can now register that justice stands in an interesting relation to the other virtues. First let us see how justice is a stronger condition than moderation. A standard way of distinguishing them is that moderation is merely agreement about the rational part's ruling and the non-rational's being ruled, while for justice each class must actually perform its proper job—thus the rulers e.g. aren't merely unchallenged in office but actually know the Good and take decisions in its light for the good of the whole. But then the city is *eo ipso* wise. And equally, if each class is doing its own the rulers are giving proper guidance to the auxiliaries who in turn are able to maintain these values under the stress of combat, so that the just city must also be brave. In fact justice turns out to be complete virtue in the sense that the just city automatically must be moderate, wise, and brave.

If the Kallipolis of Socrates really models the virtues, it must truly be an excellent city. Is it? By hypothesis, everyone has work corresponding to natural aptitude, and contributing to the well-being of the community as a whole. Everyone also wins rewards minted in the highest value they recognize (521a on the case of the rulers is especially striking).

The main worry for us has to do with the amount of control the rulers exert. First, though, note that it is far from clear that being responsible for the decisions of the city as a city will require the rulers to determine such fine-grained issues as the match-ups of particular jobs and spouses to individuals within the producer class.

When it comes to state decisions like whether to embark on the Sicilian Expedition or invade Iraq, there may actually be some appeal in having them made on our behalf by wise rulers. Of course, there is a concern in the "real world" about whether we can get rulers who have the wisdom with which Plato can credit the philosopher-kings and philosopher-queens of his Kallipolis by stipulation. But even in considering the scenario in which wise rulers are stipulated, some today think that the lack of autonomy for most of its citizens renders Plato's Kallipolis hideous.

Of course, even we readily countenance the corresponding thing in the case of children: they do not understand their own good and so are better off under the guardianship of parents who apply superior understanding in taking decisions for the good of the children. Socrates applies the idea not just to children, since the bulk of the population won't be able to meet the stringent requirements he has set for knowledge (590c–e). The problem we struggle with in considering this is how to weigh the dignity of getting to make policy decisions against the drawback of making worse choices than others might make for us. We will soon see that the analogue of this worry will be much less acute when we return to the dialogue's originating question. Remember that we looked at virtues on the bigger canvas of the city for the purpose of helping us see them on the smaller scale. We are now ready to carry out that strategy.

Virtues in the individual

Is a just individual one whose constitution corresponds to that of Kallipolis? That is what the strategy of using our identification of justice in the city to help us see justice in the individual now suggests we consider. Of course, this can only be a possibility if the individual has constituents corresponding to the three classes in our state. Socrates points out (435e–436a) that when a larger group is thought to be spirited, knowledge-loving, or skillful at material gain, this is obviously due to the presence of those traits in the individuals making up the group. But this still does not settle whether distinct elements in the individuals have these traits—and now comes the inquiry into the parts of the soul that we looked at in Chapter Six.

The attractiveness of that discussion simply as a contribution to ongoing thought about the soul shows it is wrong to see the divided soul as an artificial construct produced solely to correspond to the class structure of the state. Rather, as we have seen, the psychological scheme of the *Republic* improves significantly on previous understanding; its analogues continue to appear in thinkers from Aristotle to students of psychology and mind today who have no investment in anything corresponding to the Kallipolis of our text.

Since we have taken up this topic already, we may simply remind ourselves of our earlier results. The soul has distinct parts: one is rational, one spirited, and one appetitive. The rational part is naturally suited to come to grips with the Good and all other real natures. In addition to its characteristic desire for such understanding, it desires what it takes to be the good of the whole soul; in practical matters its assessments, choices, and operations can be informed by the understanding of real natures it has achieved. The spirited and appetitive parts by contrast go with how things simply strike them. Spirit is concerned with prestige and honor and the competitive values, and gets angry when it takes these to be violated. The appetitive part is concerned with pleasures, typically those of food, drink, and sex. In the context of human society, our appetitive part develops an interest in money and gain.

So drawing on our earlier study of the parts of the soul and their different possible ways of developing, let's take up the dialogue's proposals concerning the cardinal virtues in the individual (441c–444a). For the first three, the analogues of what we said about those virtues in the city seem spot on. A person is wise in virtue of the knowledge of the rational part of the soul, applied on behalf of the whole person. A person is brave whose spirit rallies so as to maintain the appropriate decisions of the rational part about what to do even in fearful and threatening circumstances. As we saw, moderation (*sōphrosunē*) in the individual was actually moved up to help in the discussion of the virtues of the city. It is the condition in which the parts of the soul agree about ruling and being ruled: the rational part is in charge and the lower parts agree to follow.

So finally, what is justice in the soul? Since on the large scale we identified it as the condition in which each of the three classes did its proper job in the city, the analogous thing in small would be for each of the three parts to do its own work in the soul, and this is what our text proposes (441d–e, 443b). What would that amount to? The rational part must acquire knowledge including knowledge of the Good, all of which it can then apply to determine (and desire) what is good for the whole of the soul. Spirit and appetite should each have developed so that the things they desire under their own proprietary descriptions are in fact appropriate. We should appreciate that when the spirited and appetitive parts are doing their jobs properly, they do important work in providing quick awareness of and motivational impulses toward things that we really should go for.

It is important that the work of the three parts of our soul isn't just a matter of three separate jobs going on independently. Plato makes this clear when he describes how the just person "regulates well what is really his own" (443d). He:

> puts himself in order ... and harmonizes the three parts of himself .... He binds together those parts and any others there may be in between, and from having been many things he becomes entirely one, moderate and harmonious.
>
> (443d–e)

On the Greek conception, harmony derives from concord (sumphōnia, also translated "consonance"), the desirable condition in which different notes make a unity (Barker 1994). So the just person is a unity, a well-functioning single soul constituted by psychological parts each functioning appropriately to make its distinct contribution to the whole.

As with a city, a human being in the condition that justice is will eo ipso have the other cardinal virtues (441e–444a). In this sense, Platonic justice is complete human virtue. We might think this revisionist theory of justice incidentally explains why dikaiosunē and related terms in some occurrences in ordinary Greek can elicit translation in terms like "righteousness"—"justice" in English as some of us start out understanding it doesn't always stretch quite far enough.

Plato now draws our attention to the parallel between just and unjust actions on the one hand, and healthy and unhealthy ones on the other (444c–d). Healthy actions contribute to health, the condition in which the way the elements in the body control one another and are controlled is in accordance with nature (*kata phusin*); unhealthy actions promote disease. In parallel, just actions contribute to justice, the condition in which the way the elements in the soul control one another and are controlled is in accordance with nature; unjust actions promote injustice. The immediately preceding passage licenses us to read this talk of the elements in the soul controlling and being controlled "in accordance with nature" as gesturing towards the interaction in which each part performs its natural work contributing to the function of the whole.

The claim about the role of our actions in our development is itself of considerable interest. The pattern applies broadly: in Aristotle's famous warm-up for the ethical cases, we "become builders by building and lyre-players by playing the lyre" (*Nicomachean Ethics* 1103a).

The present analogy also makes an important point about value and disvalue. Socrates in the *Gorgias* had drawn attention to the parallel in the aims of those who paint from live figures, house- and ship-builders, doctors and trainers: they all place what they are working on in "a certain organization" and compel "one thing to be suited for another and to fit to it [*harmottein*] until the entire object is put together in an organized and orderly way." Thus a good house is one that is organized and orderly; so too with a ship; so too with our bodies—and so too with the soul. This condition in the body is health and strength; in the soul it is justice and self-control (503d–504d).

What are the elements in the body here? The *Gorgias* formulation, like that of our *Republic* passage, is abstract enough to accommodate a theory in which health involves a harmony of such elements as the wet and the dry (as Eryximachus has it at *Symposium* 186d), or the Hippocratic approach in terms of the four humors; we might also consider the sort of parts of the body that, in the *Republic*, illustrate the principle of opposites in leading up to the argument for the divided soul (hands etc.).

If one takes the elements in the body to be organs, *Republic* 444d would be claiming that we are physically healthy when all our bodily organs are working well together, each in good shape and performing its natural function. Or to leave the claim abstract, health would be the condition in which the "things" (to translate most neutrally) in the body work well together, each performing its natural function. Either way, the claim seems reasonable. For the case of the soul, our dialogue has done considerable study of what the relevant elements are, and what their jobs are. The rational, spirited, and appetitive parts are the ones in question, we have learned a lot about their proper functions, and we have seen that Plato has identified justice as the condition in which these parts of the soul work well together, each performing its natural function. So we can indeed see that justice stands to the soul as health stands to the body.

Socrates sums up this part of his argument: "Virtue, then, as it seems, would be a kind of health and beauty [kallos] and good condition of the soul, and vice would be disease, ugliness, and weakness" (444d–e, tr. Shorey 1961). He has met Glaucon's challenge to show that justice is the kind of good that health is. And indeed, Glaucon soon answers his own original question, saying:

> Even if one has every kind of food and drink, lots of money, and every sort of power to rule, life is thought to be not worth living when the body's nature is ruined. So even if someone can do whatever he wishes, except what will free him from vice and injustice and make him acquire justice and virtue, how can it be worth living when his soul—the very thing by which he lives—is ruined and in turmoil?
>
> (445a–b)

This will be confirmed fully when review of the degenerate character types leads to the overall, comparative result. Socrates tells us:

> Shall we hire a herald, then, said I, or shall I myself make proclamation that the son of Ariston pronounced the best man and the most righteous [dikaiotatos] to be the happiest … and declared that the most evil and most unjust is the most unhappy …? … Shall I add the clause "alike whether their character is known to all men and gods or is not known"?
>
> (580b–c, tr. Shorey 1930)

Glaucon, here addressed with his patronymic alone, approves this formulation of the verdict of "the son of Ariston." Note here a subtle effect of the way Plato has composed the query Socrates makes of his interlocutor. Just as the bare family name "Kennedy" can in some particular context refer to Chris Kennedy, the former chairman of the University of Illinois Board of Trustees, but most naturally puts us in mind of JFK, so Plato is himself is the most famous son of Ariston. Thus the extract I just quoted also reads as telling us that this is Plato's verdict (Sedley 1995).

To complete our review of Plato's comparison of justice with injustice, we should note that after finishing this main discussion, Socrates goes on to two arguments to show that, after all, the life of the just person is actually more *pleasant* than that of the unjust (580d–588a). Part of this involves the important claim that appetite and spirit both carry out their proper functions best and get the best and truest pleasures available to them when they follow the guidance of reason; when one of the other parts gains control, it actually "won't be able to secure its own pleasure" (587a). Indeed, it was part of the study of the most unjust type, the "tyrannical" soul, that in such an individual, whose appetite is uncontrolled, it becomes so excessive that it *cannot be satisfied*. Such an individual is actually "in the greatest need of most things and truly poor" (579e). Thus the non-rational parts of the soul are better off under the guidance of reason than without it (586a–587a).

To drive home the point that there is no profit in being unjust, Socrates asks whether it can:

> profit anyone to acquire gold unjustly if, by doing so, he enslaves the best part of himself to the most vicious? If he got the gold by enslaving his son or daughter to savage and evil men, it wouldn't profit him, no matter how much gold he got. How, then, could he fail to be wretched if he pitilessly enslaves the most divine part of himself to the most godless and polluted one and accepts golden gifts in return for a more terrible destruction than Eriphyle's when she took the necklace in return for her husband's soul [*psychē*[11]]?
>
> (589d–590a)

Far from injustice paying if we can escape detection and punishment, it turns out that injustice itself is against our interest; escaping punishment just makes things worse (591a–592b). After all this, Socrates adds for good measure that we should restore to the just man the benefits of appearing to be just, which ordinarily at least will accrue to him over his lifetime. Finally, according to the myth of Er, a just life will help us do better after death as well (612b–621d).

How good an account is this?

We have traced Plato's proposals about what justice is and why it is of paramount importance in securing the good life for an individual. We can now deepen our understanding of these proposals by entertaining some issues that arise in connection with them.

What if someone objects that considering spirit and appetite worse and lower than reason simply manifests academic bias? Here we can confirm the special authority of reason by recalling a simpler case. If we were seeking for gold we wouldn't want to content ourselves with grabbing whatever happens to strike our ignorant selves as gold—we would want to get what satisfies the scientific account of what Gold *really* is. So too, if fundamental reality contains such things as Goodness and all the others Plato has mentioned, understanding them will have significant application in our project of living well. Thus reason deserves to rule in us because it is the part of our soul which is equipped to understand the things that are real and to apply that understanding in our lives.

This is not a picture according to which the rational part is in control in the domineering sense that it forcibly determines the course of the whole person while systematically frustrating the other two parts. Our text clearly argues that the lower parts of the soul do better both with regard to function and even with regard to pleasure under the guidance of reason than they could do on their own (586a–587c). Because there is an inherent tendency of appetite to grow to want more (442a–b, resulting in the extreme case in the tyrannical soul at 579e), reason and spirit have a maintenance role in managing appetitive urges even in a virtuous person. This is what the beneficent agricultural image we looked at in the final section of

Chapter Six is in fact describing (589a–b). Overall, Plato envisages as the just person one in whose soul proper upbringing and self-maintenance result in the lower parts actually desiring the very things that reason recognizes as good for them to want.

Now we can see an interesting difference between the case of the city and that of the individual. When considering Plato's Kallipolis, we noted that many modern readers find problematic the lack of autonomy of citizens not in the ruling class: the bulk of the population lives under good policies but is excluded from the process of setting them. But notice that concern for autonomy could be thought to tell in favor of Plato's preference in the case of the individual. In the person with psychic harmony, the rational part's own desires are formed in light of this person's understanding of what Goodness etc. really are, and this part tends to and approves the impulses that healthy spirit and appetite have. Considered as a person this individual could be thought to be maximally autonomous. And the person has a claim to be the relevant unit.

So while, to consider the obvious example of state censorship, we tend to be extremely skeptical of Big Brother deciding what we individual citizens can watch and not watch, it is much less unpalatable to suggest that within a human being, a person's reason should decide for that person. It is not at all clear that it would be desirable to let oneself develop and cater to tastes that one's own reason is trying to resist. That would certainly be undesirable if Plato is correct that such catering results in the hypertrophy of the many-headed beast, until the multiplying wild heads become literally insatiable and so wretched.

Let's return to the big picture and consider how well Plato has answered the dialogue's main question. Is it a problem that, having undertaken to defend justice, he has come up with this notion of psychic harmony and defended that (what Sachs 1963 stigmatized as the "fallacy of irrelevance")? Since Plato did show the inadequacy of the ambient culture's understanding of justice, providing a revisionist account is certainly in order, but we should still ask ourselves if he has identified a reasonable candidate. Someone who replaces the old "yellow metal" account with an atomic understanding of Gold has to do something to connect this underlying structure with (at least a significant number of) our usual samples of gold, even if we can tolerate or even expect the odd lump of iron pyrites to be discredited. There can be correction in the other direction too: to change the example, we can categorize avocados as fruit once we have a scientific basis for the classification, even if we used to think of them as vegetables.

Plato is providing the requisite assurance when he checks that the person in whom each part of the soul does its own would be least likely to steal, embezzle, commit adultery, etc. (442e–443b). This is reinforced by what we learn at 485d about the impact on our other interests of even an initial attraction to wisdom. Putting all this together, the inner constitution Plato has identified as justice does generally manifest as the just person's refraining from pleonectic behavior: the condition in which each part of the *psychē* does its own indeed accounts for the human being's "having his own" and not "wanting more." Since the desires of the spirit and appetite of the person with psychic harmony are well-directed and moderate, they do not provide the motivation that typically leads to transgressions. The discussion of the perverted character types in Books 8 and 9 is also relevant to the flip side i.e. injustice. Some of them will be very likely to do conventionally forbidden things.

So far we have determined that people with Platonic justice understand the Good and everything else real and apply that understanding in aiming at the good of the whole—but note that this only has the force of "the whole *soul*" (my emphasis, 441e, cf. 442c and 589b). We may still wish to ask how certain it is that these happy few will show concern for others—which we may consider a key attribute of truly excellent human beings.

In fact, we have seen that just people in Plato's sense must be brave, and none of the interlocutors question that bravery involves risking life and limb in defense of others. Again, Glaucon is brought to agree that the philosophers nourished by Kallipolis will be willing to give up (temporarily) the delights of contemplation for the chore of ruling because that is a just demand and they are just people (519e–520e). In fact, the unfolding dialectic of this passage shows the total success of Socrates' realignment of Glaucon's motivations. Plato's historical brother was highly ambitious politically; here the fictional Glaucon has been so taken by enthusiasm for the value of philosophy that his initial reaction is to protest the institution of philosopher-rulers on the basis that ruling makes their lives worse!

Note though that even if a life in which the demand to rule never came up would be better, it does not follow that philosophers for whom ruling is a just demand are better off flouting it.[12] The philosopher-kings and philosopher-queens tasked with ruling give up a little time that could be spent in contemplation, but this does not make their overall lives wretched: they have achieved and enjoyed the activity of all the human excellences including that involved in contemplation, after all. While if they refused a just demand they would have to be flawed morally and we know from the main argument that would ruin their lives. Or to take a parallel case, those who turn away from close relatives needing care may seem to consult their own advantage, but to act this way in these circumstances shows that one is a wretch who cannot truly have a good life.

Thus our Platonically just agents, who maintain themselves as excellent through their choices, will show a concern that makes their actions other-regarding in the sense that matters for the relevant others. Platonically just agents are sensitive to others' needs. This is not in tension with the idea that justice is good for its possessor. In the concrete circumstances in which such agents find themselves, the demands of justice, say, might call on them to give up some of their time for the sake of another—an action that, so described, looks like something they might be better off not doing. If circumstances were different, their preferred way of using this time might be for contemplation. But in the unfortunately constraining circumstances that obtain, the action justice requires does not conflict with the just agents' own interests. Insofar as giving up their time is (in these concrete circumstances) being responsive to the demands of justice, they are choosing the one among their options that is honorable and excellent, and so doing the best for themselves that is possible at this moment.[13] People who are going to be Platonically brave and just will have motivations that are other-regarding in this sense.

Of course, we ourselves cannot spell out now just from reading the Republic all that Platonically virtuous people will be thinking when they act, any more than we can spell out all they will be thinking in their contemplative moments. After all, Socrates claims that no one will command true understanding unless he understands everything in the light of the Good. And in our text he has handled the Good only with simile and analogy (435c–d, 504a–e).

The role and presentation of Forms in the argument of the *Republic*

Finally, let's consider the characteristic way in which Plato's detailed views in ethics and politics are grounded in this dialogue by presentation of his views about Forms. While our dialogue—and even each of several passages in it—was once regarded as the locus of an official and determinate "theory of Forms," there is growing awareness that Plato is not presenting views on Forms that are as worked-out, fine-grained or dogmatic as this phrase suggests. The extremely wide scope of its inquiry prevents the *Republic* from giving every single subject it includes a detailed and sophisticated presentation. Even attempting that would make the dialogue unassimilable by a human being! Various topics are brought in and developed to the extent that is needed for the primary discussion.

Why would Plato in the *Republic* sketch views about Forms without presenting a fully worked-out theory of these entities? Analogously with what we saw in the *Phaedo*, he is motivating us to go on to the difficult work of his "metaphysics seminar" by showing us the connection between making progress on a topic we already care about and engaging with Forms. But that does not require him to tell us all there is to know about them here. Further development of the "theory of Forms" will require hard work and our full attention; for now Plato sketches the importance and outlines of views he will go on to develop (or rather challenge us to develop) in later works.

As we conclude this chapter, let us assess how much about Forms is necessary for the main ethical, psychological, and political argument of our text. For if it does not contain an official "theory of Forms," the *Republic* is most definitely committed on some points about them, which will be the minimum common basis of all the more determinate versions we can go on to give the theory. This minimum includes importantly that there are fundamental natures to which we have access through thought; Justice and Goodness are among them. Dialectic has the job of giving accounts that say of each thing what it is; that is, it has the job of answering the "What is it?" question about each of the real things and giving the account of its nature (532a–b, 533a–b, 534b). Thus the inquiry of the dialogue into justice has all along been about the Form, Justice. But in the early books it was not necessary to think of this special status, hence lower case in English has been more natural. Note that this *does not* mean different entities are in question: just that it is sometimes but not always natural to have in mind their special status.

This minimum common basis rules out a picture of the devotee of Forms as an intellectually vacant mystic. Nor is it right to think that Plato's picture makes knowledge easy—as if all we need to do is *posit* Forms and by this quick step we're done! For to suppose there are Forms (in general) or to revere them is not yet to begin to know which ones are genuine, let alone to know the accounts in question. To have wisdom, it is not sufficient to posit that Justice, for example, is a Form. Rather, one must be able to give and defend an account of Justice in light of understanding of the Good; similarly with Courage, with Beauty, with the Double, the Equal, and so on for as many Forms as there are. Knowledge of Forms, far from being too easy, will actually be extremely hard; exactly as hard as the sum of all mathematical, aesthetic, ethical, and scientific knowledge that it in fact is. It is part of the minimum common basis not only that there are such things as what Justice and the Good really are, but that these are not to be read off from ordinary experience or taken in by osmosis from one's ambient culture. We will see why this is in Chapter Eight.

The *Republic* does not make clear either the extent of Forms or how they "do their jobs." In particular, it does not settle whether or not each must be a perfect instance of the property that it is. In Chapters Nine and Ten we will consider later works in which Plato pursued Form theory in much greater detail. But to inculcate all those details is not necessary for the immediate purpose of the *Republic*. The minimum common basis is all that is needed for Plato's argument about why we should want our lives and practices to be grounded in more than what a person of common sense and practical experience—or ordinary culture—has access to. Just as an expert on the nature of Gold is highly desirable if we want to acquire gold, so too an expert on the nature of the Good is in order if we want to live well. It is the claim that there is a real Good, a real Human Excellence, and the rest that does the work here, not any further claim that they display themselves perfectly or that they do their jobs in some other way. If only one who grasps Forms has accounts of the fundamental realities that are responsible for all else, we can already see that such a person must command a drastically improved basis for life and practice. This is what it takes if we are skillfully to navigate our course in life. Thus, the *Republic* shows readers who initially wanted to find out about the good life that they need to come to grips with Forms. The contrast the *Phaedo* and the *Republic* make between these special entities and sensibles will be our subject in Chapter Eight.

Further reading

Laws. Another text on the topic of founding a city; Plato's latest, unfinished at his death. Long left aside as not very interesting, this work has recently been the subject of renewed attention (see Bobonich 2002; Scolnicov and Brisson, eds, 2003).

Secondary literature

See Bibliography for full details of the works listed below.

On *Antiphon the Sophist*

D. Furley (1981) "Antiphon's Case Against Justice."

On the Republic

J. Adam (1963) *The "Republic" of Plato*. (First edition 1902). Adam is still useful for those who want a Greek text with line-by-line remarks, especially since some of his points are starting to get lost from view.
J. Annas (1981) *An Introduction to Plato's "Republic."*
G. Ferrari (ed.) (2007b) *The Cambridge Companion to Plato's "Republic."*

M. McPherran (ed.) (2010) *Plato's "Republic."*
N. Pappas (2003) *Routledge Philosophy Guidebook to Plato and the "Republic."*
C. Reeve (1988) *Philosopher-Kings.*
G. Vlastos (1973a) "Justice and Happiness in the *Republic.*"

Notes

1   By Hellenistic times there is acute interest in the further, fine-grained, question whether virtue by itself guarantees a good life or whether it is only the most important component, requiring some amount of external goods. We may take Plato at this early stage to be concentrating on the basic claim that virtue is paramount in living well, and not yet to be giving any great attention to the fine-grained determination.

2   The climate in Egypt is highly favorable to the preservation of papyri.

3   Cf. 428d: the rulers of a wise city use knowledge on behalf of the whole how it should best conduct itself towards itself and towards other cities.

4   A Platonic variation on a story in Herodotus 1.7 about how Gyges, the ancestor of Croesus, came to the throne of Lydia. In the *Histories* there is no ring.

5   There is controversy about exactly how to understand Glaucon's three-fold division of goods at 357b–358b, which in turn affects which parts of the dialogue correspond to which parts of his challenge.

6   The methodology is that we must get an account of each that is independently plausible, and they must match—if not we must go back and look some more (see 434d–435a). The reason for the matching is of course the ongoing demand that F-ness be the same in all cases we call F. (Of course, this only applies when F-ness is intuitively univocal.) Also notice that Plato does not apply this rule flat-footedly—just actions are those that promote the agent's internal state of justice (443c–444d), not actions that directly satisfy the account of justice.

7   Notice that from the point of view of the dialogue as a whole this community does not promote our overall well-being as humans; so Glaucon's appellation of "city for pigs" turns out to be quite appropriate.

8   See the Divided Line, the Cave and the discussion of higher education (from 509d to end of Book 7). Burnyeat (2000) and Denyer (2007a) are helpful here.

9   People have these natures in the weak sense that these are the natures responsible for the features they have. As we will see later, while Plato's metaphysics is in one sense "essentialist," it is so only at the level of Forms: there is a strong, internal connection between *Justice* and *Virtue*, but no such relation between *Socrates* and Baldness, *Socrates* and Virtue, etc.

10 Of course the text still shows many sexist slurs such as the allusions to "womanish" behavior (e.g. at 605e). We can explain how this happens by using the *Republic*'s own picture of moral development, in terms of which it is

easy to see how a person can realize intellectually some truth but still have emotional reactions (formed earlier and ingrained in the lower parts of the soul) that are not in harmony with the intellectual progress.

11 That is, his life; this refers to the participation of Eriphyle in a plan that led to her husband's death.

12 For a recent treatment of the question (currently enjoying a vogue in the secondary literature) whether and why the philosophers will be willing to serve as rulers, see Smith (2010).

13 Thanks to Will Small for help with articulating this.

Part III

Eight
Why sensibles are not fully real

La métaphysique aussi a une histoire.

(Luc Brisson 2011: 73)

Plato is famous for thinking that sensibles are not fully real—the Form is the real soufflé! Or to go with serious examples, the real good, the real double, the real ox, and so on are all Forms in Plato's view. He is not saying that sensible particulars don't exist, or that we can't taste, acquire, or have correct beliefs about them. His point rather is that neither sensibles nor observations about them are fundamental: sensibles are derived from and explained by Forms. We have begun to see how central this tenet is in Plato's thought. But *why* does he think this? In this chapter we will see more about what motivates this whole picture.

Aristotle offers discussion of the development of Plato's thinking about Forms that contains useful elements of an answer. One of the influences on Plato he identifies is Socrates' project of inquiring into ethics and seeking the universal. We saw in Chapter Three that Aristotle's characterization of Socrates' project applies well to Plato's Socratic dialogues. Interlocutors were challenged to say what piety, bravery, and so on each is, where this had relevance to their life situations. We also saw that all concerned engaged in the relevant discussions without any particular self-consciousness on the score of the character and status of the objects of their enquiry. According to Aristotle, Plato then became concerned with that issue. Plato thought sensibles could not be objects of knowledge because they were always "changing" (*Metaphysics* 987a–b, with 1078b–1079a, 1086a–b). This gives us a snapshot of Plato's thinking as he started to develop his distinctive theory of Forms.

To avoid confusion, let me clarify two points. "Change" in ancient texts sometimes has a broader sense than we are used to. We are used to thinking a thing changes if it is in different conditions at different times. Ancient authors can also count as changing anything that both is and is not F (for some property F), possibly in different respects, relations, or contexts. Also, it will turn out that "sensibles" in this connection are not confined to sensible particulars—sometimes "perceptible universals" or "sensible properties" are also under consideration.[1] In fact, what Plato is often getting at with the idea of the visible/sensible domain is a matter of "sensibles" very broadly construed—something like what is patent to superficial observation.

But these broadenings of the notions in play do nothing to allay—indeed they may even make more pressing—our questions about Plato. He often draws attention to sensibles' being e.g. beautiful and ugly, equal and unequal, just and unjust, one and many. But we want to ask: If Chicago is cold (in winter) and hot (in summer), so what? If bright color is admirable (in a playroom) and garish (at a funeral), so what ? Those are perfectly good facts that everyone knows, as long as we put in the necessary qualifications. Nor is it immediately clear to us why this pattern shows that Chicago (a sensible particular) and bright color (a sensible universal) are not truly real.

Some awareness of the underlying Greek is relevant here. In English a variety of terms including "what is," "being," "the real," "reality," and "real nature" are dragooned in order to represent Greek expressions including *to on* and *ousia* that derive from *einai* ("to be.") So Plato's claim that sensibles are not fully real is supported by demonstration that they both are and are not, that they are between what fully is and what purely is not, that they mix being and not-being. What does all that amount to, and why does it matter? We will address those issues in the present chapter.

We will first consider the dialectical situation in Plato's historical context. I already indicated briefly that it helps in understanding the affinity argument in the *Phaedo* to locate Plato's program in relation to a family of two-tiered theories that came before his (Chapter

Five). The character and motivation of this family is what we will be exploring more fully now.

Our starting point will be the work of Parmenides of Elea. We will look at the refutation he offered for anyone who tries to speak or think of generation, destruction, or change: these all violate his demand that we cleave wholly to what is; they involve mixing being and not-being. He put it that, unless we knew what was wrong with his argument, we should acknowledge that the multitude of distinct individuals we ordinarily recognize and their histories must all be completely illusory.

Then we will turn to the two-tiered philosophies of nature developed in response to this. These theories tried to observe Eleatic constraints at the level of fundamental entities—*those* should not be subject to not-being. Ordinary objects and their histories, while not fundamental, still got some standing, as derived from and so partly intelligible in terms of things that are. Ancient atomism as well as the work of Empedocles and Anaxagoras were theories of this type. We will see how, with respect to the key issue, the theory of Anaxagoras is the most scrupulous of these.

When we return to Plato with this background in place, we will be in a position to see that he is offering a successor-theory to that of Anaxagoras (Furley 1976). Plato's general set-up is isomorphic with that of his predecessor. Of course, instead of focusing exclusively on philosophy of nature or cosmology, Plato's theory was meant to encompass mathematical, ethical, and aesthetic reality as well. And this makes Plato especially aware of a certain problem in the original, Anaxagorean, theory. Plato recognizes the need to find a new interpretation of participation in (having a share of) something fundamental. So roughly the first half of the chapter will show that Plato shared the estimate of sensible particulars of the philosophers of nature, but that he thought their best work on what *is* could not succeed in accounting for all that he wanted to comprehend.

Then we will turn to the central discussion distinguishing opinion from knowledge in *Republic* Book 5. We will see that Plato's Presocratic legacy is foundational for this text as well: opinion, the lesser cognitive state, has objects that both are and are not; for knowledge we must come to terms with what purely is. While the official discussion of cognitive short-coming is framed in sufficiently abstract terms to take in a whole variety of people who don't succeed in grasping pure being, we will see that one particular group is centrally targeted: the kind of person who is educated and civilized in a way conventionally recognized in contemporary Athenian society. The chapter will end with the *Republic's* figurative treatment of the sensible domain in the famous parable of the Cave, with its associated figures the Sun and the Divided Line.

So in the chapter as a whole, we will see how Plato's program developed out of the work of the Presocratics combined with Socrates' investigations in ethics. And we will trace why he thought one could not simply rely on the natural science and surrounding culture of his day. Many people with a passing awareness of Plato's proclamation that the ordinary domain of everyday experience is not fully real take him to be the historical figure who is maximally hostile to it. Yet viewing him in his true place in debate on these issues gives us a very different sense. Parmenides the Eleatic is the maximally hostile one. Against this baseline Plato's approach—like those of the philosophers of nature—is designed to rehabilitate the ordinary domain as much as possible. Just as a still taken from a movie that looks at first glance like a man who has fallen halfway down from a building might be revealed in context to be someone with superpowers zooming up, this assessment gains much from putting snapshots from the *Phaedo* and *Republic* in their setting of the ongoing dialectic of Greek philosophy.

The Eleatic challenge

Our story starts with the awesome figure of Parmenides the Eleatic. If being a philosopher is a matter not of having a special topic but of a characteristic way of proceeding and in particular a characteristic attitude to argument, then Parmenides has a claim to be the very first philosopher of the Western tradition. We are lucky that the essential core of his thought survives in fragments giving his own words; these fragments are extracts quoted by later philosophers including Plato himself. We have the opening of his work and the argument of its "Truth" section. (We don't have all that Parmenides offers after the "Truth," but whatever he gives as his contribution to mortal opinion must have a lesser status.)

Born in the sixth century BC, Parmenides was the author of a hexameter poem that "proved, by an argument that nobody could fault, a conclusion that nobody could believe" (Annas 1986: 235). He presented it as an *elenchos* (that is, as an examination, or refutation, or challenge) for all those who subscribed to a world of change and difference. As an (unnamed) goddess supposedly tells the narrator of the poem, "judge by reason the strife-encompassed refutation spoken by me" (fragment 7, tr. Kirk, Raven, and Schofield 1983[2]). Parmenides' basic stance (and that of his pupil Zeno) was: unless you can work out how to evade my argument, reason requires you to accept the position that there is in reality only a single unchanging thing.

The position supposedly revealed by Parmenides' argument is one peculiarly incompatible with the narrative of his poem and the drama of his address to us. The narrator's reported initiation into the argument by the goddess, our hearing the challenge and potentially profiting from it are all events that could not happen according to the conclusions to which Parmenides is apparently driving us. Yet the *issue of this challenge* was a major intellectual event for the Greeks: without some way of responding to it, pluralists were not really in a position to hold their views; intellectual respectability required everyone to shore up their foundations.

The primary weapon of Parmenides is the blank incomprehensibility of what is not, or not-being: "for you could not know what is not—that cannot be done—nor indicate it" (fragment 2). Why is what is not unmanageable? To start by quoting what we will then interpret: "What can be spoken and thought of [alternatively: known] must be: for it *can* be, but nothing cannot [alternatively: and it is not nothing]" (fragment 6, my combination of various translations).

There are several different ways of reconstructing how fragment 6 gets Parmenides to the conclusion announced in fragment 2 that are appropriate for our present project. I offer informal reconstructions instead of the hyper-formalized type because the latter, building in as they do precision and commitments foreign to the original context, are not to our present point, which is to trace an important strand in the historical reception of the work of the Eleatics.

One reconstruction of the argument is as follows: What can be known and spoken of *can be* and is not nothing. Add unexpressed disjunction: "Either it is, or it is nothing." So *it must be* (Furley 1973). An alternative reconstruction: What can be spoken and thought of at least *can* be; nothing by contrast *cannot be*. So our subject differs in its pattern of attributes from nothing, so it is not nothing; if not nothing it is a thing that is (following Owen 1960[3]). If these reanimations of fragment 6's argument seem to turn on too simple and easily avoidable mistakes, those who are interested in such matters may like to consider the suggestion that the basic claim of fragment 2 results directly from Parmenides' "hyper-denotationism" (Furth 1968).

However we reconstruct the details of the thinking that gets us to this, Parmenides clearly maintains that what is not fails to meet the criterion for being a viable object of knowledge/thought/inquiry/speech and is wholly unmanageable. This gives him the blunt instrument he will employ for the rest of the "Truth."

Once Parmenides has ruled out the way "it is not" (he calls it "a track beyond all tidings," fragment 2, tr. Barnes 1982), he shows how the mixing of being and not-being that the ordinary person is committed to is equally hopeless. Consider our belief in generation and destruction (fragment 8). Generation is supposed to be the coming into being of what formerly was not; we can now see that, with its crucial appeal to not-being, this will be incoherent. Similarly, for destruction, a thing that is would have to make the transition to not-being—again forbidden. Likewise, for change (in the narrow sense), something like Toto's running (or the fact that Toto is running) would have to make the transition between being and not-being. Finally, to distinguish one thing from another is hopeless. Whichever object I take first, it can never leave off: that would require a contrasting time or place where it *is not*. If I start with Toto, he ends up as the totality! Notice that the mixtures of being and not-being that Parmenides is challenging here are not on their face contradictions. Rather, the problem is the putative involvement of *what is not*.

Parmenides' challenge is that, unless we can see how to elude the refutation given by "the goddess," reason requires us to accept that reality is a single unchanging thing. To continue to describe the world as our senses report it—with its vast and ever-changing population, all of varying colors, sounds, and flavors—is hopelessly to mix not-being with being.

The pluralist response: philosophy of nature

Importantly for the history of what would come to be science as well as for philosophy more generally, in the immediate aftermath of Parmenides' challenge the proto-scientists we call philosophers of nature did their best to live within Eleatic strictures. As we saw briefly in Chapter Five, they did this by developing two-tiered theories: they thought to afford themselves the possibility of explaining the generation, destruction, and change we ordinarily speak of in the world around us as not involving the generation or destruction of anything real (i.e. fundamental).

On this type of theory, the artifacts, seas and mountains, animals and plants of our everyday world are not fundamental beings, but neither are they and their vicissitudes wholly illusory as Parmenides was pushing us to admit. Rather, everyday objects of this sort are derived items, temporarily made up as typically shifting composites of fundamental entities or portions thereof. As we will see in more detail in this chapter, the strategy of the cosmologists was to obey Eleatic constraints by eliminating not-being in connection with their fundamental entities. Their program was to explain what people *ordinarily* call the generation, destruction and change of the objects around us in terms of recombinations of the invulnerable basic entities. As we might put it: talk about what is and is not (among ordinary objects) can always be translated into talk about the fundamentals, and in such a way that we do not have to speak at that level of what is not.[4] So the cosmologists don't throw out the "generation", "destruction," and "change" of ordinary life entirely—but neither do they allow not-being at the level of what is fundamental.

Each such theorist allowed himself a plurality of beings which were unchanging except in location. Did they have a principled reason for relaxing Eleatic strictures in exactly this way? They may have thought their beings were sufficiently distinguished by their *positive* characteristics. And perhaps, since the conclusions of

Parmenides' "Truth" are impossible to live with, the pluralists simply tried to respect as many of the constraints as they could while making the minimum change they needed to get to some view that works. Each had a proprietary version of the shared basic strategy.

Interestingly, atomism originated as one realization of this. What we see around us are temporary combinations of (unsplittable) atoms whizzing around in the infinite void. In fact the atomists, in positing the void, were in a way committed to making not-being basic. The other pluralists avoided any hint among their fundamentals of what is not.

So Empedocles, the originator of four-element theory, operated with elemental earth, air, fire and water (sometimes called "the four roots") combined in different ratios. To get a feel for his theory, we cannot do better than to look at some fragments from his poem. He tells us that when the elements:

> are mixed in the form of a man and come to the air, or in the form of the race of wild beasts or of plants or of birds, then they [i.e. ordinary people] say that this comes into being; but when they are separated, they call this wretched fate.
>
> (Fragment 9)

Empedocles rejects the views of those who countenance real generation or destruction, for Eleatic reasons:

> Fools—for they have no far-reaching thoughts, since they think that what before did not exist comes into being, or that a thing dies and is completely destroyed. / For it is impossible for anything to come to be from what is not, and it cannot be brought about or heard of that what is should be utterly destroyed; for wherever one may ever set it, there indeed it will always be.
>
> (Fragments 11 and 12)

Empedocles was happy to suppose that more characteristics could show up at the level of the derived entities than among his four "roots," and illustrated how this could be with a lovely analogy.

As when painters are decorating offerings ... men through cunning well skilled in their craft—when they actually seize pigments of many colours in their hands, mixing in harmony more of some and less of others, they produce from them forms resembling all things, creating trees and men and women, beasts and birds and water-bred fish, and long-lived gods, too, highest in honour: so let not deception overcome your mind and make you think there is any other source [than the four roots] of all the countless mortal things that are plain to see, but know this clearly, for the tale you hear comes from a god.

(Fragment 23)

In the case of pigments, we are familiar with the procedure in which one can start with a limited number of colors and then mix them in different proportions to produce an infinite variety, so reproducing the full range of hue, brightness, and saturation we see around us. We can for example mix some blue and yellow to get green; then we can add white and more blue to get aquamarine, and so on. The green and the aqua each presents a look different from the other and from the original primary colors. So too Empedocles would have it that when the four elements are mixed in the ratio 1:1:1:1, blood results; a different recipe yields bone; each shows characteristics different from those of the original earth, air, fire, and water. Thus the whole panoply we see around us of animals, minerals and vegetables comes about from the basic elements, just as representations of them all can be made from the basic paints.

For Anaxagoras of Clazomenae, this emergence of new characteristics not found among the elements would vitiate the entire program.[5] "How could hair come from what is not hair or flesh from what is not flesh?" he is reported to have demanded (fragment 10; in reconstructing the theory of Anaxagoras I rely on important points in Strang 1963; Furley 1976, 1987: ch. 6[6]). He accordingly posits the maximum variety in his fundamental beings, and uses them in the now-familiar shared pluralist strategy. As he puts it:

The Greeks are wrong to recognize coming into being and perishing; for nothing comes into being nor perishes, but is rather compounded or dissolved from things that are. So they

would be right to call coming into being composition and
perishing dissolution.

(Fragment 17)

This way of understanding "coming into being" and "perishing" is
very close to what we saw in Empedocles. The most important
difference is that Empedocles thinks it enough to avoid anything's
coming about from "what is not" in the sense of "nothing."
Anaxagoras interprets the Eleatic proscription much more strictly:
he maintains that *nothing F can come about from what is not F*. Thus for
Anaxagoras, a chocolate cake owes its salient characteristics to its
significant shares of the sweet, the dark, the wet, etc. (pure stuffs,
portions of which are present as ingredients in the mixture). No
characteristic of the cake is springing into existence from what is
not that. But these are not its only constituents. Anaxagoras' reading
of Eleatic reasoning requires that, if our flesh and bones can be
nourished when we eat bread, there must have been flesh and bone
in the bread. Since these are not apparent, the portions in question
must be latent, hidden by a predominating competitor (testimony
in Kirk, Raven, and Schofield 1983: 374–5).

We have now come to a pair of principles special to this theory:
Anaxagoras' principles of latency and predominance. Anaxagoras
saw "everything arising out of everything" (as reported by Aristotle
Physics 187b) if not immediately at least by transitivity over the
course of cosmic history, as algae may contribute to a fish which
fertilizes a bush whose berries are eaten by a bear who returns to
dust and so on and on without limit. In order to account for all this,
in Anaxagoras' theory everything around us is a mixture containing
portions of everything. But not all these portions in a given
composite have to be equal—some can be present in trace amounts
and then others predominate over them.

Just as in our view a gold bracelet is one in which there is enough
pure gold compared with base metals for the piece to be called gold
or golden, so for Anaxagoras, the evident characteristics of any
mixture are those of its dominant ingredients. Because anything that
can become manifest in the world around us must correspond to a
basic ingredient (for how could it come from what is not?),
Anaxagoras is committed to treat a much longer list in the way we

treat gold. He is committed at least to the hot, the cold, the wet, the dry, the bright, the dark, the large, and the small, as well as the tissues of living creatures.

Change is simply the exchange or acquisition of portions of these basic stuffs. Thus, an Anaxagorean analysis of the "Chicken Soup Game," in which the quarterback Joe Montana, rendered hypothermic by illness and weather, was revived in the locker room by the homely remedy, would go as follows. Hypothermia is obviously a condition in which one's body has an insufficient amount of the hot (thought of as a stuff, the totality of heat in the world, as caloric once was). The soup however contained a significant portion of the hot, which was integrated into Montana's body when he drank it; when this new portion joined with whatever modest amount of the hot was already present, he was sufficiently restored to return to the game, leading Notre Dame to victory in the final seconds. Or consider how the addition of anchovies affects a pizza. The anchovies have a huge portion of pure salt, which in combination with whatever salt was already in the crust, sauce, and cheese make the finished pie extremely salty as well.

Since everything will always contain a portion of everything, no basic stuff will ever be physically isolated—the true beings will never lie evident to the senses. But "Mind ... has all knowledge about everything ... the things that are mingled and separated and divided off, all are known by Mind" (fragment 12). In other words, this theory no less than atomism explains the world accessible to our senses by means of more fundamental theoretical entities accessible only in thought.

We have now studied in some detail a strategy developed in the philosophy of nature for explaining the vicissitudes of the derived items accessible to our senses by invoking fundamental theoretical entities themselves not subject to generation and corruption. We have seen how this was motivated by the Eleatic challenge, and we have seen how Anaxagoras is the most rigorous of the pluralists in his procedure. He stands out as "a kind of Ajax among the Presocratics ... heroically adhering to the strictest interpretation of the Parmenidean code" (Furley 1976: 83).

Plato as a successor to Anaxagoras

On the reading I have presented of the theory of Anaxagoras, things around us are gold because they *have a portion of* elemental gold (a portion large enough to dominate competitors) and wet because they *have a share of* the wet. The italicized phrases are two variant ways of rendering the Greek in question. In fact, the "participation" we often find in translations of Plato is simply another possible—and more Latinate—translation (Anaxagoras and Plato each uses *metechein* along with other terminology for this relation). We can now see the striking isomorphism between Plato's theory and that of Anaxagoras. For both of them:

> Derived things of lesser status can be called F at some times because they have a share of/have a portion of/participate in the F itself.

> The F itself is F.

Translational practice (if it makes "participation" seem to figure in Plato's theory alone) can have the very unfortunate side-effect of obscuring this isomorphism—even if it does have some use in marking the fact that Plato recognizes the need to rethink the relationship of *having a share* that holds between the derived items and the basic entities. (This turns out to go with rethinking what sort of things the basic entities are, and what sort of fact "The F itself is F" concerns. Plato's variant of the theory will not need principles of latency and predominance.)

The physical-ingredient interpretation that is the Anaxagorean understanding of participation works well—but only in a certain range of cases. What if we move on from what makes a bracelet gold to what makes it beautiful? Obviously elemental gold will not account for that, since plenty of beautiful objects are not golden, and plenty of golden ones are hideous. Can we understand "the beautiful" as another thing analogous to elemental gold, as a homogeneous stuff portions of which can figure among the ingredients in mixtures? We can see on our own that no such stuff, detachable from the composites it temporarily forms part of and transferable to others, can account for things' being beautiful in the way elemental gold can account for things' being golden, or water for their being wet. To play this role, a candidate would have to be some homogeneous ingredient lost by a fresco that is exposed to air pollution, and gained by the Los Angeles Philharmonic as its playing becomes more beautiful.

Moreover, it seems an Anaxagorean would have to approve of matchstick potatoes as a diet regimen. Since each matchstick has a dominant portion of "the thin," the Anaxagorean approach predicts that a regime of ingesting many, many of them would supply an overwhelming amount of the thin, easily able to predominate over competitors and make the eater thin. Experience tells against this.

In a passage in the *Phaedo* commonly referred to as the "intellectual autobiography" of the character Socrates (96a–102a), he mentions Anaxagoras by name (97b, d). But even earlier in the passage, Anaxagoras is relevant. Socrates tells of an early passion for natural science and how he gave up this form of inquiry when he realized that it confused him about even things he had formerly thought he understood. His mention of when flesh is added to flesh (96d) is recognized to evoke Anaxagoras in particular within the general corps of philosophers of nature Socrates has mentioned explicitly. What sorts of confusion did Socrates fall into? For us the puzzles he relates are more *meta*-puzzles: our challenge is to see why anyone should ever have been confused in the ways Socrates indicates (Vlastos 1969: 308–9). The key is to see the puzzles as trading on the way an Anaxagorean must approach the situation (Brentlinger 1972).

Let's quickly review: we have been considering the Anaxagorean picture on which characteristics of things are due to their portions of elemental stuffs, and on which change occurs through rearrangement of such portions. A sufficiently increased share of an elemental stuff accounts for an observable change in a composite (as when soup brings its portion of the hot to be added to our body, making our body hot, or when the anchovies bring their portion of salt to make a pizza salty).

Now we are ready to (re)turn to our passage. When a large/tall man stands next to a short/small one, what makes the one larger/taller than the other? (Forms of the Greek *megas* underlie forms of "large," "tall," and "great" in translations of different examples in Plato, depending on the cases in view; there is an analogous phenomenon with "short"/"small." For Plato's characteristic assimilation of positive and comparative, see Chapter Ten.) Why are ten units more than eight? Why is a two-cubit length greater than a one-cubit one (96de with 100e–101c)? In cases like these, it is impossible for Anaxagorean explanation—in which the physical addition of something contributes its share of the relevant elemental stuff—to get off the ground.

To see this, consider two piles of books that are exactly the same height—until I add a paperback mystery to one of them. Here I can say that one pile is taller than the other "by a book" and in a sense the addition of this book does make one pile taller. Or again, two cities each have a sky-scraper of exactly the same height—until the one more hungry for a win in the *Guinness Book of World Records* affixes a spire to the top of its structure. Now this building is taller "by the spire." These cases help us have some sympathy for Socrates' old idea that one man is taller than another "by a head" (96d–e).[7]

The problem with treating this in an Anaxagorean way is that one has to assimilate these cases to those of the hot chicken soup and the salty anchovies. But a book cannot stand to a tall stack (or a spire to a tall building, or a head to a tall man) as the anchovies do to a salty pizza. This is due in part to the circumstance that, because the largeness of any given thing is necessarily connected with the sort of thing we are considering it as, there is nothing that is transferable in portions that could account for all cases of largeness. And even if there were such largeness-stuff, it is problematic how the head, itself small, could be responsible for bringing it to the person (see the return to the puzzle case when Socrates tells how he avoids it, 100e–101b). Similarly with a small book or small design element.

This sort of problem may have escaped the notice of Anaxagoras himself since his model of participation does work for most of the features he mentions. But for many of the properties Plato is most interested in (such as beauty, goodness, and unity), the Anaxagorean model of real beings as stuffs, portions of which are ingredients in derived entities, does not work. However, it would be an incorrect diagnosis to conclude from this that Plato's topics of interest are just not scientific enough to be respectable. After all, the problem occurs in plenty of cases that natural science would hardly wish to reject, including largeness, unity, and equality. Thus Plato concludes correctly that we should give up the physical-ingredient interpretation of participation.

But that is the only change he announces. In the very passage of the *Phaedo* in which Socrates gives up the causal accounts of the natural philosophers, he immediately and famously puts his own simple and safe explanatory pattern as follows:

> I think that, if there is anything beautiful besides the Beautiful itself, it is beautiful for no other reason than that it has a share of/participates in [*metechei*] that Beautiful, and I say so with everything … I simply, naively and perhaps foolishly cling to this, that nothing else makes it beautiful other than the presence of, or the communion with [*koinōnia*], or however you may describe its relationship to that Beautiful we mentioned, for I will not insist on the precise nature of the relationship, but that all beautiful things are beautiful by the Beautiful.
>
> (100c–d, my translation, based on Grube in Cooper, ed., 1997)

Against the background we have been studying, it is clear that Socrates is endorsing the same general set-up as Anaxagoras, in which ordinary things are F because they have a share of/participate in the F itself; however since he must reject the interpretation of participation as having a portion of a physical stuff as an ingredient, he flags that he is leaving open the precise nature of the relation. The importance of embracing this scheme is underscored by the length and layering of the portion of our text in which agreement and approval are expressed for the method of hypothesis which has resulted in it: first in the quoted words of Simmias and Cebes, next by the reported agreement of "all those present" and finally by discussion in the frame, with approving comments by both Echecrates and Phaedo (102a). This approval in effect creates the ending of a section of text before Socrates goes on.

So when Socrates sets out his new approach as he makes the transition from his "intellectual autobiography" to the final argument in the *Phaedo*, he brings into the open his inauguration of a successor-theory to that of Anaxagoras: one that is isomorphic but seeks to avoid problems with certain cases by committing to find a new interpretation of participation. Seeing what these theories share and how they respond to Eleaticism gives us a deeper understanding of the significance of the following claims in Plato:

1   Sensible Fs both are and are not F.
2   Sensible Fs are to be explained by the F itself. This is what makes F things F; it is that by which F things are F.
3   An account of F-ness must separate it from its opposite (if it has one)—not muddle them together.
4   The same cause cannot have opposite effects; opposite causes cannot have the same effect.
5   The F itself always "deserves its own name" (to use the language of *Phaedo* 103e); it is purely F.

So what we've now seen about the *Phaedo* is two-fold. First, its insistence that sensibles are derivative from and to be understood in terms of *things that are* is part of a broader tradition with a shared strategy for coping with the challenge of the Eleatics. And second— given the full range of features of ordinary objects Plato wanted to account for—he found that the best philosophy of nature would not work. Of course, some may assume that dealing with such matters as the just, the beautiful and the good is the job of a different group of people than scientists, carrying out a very different kind of project. We will now turn to the *Republic* to see Plato's demonstration of problems with relying on what they had offered.

Lovers of pseudo-learning

We now turn to the characterization of the sensible domain of opinion in the central books of the *Republic*. Here as well, the metaphysical and the epistemological are inextricably intertwined. A huge role is played by the idea that to have knowledge, the highest cognitive state, one must come to terms with what is (477a—the phrases I quote in this paragraph have variants that occur throughout 477a–480a). By contrast opinion, a lesser cognitive state, is assigned to what "both is and is not" and so occupies a position "between that which purely and absolutely is and that which wholly is not" (478d, tr. Shorey 1930).

We have already seen that Plato's basic argument in the Republic turned on the claim that the rational element has special access to wisdom concerning ultimate realities that other parts of city and soul have no inkling of (Chapter Seven). But I postponed until now discussion of this claim. The key passages are of two very different kinds. Firstly, the Republic contains straightforward discussion of its claim that many people we might initially take to be lovers of learning in fact fall short of the highest cognitive state. Then the theme of the lesser status of the sensible domain is conveyed in a literary manner by the famous figures of the Sun, the Divided Line, and the Cave. A rough way to think of the division of labor here is that the initial discussion and argument are for the rational part of the soul, while the Cave figure is to reorient the rest—since we are informed at 518c that the *whole soul* must be turned around for progress to occur (following J. Lear 2008).

We will begin with the straightforward discussion (underlying scholarship in Meinwald [forthcoming] from which some formulations in this section are taken). This itself has two parts. In the first, Socrates and Glaucon agree third-personally that certain *other* people are missing the mark; it will be worth our while to spend some time getting as much as possible out of this passage (475b–476d). Then we will go on to the official argument whereby Socrates offers to persuade an imaginary representative of the group he claims does not have knowledge that this is in fact the case (476d–480a).

The way in to all of this discussion is the question of who we should really take to be lovers of learning—and so suited to rule. Socrates points out that for the same reason that a picky eater is no lover of food, the lover of wisdom is an omnivore of learning. However, the tribe of people who seem to satisfy this description strikes Glaucon as a bizarre motley, including those who love being spectators and audience-members [*philotheamones* and *philēkooi*], who rush around from one dramatic festival to another; others who engage with "similar things;" and students of "petty crafts"—none of whom could tolerate a philosophical discussion. The drama-fiends are mentioned first and get the longest description—with the somewhat insulting characterization that they behave as if they had rented out their ears, and run around even to minor country festivals, reluctant to miss any.

Socrates distinguishes the lovers of learning he has in mind from Glaucon's avid spectators by saying that philosophers are lovers of the spectacle of the truth (475e). We saw in the *Phaedo* that Plato can use "the truth" to refer to fundamental entities, and we find that usage here again. Spectators of the truth engage with the single thing that is the nature (*phusis*) of Beauty itself (and similarly with other Forms), while the original avid spectators are engaging only with "the many beautiful things" (this phrase is used in 479a ff. to pick up on what has been discussed in this initial passage). This limitation of Glaucon's avid spectators presumably connects in Socrates' view with their inability to tolerate philosophical discussion. They find many different things beautiful, and don't care about asking whether there isn't really some one thing common to the different cases; even if they come across someone who tries to get them to engage, they are not able to see and delight in Beauty itself: *auto to kalon* (475e–476c).

Before proceeding from this opening, third-person discussion to Socrates' imagined direct engagement with a representative of the avid spectators, we should ask ourselves why this group should have been the first pseudo-philosophers to occur to Glaucon, and would do well to remember the cultural context. We have already had occasion to touch on the centrality of poetry in the transmission of culture—in the broadest, not the narrow sense—in Plato's time. According to a large-scale theme of the *Republic* itself, artful presentation is specially influential in shaping us.

What one learns from artistic productions on this view concerns what is to be done and avoided in life: the conduct of a man, a warrior, etc. (On this point in connection with Books 2, 3, and 10, see Burnyeat 1999 and Moss 2007.) The impact of such works is suspect for Plato because it is independent of their content's being true, and important because it influences us beyond the narrowly aesthetic, in matters ethical in the broadest sense. This is why Homer is thought by some to have educated Greece (606e). And that in turn is why it is apposite for Plato to cast in Homer's teeth that he does not understand how to win wars, run cities, and make men better.

The present passage has the potential to make an important

contribution to the development of this theme, if we can read the *kala* (beautiful/admirable/honorable/splendid/noble/fine things— see Glossary) audience-members believe in and admire to include splendid actions presented in the theater. On this reading, the interest of our avid spectators is not, as the secondary literature tends to suppose, confined to what is beautiful in the narrowest English sense.

Let's now think carefully about this key part of the discussion between Socrates and Glaucon. Socrates says:

> Well, I imagine that audiences and spectators take pleasure in beautiful *phōnai* [voices/speeches/sounds], colors, shapes, *and in everything crafted out of such things*, but that their thought is incapable of seeing, and taking pleasure in, the nature of the Beautiful itself.
>
> (476b, my translation; emphasis added)

In interpreting this remark, a crucial decision is how to take the reference to "everything crafted out of" speeches/voices/sounds together with colors and shapes. It could of course be such things as special effects, scenery, and costumes: a special-effects storm is a metaphysical composite of certain sounds, colors, and shapes. But I propose we take the composites in question to include centrally the *actions* the characters perform. Book 3 treated extensively of the use of voice/speech and shape/gesture in imitating the action of characters. Thus I propose that we understand Socrates to be saying that those who love being spectators/audience-members, receptive as they are to beautiful/fine voices (or speeches), colors, and shapes, are also accepting as beautiful/fine the behavior shown in the production.

Is there any connection between these different parts of their reaction? While it is not necessary for my main claim, I find it plausible to think that Plato is already anticipating a point he will make explicitly in Book 10: that the beauty of the voices, colors and shapes is relevant when the avid spectators learn to see as beautiful the behavior shown. To see that this point is reasonably intuitive (i.e. accessible at this point in the text), consider the climactic scene in *Don Giovanni*. The title character has disrespectfully invited the statue of the Commendatore (recently killed by himself in a duel over the honor of that dignitary's daughter) to dinner. The statue shows up and issues a reciprocal invitation! With his servant Leporello groveling in fear, the Don says to himself that though he did not expect this, he cannot allow his honor to be stained by any cowardice. The Commendatore—who we now realize has the fundamental powers of the universe on his side—prepares to drag the rake off to Hell unless he repents, but our hero, minor scales swirling around him, resists. As the statue repeatedly demands he repent, Don Giovanni continues to shout his refusal "No, no! No!" and with a final scream he falls into the inferno.

My thought is that our response is not solely a matter of admiring the vibrato, portamento, rubato, etc. we have heard; we audience-members admire the way Don Giovanni stands fast; we say to ourselves "Splendid!" or "*That* is courage!" Clearly, without the music of Mozart, the text of Da Ponte, the costume with its high boots and tight breeches, the tension of the three intertwining bass/baritone voices, the theatrical storm and hellfire, we would find nothing to admire in a libertine's refusal to repent. So the beautiful voices, shapes and colors really do seem to be relevant. Our perception of the beautiful elements from which the action in the opera is made up predisposes us to judge the action itself as being beautiful. This connection is uncontroversially a concern of Plato's elsewhere in our dialogue (cf. 568c about hiring voices that are beautiful, big and persuasive). It is the theme of much of the discussion of art in Book 10. 601a–b starts with the painter whose depiction of what looks like a shoemaker takes in those who "judge things by their colors and shapes." Plato then goes on to his real target: the poet who "uses words and phrases to paint colored pictures of each of the crafts" for people "as ignorant as he, who judge by words;" the passage makes explicit the role of the "natural charm" of meter, rhythm, and harmony.

Whether or not we adopt this additional view, that the beauty of the voices etc. is relevant to our reception of the actions depicted, my suggested reading of the Book 5 passage is that the many beautiful things under consideration there would by now include what audience-members admire in the *Iliad*, what we admire in the *Antigone*, what we admire in *Henry V*, what we admire in *Don Giovanni*, what we admire in La Traviata, what we admire in Lawrence of Arabia, The Godfather, Titanic, etc. (Readers: you can and should update the list!) Thus, an audience-member of the type Plato is envisioning is not only something of a connoisseur of aesthetic presentations. The passage is delineating a person of traditional cultivation who assumes one learns about life by assimilating this cultural lore and by coming to appreciate the fineness of the many great actions shown in these dramas, so that there is no further role for theorizing about the Beautiful itself.

We come now to Socrates' imagined direct exchange with the avid spectator, which is the official argument about the objects of knowledge and opinion (476d–480a). The basic framework of that central argument is that knowledge must concern what is; ignorance what is not; and so opinion—a faculty distinct from knowledge—must be set over what is intermediate between what purely is and what in every way is not. Much scholarship has converged on identifying here the Greek use of "is" that allows completion—the use familiar to us from Anaxagoras' reading of Parmenides' talk of "being" or "what is."[8] So read, the framework has it that knowledge is of what is [just], what is [good] and so on; ignorance wholly misses the mark of justice and goodness; and the domain of opinion is what somehow is and is not [just, good, etc.].

This framework will not seem strange in the light of our review of Plato's predecessors: we have become familiar with the legacy of the Eleatics that what is not is unmanageable, and that for knowledge we must cleave to what is. For Plato as for the natural philosophers we have surveyed, what the ordinary person takes to be reality is in fact a region intermediate between the fundamental ("what purely is") and the unheard-of ("what in every way is not")—not wholly illusory as Parmenides had claimed, but still disallowed from basic status.[9] The argument is to convince the imaginary interlocutor that the objects he engages with are not fundamental.

Thus our present passage needs to determine what to take as intermediate between being and not-being, and why. (Readers of Plato's previous work may of course have some idea of the answers, but since a dialogue is the fundamental unit of interpretation, we need to glean whether the Republic is taking the same line.) Socrates imagines the following conversation:

> I want to address a question to our friend who doesn't believe
> in the beautiful itself or any form of the beautiful itself that
> remains always the same in all respects but who does believe in
> the many beautiful things—the lover of sights [philotheamōn[10]]
> who wouldn't allow anyone to say that the beautiful itself is one
> or that the just is one or any of the rest: "My dear fellow," we'll
> say, "of all the many beautiful things, is there one that will not
> also appear[11] ugly? Or is there one of those just things that will
> not also appear unjust? Or one of those pious things that will
> not also appear impious?"
>
> (478e–479a)

(Please remember that variation among scholars concerning
whether and how to capitalize when naming Platonic Forms is
something that one has to learn to live with!) Socrates imagines his
interlocutor agreeing with him, and continues in this vein with
double and half, big and small, light and heavy. Thus the many Fs the
pseudo-learners engage with fit the bill of objects of opinion: they
can be said to be and not to be, they no more are than they are not.
In perhaps the best formulation: they are *between being and not-being*.

Nothing important seems to me to turn on the question whether
the many Fs of 476e4–480a13 slide over to include all the "many
Fs" of all the targeted pseudo-learners, or are confined to the objects
of thought of the drama-fiends. The line of thought we are pursuing
will make it possible for us to see that the status of the drama-fiends'
many Fs will be shared by the others.

I have proposed that the avid spectators are people who believe
they learn about life from art; they were the primary target of the
pseudo-learners discussion. The people who engage with "similar
things" were thrown in as well—perhaps they like to listen to
speeches in other contexts, such as lawcourts and political assemblies. Glaucon also appended students of the petty crafts—Socrates
called them craft-lovers in 476a. Perhaps these are the sort of people
who in the seventies hung about the tables at craft fairs, or in the
present day watch competitions like *Project Runway* and the cooking
shows. Or if they are learning actually to practice the minor crafts,

they do so without any willingness or ability to achieve under-standing of the relevant first principles. And why not throw all these in, for surely they are all in a sense learning, and their addition is bound to lower the tone of the group in the mind of the aristocratic Glaucon. The basic characterization of the people in this ill-assorted crowd is that they deal with the many Fs but don't try to identify the F itself. We need now to get a sense of how the imaginary inter-locutor can be brought to agree that his many Fs no more are than they are not.

Why does the avid spectator agree that the many beautifuls will also appear ugly? It has plausibility that the behavior we admire in *Don Giovanni* will look very different in the cold light of day. (No wonder, if we gave a role to the beauty of the dramatic elements when we came to admire him in the first place.) Similarly if we have been to a tragedy dealing with Agamemnon's sacrifice of his daughter Iphigenia in order to get the Greek army to Troy. Such a thing can be presented as sublime in its patriotism. We can also see it as monstrously misguided.

Plato can trade on the idea, his subject in numerous other passages, that changing the context will typically reveal beautiful things to be ugly in some way, at some time, in some respect, etc. Thus they are indeed things that are and are not [beautiful]. But should we take the many Fs to be particular or general? Tokens or types? Instances or universals? Plato's previous examples have been of two different kinds, so that commentators sometimes like to choose only a subset of them.

Many famous examples are clearly about individual sensible particulars. Socrates pointed out in the *Hippias Major* that a beautiful girl will appear/be ugly next to a goddess (289a–d, both formula-tions are used). Lest we think this phenomenon is limited to the aesthetic/moral dimension: we have the sticks and stones of the *Phaedo* that appear equal and unequal, and the discussion at *Republic* 523c–524c of how sight reports the same finger as large and as small.[12]

These passages are all saying something that can fit under the slogan that "the many Fs both are and are not." (In Chapter Ten we will review the logical respectability of these results of Plato's.) But there are passages making a slightly different point that other commentators have drawn to our attention in the present connection. It is linguistically possible for the Greek expressions represented by English along the lines of "the many Fs" to refer to the many *types* of things that (people think) are F—so here they would be the many inadequate accounts of F-ness people give. To suppose that things of this sort are in play is the best way to take Socrates' remark:

> We would seem to have found, then, that the many conventions [*nomima*] of the many about the fair and honorable [i.e. about the *kalon*] and other things are tumbled about in the mid-region between that which is not and that which is in the true and absolute sense.
>
> (479d, tr. Shorey 1930)

Someone who takes the passage to have concerned only the confused displays by sensible particulars faces awkwardness here since it is not clear what this has to do with the many conventions or customs of the many. By contrast, the many Fs read the other way actually *are* the conventions in question: customary rules about the *kalon* [the beautiful/fine], the just, and so on.

Consider 538c ff, where Socrates envisages someone, having always followed the beliefs concerning just and *kalon* things in which he was raised by his parents, being asked "What is the fine [*to kalon*]?" The imaginary youth parrots "what he has heard from the traditional lawgiver" (who presumably gave types of action that are right) and is shown that this is no more *kalon* than wretched (Gosling 1960). Another issue with an action-type came up in the exchange of Socrates with Cephalus in Book 1. Returning deposits may normally be right; but it is not right in all circumstances, for example if the owner has deposited a weapon with you when in his right mind and asks for it back during a manic episode. The customary rules mentioned in these two passages may perhaps be acquired through drama by our avid spectators, or they could belong to the least-clear of Glaucon's three deprecated groups: those mentioned right after the avid spectators as interested in "similar things," in my view the audiences for courtroom and political discourse. These notions are certainly examples of "the many conventions of the many about the fair and honorable."[13]

Now let's return to what is often considered the crux of interpretation. Is it necessary or even desirable to make a choice between understanding the many Fs of our passage as on the one hand the many instances of a universal or tokens of a type or, on the other, the many partial and superficial characterizations of F-ness? The technical notions that make them feel radically heterogeneous to us were of course not in place when Plato wrote. And as we have seen, he habitually makes points of both sorts. In any case, the present argument is so schematic and abstract that we have to supply the examples and analysis of them, regarding the present treatment as a sort of summary. If we are willing to countenance the whole variety of examples that could be in play, we may actually have a reason for the schematic presentation of our passage—precisely to allow for them all.

Our existing discussion of the avid spectators is very compatible with this. I have been careful to use formulations along the lines of "what we admire in ..." or "the behavior/action shown" that avoided deciding whether we were dealing with sensible particulars, types, or both. Is it not somewhat artificial to insist on precisifying the reaction of say an opera-goer at La Traviata ("It's so beautiful when the girl sacrifices herself for her lover!") in terms exclusively of one or the other?[14]

In addition to the drama-fiends and those interested in "similar things," our original Book 5 passage also knocked people who are mad for the crafts. I suggested that this group in our day might include fans of shows like Project Runway, Next Top Model, and Top Chef. It might also include some of the members of their judging panels. All such people spend a lot of time engaging with outstanding particulars; they also tend to employ general notions they find useful in this connection. Fashionistas may toss around terms like "edgy" and "fierce"—partial takes on beauty. Similarly, foodies typically identify such things as "the locally sourced" and " the luxurious" as delicious. But they would never try to develop an account of what it is to be delicious in general.

Whether we regard these people as engaging primarily with the displays of particulars, or primarily with the partial identifications I have mentioned, or as sliding between the two (as I find plausible), what they engage with will fail Plato's test for being fundamental. The finest *omelette grandmère* (a sensible particular) would be a hideous embarrassment in a three-star dining room—it doesn't have the refinement the context calls for. The locally sourced (a sensible universal) both is and is not delicious—or why don't Midwesterners prize locally sourced avocados and citrus? The targeted lovers of craft no less than audiences for political discourse and the central avid spectators all fall short in Plato's eyes. Whether they cherish only outstanding individual cases or come up with tags that only partially identify the real nature in question, all such people fail to grasp what is truly F. The objects of their misguided devotion are indeed "between that which purely and absolutely is and that which wholly is not" (478d, tr. Shorey 1930). Now we understand why such people don't achieve the kind of knowledge that Plato is looking for.

From shadows to sun

As our final topic before closing the chapter, let us turn now to one of Plato's most powerful images. But before we proceed, a methodological caveat. As we previewed in Chapter Two, Plato thinks literary tropes can never be the vehicle of deep understanding. Since they cannot in principle deliver the truth, their role is preparatory: to orient us towards it, and motivate us to do the further, hard work that is required to reach it. In view of this, we should avoid falling into the trap of supposing that the key to Plato's philosophy is to "solve" the figures by divining the meaning of every single detail they contain. Indeed, we should not be surprised if they sometimes leave us with questions that they provide no good materials to answer—or even contain indications that seem to pull in different directions. In what follows, I will content myself merely with noting some of the strong indications that our figure does make.

The Cave is a parable concerning "the effect of education and of the lack of it on our nature" (514a); let us start as Plato does with its lowest level. This is populated by prisoners who dwell underground, where they are chained in place. What they take for reality is shadows cast on the rock face in front of them (by statues of which they are unaware, carried by people hidden behind a wall, between the backs of the prisoners and the light of a fire). These wretches have lives calculated to appall readers as Plato would have imagined them: at a time and place where freedom and self-determination were considered necessary for a good life, the people depicted are not free. Moreover they are radically and pervasively mistaken about the world: what they regard as reality are merely flittering shadows. Note how Plato actually drafts off of Homer here: as a subterranean realm of phantasms/images (*eidōla*) and shadows/shades (*skiai*), the cave evokes the poet's description of Hades (which we surveyed in Chapter Six). Plato has embedded many snippets from epic throughout the *Republic* on exactly the theme of the wretchedness of existence in the underworld, including in this very passage a second quotation of the key line about the preferability of being the serf of a landless man on the earth above. He is counting on us to feel revulsion as we read of those who waste their lives chained in place underground—and to be struck with horror when, to Glaucon's remark "It's a strange image you're describing, and strange prisoners" Socrates gives the reply "They're like us."

It is a shock suddenly to realize that the prisoners leading this wretched existence represent us—at least as we start out. What a relief that there is a possibility of progress first to see the statues that cast the shadows; then and crucially out of the cave to see reflections of natural objects; then plants and animals themselves in the natural light of the sun, and heavenly bodies, and at last the sun itself! The possibility of this upwards progress symbolizes the benefit proper education and philosophy hold out—if we can persevere through the discomfort and hard work that are required to win through to the realm of the sun (symbolizing the Good, that on which all else depends and in light of which all else must be understood). Returning alive from the underworld had been the greatest of the heroic achievements of Hercules and of Odysseus. So, it seems, it will take a Herculean effort if any of us is able to make our way from the shadow realm up to the sunlit domain—or to translate back into literal terms, from dealing with the inadequate ways our culture construes things to Platonic Forms seen in the light of the Good.

Let's focus for now on the theme of our present chapter, the domain of opinion—the subterranean realm in terms of the Cave.

The narrative depicts two stations within this: one in which prisoners chained in place underground see only the shadows thrown on the wall of their dwelling, and another when, freed from their bonds, they turn around to look at the statues that cast the shadows. At first they doubt that the statues can be more real than their old familiar shadows, and are at a loss when asked concerning the statues what each of them is. Later we learn that the prisoners win prestige and power from identifying the shadows that pass in front of them and predicting which will come next (516c–d).[15] Moreover, they compete in the law-courts and elsewhere about "the shadows of justice" and "the statues of which they are the shadows" (517d–e).

Notice that because the subterranean realm is here subdivided, it is possible that we can now separate out the somewhat heterogeneous cluster we had in view in connection with the lovers of pseudo-learning. I offer the suggestion that at the lowest level the prisoners are dealing with such things as individual actions they take to be just, individual cases they take to be of success, etc. One up (turning from the shadows to the statues that cast them) takes them to engagement with action-types, or properties of some sort. The circumstance that what casts the shadows are statues symbolizes as is widely recognized that these are human artifacts: the canons that constitute our ambient culture.

But surely it is backwards, one may protest, to posit that what people take to be cases of justice or bravery or beauty or good living are shadows or images of cultural artifacts? We ordinarily assume that physical objects and hence their actions and the features we recognize them to have are basic and given. Anything more general (properties, universals, types) is abstracted off these basic things or constructed from them in some way. Yet Plato's idea is that it is exactly the reverse. His point is that what we are going to find beautiful reflects the canons conveyed in the surrounding culture (for us, especially advertising and the media); something corresponding is true for bravery, justice, etc. To this extent, what a person "recognizes" to be beautiful, brave, or just is actually a product of that person's cultural canons—which may represent what Beauty, Bravery, and Justice really are with a fair or perhaps not-so-fair degree of fidelity.

When partisans of terrorism see a suicide bombing as heroic, this is a direct reflection of a cultural canon along the lines of "an eye for an eye." Or to take a less violent example, a man who supposes he is living the good life because he has acquired the Scotch, the sports-car, the electronics, etc. shown in advertisements takes as his reality what are (in the terms of our figure) shadows. The notion that wealth or power are "false idols" parallels the one Plato offers here.

If we believe that reactions along the lines of "this bombing is heroic" or "this is the good life" are direct apprehensions of reality, we only show that we ourselves are still at the level of the prisoners. Plato has it that, when first turned to see the statues, the cave-dwellers cannot believe them to be more real than (i.e. responsible for the lesser beings that are) the old familiar shadows. Just as the cave-dwellers can't believe—when first turned to see the statues—that they are responsible for some of the shadows they formerly took to be independent existences, so we can hardly believe—when we become aware of standards of value—that they are responsible for some of what we took to be independent moral facts.

Let's now consider the particular case of subterranean thinking about justice—this is after all the dialogue's main topic. The inhabitants of the cave are said to argue in law-courts and political assemblies over "the shadows of justice" and "the statues of which they are the shadows." On the reading I have suggested, this refers to the circumstance that, during court cases and political debate, speakers may mention not only the particular case under discussion but also more general banners that are relevant (an eye for an eye, the enemy of my enemy is my friend, good policy aims at power, etc.) Yet these generalities (symbolized by the local and human production of the statues, which are supposed to represent but still fall short of identity with the realities of the sunlit natural world) are all inadequate. They are just some of the "many Fs" that were discussed more directly in our previous passage. Being asked "What is it?" on one of these subjects—justice etc.—is being subjected to the Socratic *elenchos*. Thus the fact that the released prisoners experience *aporia* at that stage is familiar and ties in well with the reference to the career of Socrates in the observation that the prisoners' discomfort and rage at the one who tries to set them free and take them upwards is so great that they try to kill him (517a, cf. 515c–516a).

At the end of the presentation of the Cave figure, we are invited to attach the Divided Line to it, so I will add the Line now. First let us avoid a potential confusion. In the Line, the ratios between the lengths of the segments symbolize those between the clarity and truth of the cognitive states mentioned—but talk of physical objects such as animals is part of the explanation of what is symbolized, and so is to be taken literally. While in the Cave, physical objects such as animals are part of the figure: the physical objects of the sunlit region symbolize intelligible objects—the Forms. There is also another source of trouble we can head off. We should not over-force the Line and Cave to be talking about the same things in all details. We must be guided by the text in realizing the kind of relationship Plato means between the two figures: we are told at 517b to *liken* the underground domain of the Cave to the Line's visible domain, and to take the upward journey out of the cave as the move to the Line's intelligible domain (Schofield 2007). To proceed now to the Line.

Its lowest level is *eikasia* which is said to deal with images, for example shadows and reflections of objects. (If physical reflections and shadows of visible objects such as animals, plants, and artifacts are like what the prisoners in the Cave engage with, we will need a reading of what it is to be a reflection/image/shadow of justice. I have offered one possible way to do this above.[16]) One level up is *pistis*, which deals with the originals of the images. The two of these together make up our engagement with the domain of opinion. The Line also has two upper sections representing our higher cognitive states, which deal with intelligibles. The example of mathematics illustrates *dianoia*, which proceeds from hypotheses and uses reason rather than the senses, (though summoning the assistance of visible figures, so that it uses the "real" objects of *pistis* as images of its intelligibles but only for heuristic purposes). *Noēsis* somehow travels upward to grasp an unhypothetical first principle in light of which thought that was formerly *dianoia* can become secured as we move downward again.[17]

Plato continues through the end of Book 7 to develop the idea that the conversion and ascent out of the cave is by means of mathematics. The importance of this discipline is not only that it takes us to engagement with abstract objects and accustoms us to a method of proceeding on the basis of reason alone. Of course, it is by giving proofs and not by measuring slices of baklava that one properly apprehends truths about such matters as the length of the hypotenuse of a right triangle.

But in addition to this, Plato is signing onto a program according to which the content of some mathematics is inextricably intertwined with that of aesthetics and ethics. Indeed, he criticizes contemporary harmonic theorists for starting from heard concord and simply trying to find what ratios correspond to these sensorily identified intervals. Rather he thinks they should ask which numbers are concordant [with each other] and why (531c).

Because, in this program, concord and unity are closely related to each other and ultimately explanatory of anything valuable at all, Plato makes Socrates at 531c inform his interlocutors that this task is useful for inquiry into the Beautiful and the Good, and useless to pursue otherwise (here following Burnyeat 1987, 2000). Of course none of that can be developed in detail in the images, or even in the *Republic* as a whole. Glaucon does not have enough of the mathematical background to follow such a discussion at present; moreover going into it would distort the structure of the *Republic*. The job at hand is to indicate the importance of this study, not to achieve all of its results. For now we should simply note that this advanced mathematics is meant to connect with the achievement aimed at by the genuine lovers of learning of Book 5: apprehension of the pure being of the Forms. Yet after all what does that pure being amount to? And how does mathematical research connect with it? Our final chapters will trace how Plato addressed these issues.

Further reading

See Bibliography for full details of the works listed below.

On the Presocratics

J. Barnes (1982) *The Presocratic Philosophers* is an outstanding exemplar of the very formalized kind of treatment.
D. Furley (1973) "Notes on Parmenides."
D. Furley (1976) "Anaxagoras in Response to Parmenides."

D. Furley (1987) *The Greek Cosmologists*, ch. 6 ("Anaxagoras.")
M. Furth (1968) "Elements of Eleatic Ontology."
G. Owen (1960) "Eleatic Questions."
C. Strang (1963) "The Physical Theory of Anaxagoras."

On Plato

J. Annas (1981) *An Introduction to Plato's "Republic,"* ch. 8.
D. Bailey (2014) "Platonic Causes Revisited."
G. Fine (1978) "Knowledge and Belief in Republic 5."
G. Fine (1990) Knowledge and Belief in Republic 5–7."
J. Gosling (1960) "*Republic* Book 5: *ta polla kala* etc."
T. Irwin (1977b) "Plato's Heracleiteanism."
C. Kahn (1981) "Some Philosophical Uses of 'to Be' in Plato."
G. Vlastos (1965) "Degrees of Reality in Plato."
G. Vlastos (1969) "Reasons and Causes in the *Phaedo*."

Notes

1 A landmark article on different ways of understanding the flux/change of sensibles is Irwin (1977b). Note that the secondary literature in ancient philosophy does not generally observe the distinction made by some philosophers today between universals and properties.
2 Our default translation for the Presocratics throughout.
3 Modifying "exists" in Owen (1960) in light of general agreement about the "fused" concept of being in Greek whereby the existential and copulative uses are not starkly separate.
4 Thanks to Walter Edelberg for this formulation.
5 It is unknown which wrote first, but that does not matter for our purposes. We can see why each would have preferred his own system, whether or not he was acquainted with the work of the other.
6 This is not the only possible interpretation but it is the one that makes most sense of the fragments. Since this reading was perfectly accessible to Plato and since it accounts for his engagement with Anaxagoras, it is the one relevant for our present discussion.
7 The pile and building examples show that it is not enough to dismiss the problem of taller by a head by saying it trades on confusing dative of degree of difference with that connoting cause—in my examples, the degree of difference reading does not defeat the causal one.
8 Fine (1978, 1990) is the gallant exception with a divergent and well-worked out view on which "is" in our passage is initially veridical.
9 Does this problematically credit the pseudo-philosopher with familiarity with

Eleatic reasoning and the pluralist response to it? Perhaps he's heard them too. But if not, we can take Plato to be relying on the fact that he could always add the Parmenidean *elenchos*. Since no one in generations had been able to evade that, the avid spectator is hardly going to be equipped to do so.

10 In my surrounding discussion, I adopt the formulations of Ferrari and Griffith (2000) in terms of loving to be spectators and members of an audience. The more usual and more euphonious "lovers of sights and sounds" and "lovers of spectacle" do not capture the passive role of these avid spectators.

11 The Greek rendered here as "appear" does not necessarily carry the suggestion of *merely* appearing (i.e. misleadingly or falsely); it can just as well be construed as: "be evident being," "turn out to be," or "show itself to be." Note though that the distinction as usually drawn between the "veridical" and "non-veridical" uses of "appear" when applied to the sort of cases in question here is not particularly prominent for those who hold that neither indicates true being—the whole point of the passage.

12 We sometimes read that this will not hold in the general case: there can be a particular just action, say, that would be just without qualification. However, it is not obvious that Plato had to think of matters that way. Remember he generated the result that a beautiful girl is also ugly by changing her context and imagining her by the side of a goddess. Obviously this is not something one can expect to observe; I suppose one "cuts her out" of her real situation in imagination and plunks the cut-out down in a scene with the goddess. But then, when faced with an action that is supposed to be just without qualification (perhaps paying one's taxes), suppose we "cut it out" and put it in a new context (in which the government is using these tax dollars for something horrible). Is it out of the question that Plato could have considered this to be a case of "the very same action" being both just and unjust?

13 Cf. Annas (1981: 21–2, 204), though she doesn't specify there the origin of the ideas of "unreflective people."

14 See Aristotle's idea that tragedy concerns universals, and Burnyeat (1999: lecture 1).

15 See Schofield (2007: 223–4) on how this refers to leading politicians. He cites Thucydides 1.138 for "the eulogy of Themistocles for his supreme ability to form judgements instantly with minimal deliberation, his no less impressive success at guessing for the most part the future turn of events, and his capacity to interpret what is on the city's hands at the moment."

16 And this receives confirmation in Book 10's discussion of art—there both what poets copy and what they produce are said to be images/appearances. For discussion of how this can be understood see Belfiore (1983: 42, 44, 52) and Moss (2007: 419).

17 The downward process cannot be deduction from the first principle alone. See Mueller (1992) on the method of hypothesis.

Nine

Forms I

Are forms perfect instances?

The theme *On the Forms*

In the works we have discussed so far, the theory of Forms has not been the main topic, if it has been a topic at all. In the early dialogues of definition, Socrates launched his search for the accounts of piety, bravery, etc. on the basis of the ordinary way of taking such general items without anyone demanding self-consciously philosophical discussion of their status. Euthyphro for example readily agreed that the pious is something the same in every pious action—it is the form that makes them pious. (I use non-capitalized vocabulary here because one need not at this stage have a particular theory about the special status of these entities.)

The *Symposium*, *Phaedo* and *Republic* did give some distinctive indications of what has come to be called Plato's theory of Forms (because of which vocabulary for the entities in question is often capitalized in English when translating and discussing these works). But they did not have the scope to go into this with the same detail they gave their primary subject matter. Nor did they need to. Plato was able to get interesting and original discussions of virtue, the soul, and *erōs* going without having to elaborate a full theory of Forms. His commitments included the following claims. Such Forms as the Beautiful, the Just, and the Good, to which we have access in thought, are fundamentally real: they have pure being. By contrast sensibles, which are between pure being and pure not-being, are less real than the Forms. Everyday objects may participate in (have a share of) Forms and so be called after and explained by them.

However, none of the arguments we have looked at on the main topics, the human questions, relied on any fine-grained specification of precisely what Forms there are, what the participation relation between everyday objects and Forms amounts to, or—and most fundamentally—how we should understand the pure being of Forms.

We may suppose that Plato planned this with a view to us readers: everyone who is serious about anything in life must have some interest in the human questions, so by writing on those he engaged the maximal audience. By showing us the connection between the topics we were already interested in and the more technical subjects, he motivated us to go on to his more advanced works. The ancients recognized the varying focus of different dialogues with a series of topic-signaling titles, parallel to the more familiar ones that have won out today. While the *Phaedo* in this system is *On the Soul* and the *Republic* is *On Justice*, a distinct work is crowned with the title *On the Forms*: the *Parmenides*.

A central manifestation of the pure being of Forms is Plato's commitment to sentences of the grammatical form "The F is F" or "F-ness is F," for which the secondary literature has come up with the tag "self-predication." If we interpret these along the lines we use for ordinary predications like "Socrates is brave," then Plato appears committed to thinking that each Form F-ness is itself an F thing; that it *has* the property that it is. As some today would put it, he appears committed to thinking that each Form F-ness instantiates (or exemplifies) itself. This reading suggests that each Form performs its role by being the perfect instance of itself. This thought lies behind such lighthearted locutions as when one reports the felicity of consuming "the Platonic ideal of the banana split."

We have already seen that Platonic Forms have the functional role of universals: the F is explicitly and clearly said to be what F things have in common. Yet many universals do not exemplify themselves: Bravery doesn't have the emotional apparatus that is presupposed if anything is meaningfully to stand up to fearful circumstances; Heaviness isn't the sort of thing to have a weight; Generosity has no scope for giving; Triangularity is not a triangular object; Vertebratehood doesn't have a backbone; and so on. We will need to know more about the extent of Forms to be certain what Forms there are, yet it is already clear that at least some of these problematic cases are supposed to be Forms. So if "F-ness is F" requires the Form, F-ness, to instantiate itself, Plato's theory builds in a flaw in its very foundation. Some scholars use "self-predication" in a way that builds in this interpretation.

By contrast, I am one of those who use "self-predication" to pick out the specified form of words, leaving its interpretation open. In this chapter we will see that, in the *Parmenides*, Plato showed that he associated two systematically different sets of truth conditions with sentences of the grammatical "S is P" type whose subjects are Forms: he distinguished two different kinds of facts that could make such sentences true, and so developed two radically different uses for the sentences. In fact, he developed two radically different types of predication. Because he distinguished two kinds of predication, Plato was able to maintain self-predication without being committed to nonsense.

The kind of self-predication that is always safe turns out to be the uninformative limit case of a class of predications Plato considers fundamental. Other members of this class require discovery and are explanatory once won: they are a linguistic vehicle for articulating the accounts of natures Plato has been seeking all along. In Chapter Ten we will see in detail how the *Phaedrus*, *Sophist*, *Statesman*, and *Philebus* thematize, discuss, and illustrate in detail a program sometimes called "Platonic division" or "collection and division," which envisages a particular way of mapping the structures of these natures. For our purposes in the present chapter, I will be providing a brief sketch of the program.

The division of labor I have identified among Plato's works suggests we should not try to manufacture his "final answer" on all issues about Forms from continuing perusal of the limited passages on them in the *Symposium*, *Phaedo*, and *Republic*, however famous. He himself raised and discussed such issues at length in the *Parmenides* and later works—it is to them we should look for his answers. In this chapter we will address some basic problems to do with self-predication, the extent of Forms, and participation. We will then consider the main innovation that results from the *Parmenides* as a whole: the systematic distinction I have been mentioning between the two kinds of facts and so two kinds of assertions about Forms;

we will see how the progress involved in coming to see this enables us to handle the problems we've considered.[1] Then in Chapter Ten, we will turn to exploring how Forms can admit considerable complexity in their displays of features while still retaining the unity and pure being they need; finally we will look in detail at some passages on the program of Platonic division, the late dialogues' primary way of exploring Forms.

Fundamental in discussion of Plato's theory of Forms for the last half-century and more is the question whether self-predication is not straightforwardly a mistake. Before going on to anything else therefore, let us fill in a key bit of background concerning this matter. It is important—and exciting—to recognize that, while many of Plato's texts do not actually identify their force, there indeed is guaranteed to be some viable reading of self-predication sentences.

Self-predication in the *Protagoras*

While the *Protagoras* pre-dates interest in explicit discussion of the status of Forms, it contains a passage that is increasingly recognized to show that sentences of the grammatical form "F-ness is F" must have *some* interpretation on which they are true. Seeing why involves bringing to bear sensitivity to Plato's use of different characters. In the discussion at 330c–e, Protagoras agrees that justice is just and that piety is pious as soon as these ideas are offered to him. Yet he is no intimate of the character Socrates, let alone an early adopter of Platonist metaphysics. Rather, he is a leading member of a class (sophists, by word formation "wise men") who we have come to distinguish from philosophers largely because of Plato's influence. This very dialogue contrasts the sophist's preferred mode (long-form) and subject of speech (explication of poetry) with those of Socrates, the standard-bearer for philosophy.

Notice that in the cases of justice and piety, any claim about each being the perfect instance of itself would presumably appear to Protagoras as bizarre. Piety in antiquity was thought to be a matter of showing the proper respect to the gods and their requirements. Justice according to the account Protagoras himself offers in this very dialogue consists in behaving in the way that is needed for the city to get along; the general thought is that without each of us having this, there would be a war of all against all and no one could have a decent life. Yet justice *itself* doesn't seem capable of just behavior, nor does piety seem the right kind of thing to be an instance of piety. So why does Protagoras accept the self-predication sentences?

We have ruled out answers deriving from special fealty to a Platonic theory of Forms or from the content of Protagoras' notions of piety and justice. What is left is his expertise with language—a core attribute of all sophists. There is in fact a purely formal reason to accept that there must be some reading of self-predication on which each sentence of the grammatical form "F-ness is F" expresses a truth. To see this, remember how we went back (in Chapter One) to the original Greek and saw that expressions along the lines of "the beautiful" actually had two distinct types of use: to refer to something, such as an urn, that happens to be beautiful (or to all such things); or to pick out *what it is about those things that is beautiful*. As we saw, abstract nouns came into increasing use in Plato's time to disambiguate and refer clearly to what the second use of the older type of expression picked out: not an urn or Helen but something they have, namely, beauty.

The key point derives from reflection on the gloss I gave above of "beauty" and "the beautiful" in the use now relevant: "what it is about those things *that is beautiful*." To say

The beautiful is beautiful

or

Beauty is beautiful

is to say something tantamount to

[What it is about those things (the urn, etc.) that is beautiful] is beautiful.

The predicate has to apply as long as the subject term refers.[2] To see this, simply look carefully at the last bit within the subject term, and compare it with the predicate. (Remember that we are not yet trying to spell out our interpretation of the sentence. In particular, we are not building in that the subject *has the property* associated with the predicate.)

The analogous point holds for "justice" and "the just," "piety" and "the pious," and in general for "F-ness" and "the F." Given that "F-ness" and "the F" in the use we are focusing on are to be glossed "what it is about F things that is F", and that

[what it is about those things that is F] is F

must hold,

The F itself is F

and

F-ness is F

must hold as well. The reason I called this consideration purely formal is that it does not yet tell us how to interpret any such self-predication sentence; it shows that each must express a truth without specifying the truth in question. (The possibility of knowing that a sentence expresses a truth without yet being in a position to identify which truth it expresses is an interesting one by no means confined to this case—I leave it as an exercise for each reader individually to consider this!) If it is false that justice instantiates justice and that piety exemplifies piety, what that shows is that more work will be required to find out the true interpretation of ancient Greek self-predication sentences: since these universals don't have the property that they are, the subject-predicate grammatical form must be capable of a distinct use from the one that is most obvious to us.

To sum up: Plato was able to rely on linguistic competence's enabling his contemporaries to see that there is guaranteed to be an interpretation of each of his self-predication sentences on which it expresses a truth. And that bears immediately on his willingness to sign on to a theory isomorphic with that of Anaxagoras: a theory containing "The F itself is F." Equally important is to recognize that Plato's confidence (and his relying on the confidence of readers) in this regard is completely independent of readiness to specify what the force of the sentences in question is; thus we should not assume that every one of Plato's texts that contains commitment to any particular self-predication or to self-predication in general should have assigned to it a fine-grained interpretation of the pure being of Forms.

However, anyone committed to Plato's theory obviously needs to work on developing such an interpretation. In this chapter, we will see that Plato himself provided texts to help us come to an understanding of this, an understanding that worked better for his purposes than the Anaxagorean one. His theory so understood provided, in its own way, the explanatory capacity that is the general motivation for the shared program.

Socrates in the *Parmenides*

We now turn to the *Parmenides*. In this section we will see how Plato handled the literary elements of the dialogue in such a way as to point out limitations in his previous presentation of Forms, while also indicating that his theory was capable of successful development. In the dialogues we have discussed so far, Socrates has been the most philosophically active character. Even if his role was formally to question, he was the one who guided the course of the conversation: he often introduced into his questions novel thoughts that felt to the interlocutor and to the reader like suggestions, though of course it was open to us to reject them. In the lengthy and elaborate *Phaedo* and *Republic*, Socrates contributed not only well-developed ideas on the main topics, but also the more sketchy ones about Forms which he claimed were foundational to all else. So it is no surprise as we turn from these works to the dialogue that takes on Forms as its main focus that Socrates is a character. The novelty is that his function in the dialogue has changed.

In the reported and triply framed conversation that has made the first part of this work famous, we find the tables turned on the character Socrates. The conversation is formally in the pattern of his namesake *elenchos*, but this time *he* is the over-confident victim who proves unable to sustain his position when questioned by the dialogue's guiding philosophical presence. The occasion is a visit to Athens by the venerable Eleatic Parmenides and his onetime student Zeno. We learn that Zeno had given a reading from his book (a historical reality, from which fragments, famous paradoxes about plurality and motion, survive today). Socrates, though still a youth, speaks up from the audience with a rude attack on Zeno. He accuses the celebrity, who the innermost narrator has reported was said to have been Parmenides' *paidika* (boytoy), presumably well in the past, of trying to regain the favor of his master (128a), and of trying to impose on others with pretensions to advance something new while in reality saying the same thing as the senior Eleatic.

In the philosophical core of this attack, Socrates claims in effect that Zeno is attempting the *reductio ad absurdum* strategy with arguments that lead to no significant absurdity. According to Socrates (127d–128a), the general form of Zeno's arguments is:

1   If the things that are are many, they are like and unlike, and so on.
2   But that is impossible.
3   So the things that are cannot be many.

Socrates takes "the things that are" in Zeno's usage to be "visible things" (130a); examples are Socrates himself and "stones and sticks and such things" (129c–d; cf. 129a). He distinguishes these visible things from Forms, which reason grasps. Socrates claims that there is no absurdity if objects in the visible domain are like and unlike, one and many, and so on. Of *course* they are one and many: each of us is one human but many limbs (129c–d). Of course visible things are like and unlike: presumably each is like some things and unlike others. We are familiar with this sort of point from Plato's previous works.

As we saw in Chapter Eight, those works took the circumstance that sensibles figured in such patterns to show that they could not be fundamental; sensibles had some standing nevertheless owing to their being derived from and called after the fundamental entities, the Forms. And here too Socrates contrasts sensibles with Forms, to which he gives a different status (129a–b). Here too, sensibles participate in Forms (*metechein* and *metalambanein* occur throughout), and so are called after (130e) them.

Socrates in the *Parmenides* sees Zeno as trying to confute his opponents by driving them to claims about their many—such as that the many turn out to be like and unlike—that are impossible. In fact and in the opinion of Socrates though, these results are not impossible, as we will confirm in Chapter Ten. While the confused sort of display in question cannot be a locus of Eleatic being, it is no violation of the principle of non-contradiction. (Plato is writing before the development of formal logic, but for us it can be useful to put the point this way.) Socrates himself does grant that ordinary things are not fundamentally real. But that's no skin off his nose. His theory *takes off* from that.

Plato's Socrates can afford to accept Zeno's description of sensibles because he has already moved on from taking everyday objects to be fundamental reality. Thus he announces that the description from which Zeno expected to produce consternation is actually fine. Zeno's results are nothing notable; what Socrates *would* be struck by would be if the Likes themselves [i.e. Likeness] came to be unlike, or the Unlikes [i.e. Unlikeness] like; or if someone should demonstrate "this thing itself, what one is, to be many, or, conversely, the many to be one" (129b-c). (Again, one has to take in one's stride that different scholars follow different conventions about whether or not to capitalize vocabulary for Forms.) In fact, as we will see in Chapter Ten, this challenge from Socrates will be met by the respective senior Eleatics in both the second part of the *Parmenides* and the *Sophist*.

We've seen that the statements of Socrates in this section of the *Parmenides* are reminiscent of those of the character Socrates in the *Phaedo* and *Republic*. But our present dialogue has a special feature that depends on the new *dramatis personae*. When reading previous works we may occasionally have felt that the character Socrates had it too easy: his primary interlocutors did not push back very much. Plato now will cater for our critical wishes by subjecting the familiar sketchy but confident presentation of Forms to serious scrutiny by a most able questioner. For in making theoretical commitments the basis of his attack on one of the guests of honor, Socrates has put himself in the position of the interlocutors of the early dialogues. That is, since he has made his claims about Forms the basis for his arrogance towards

Zeno, he had better be an expert on the relevant theory. And the familiar technique of elenchos is now brought to bear to test him.

The senior philosopher present, Parmenides himself, now examines the youth, taking on the role that the character Socrates had had in Plato's earliest works. Since Socrates in the *Parmenides* personifies the previously existing presentation of Forms, his level of understanding should not automatically be identified with that of Plato, the author of the *Parmenides*. Rather the author now uses the new leading character Parmenides to make a comment about his earlier spokesperson and so in effect about his own earlier presentation. This new leading character is by no means a literal avatar of the actual Eleatic. He has historically impossible awareness of Plato's theory (e.g. 130e on eponomy—sensibles' being called after Forms) and acceptance of it (135a–e). But this character also personifies the legacy of the historical Parmenides, whose importance Plato is crediting by this fictional creation.

As we will see, Socrates will prove unable to maintain his position: he will fall repeatedly into perplexity. So is Plato now showing that his theory of Forms should be rejected? It is important to recognize that we need not go to this extreme. After all, as we saw in Chapter Three, the *elenchos* is in the first instance a test of the expertise of an individual: if he contradicts himself, he clearly does not have expertise. Whether the problem originates in his core tenets or merely in his incompetent way of handling them may well require further investigation to determine.

In this case, I believe it will turn out that the dialogue presents Socrates as advocating in an immature way a promising theory that can be developed successfully. On this reading, Plato's choice to make Socrates much younger than he had been in the *Symposium*, *Phaedo*, and *Republic* is a significant touch. In Plato's previous works, Socrates had been portrayed as senior, and authoritative on the main topics (compared both with his interlocutors and with himself in the *Parmenides*); now his age being put back brings out the fact that on the topic of Forms, the middle-dialogue presentation was far from developed. The immaturity of Socrates here has several manifestations besides his brash arrogance. He is brought to confess that he is unsure on some points. Most importantly, he embraces the formalism of his theory without knowing its true interpretation, and so he is vulnerable to being led into unviable readings and disastrous inferences from them.

The persistent sniping of Plato's student, Aristotle, together with concentration on the first part of the *Parmenides* can create the impression that Platonic Forms are definitively exploded by arguments such as the "third man" (the name derives from Aristotle's repeated reference to his own formulation of the argument; we will soon look at Plato's presentation at 132a1–b2). Yet scholars who read the *Parmenides* as a whole tend to find a more constructive moral to the story. The resources of the dialogue are not exhausted by those of the character Socrates. We must give its full value to the fact that venerable Parmenides praises Socrates for positing Forms, says that is necessary if one is not to destroy the power of *dialegesthai* (which can mean anything from conversation through dialectic), and prescribes an exercise for the young man without which, he says, the truth will elude him (135b–d).

Parmenides is prevailed on by the company to demonstrate the exercise, which he does taking as his interlocutor a certain Aristotle (a character based not on "our" Aristotle, but on someone else of the same name). This demonstration, the longest stretch of argument in Plato's entire corpus, constitutes the second part of the dialogue. It is in effect directed at us: once it has started, there are no resumptions of the frames or words from the narrators; nothing at all but the direct speech—as in a play—of Parmenides and his young interlocutor. We have seen in connection with the *Symposium* that this technique involves us directly as the real audience of this part of the work. So in the *Parmenides*, it is on us to benefit from the demonstration and apply the lessons of the exercise to develop our thinking on Forms (McCabe 1996; Meinwald 2005). To prepare first though by seeing the problems of Socrates, let us examine some of the famous passages in the first part of the dialogue. We will see that Plato is raising here some of the issues about Forms we have been worried about.

The extent of Forms

With respect to the first topic that comes up, no argument is needed to show the limitation of the character Socrates. While he is confident in positing Likeness and One and Many and "all the things you heard Zeno read about a while ago;" likewise the Just, the Beautiful, and the Good, and "everything of that sort" (130b); he confesses doubt concerning a Form of human being, or fire, or water. He rejects Forms for hair and mud and dirt "or anything else totally undignified and worthless" (130c), only to have Parmenides remark, "That's because you are still young, Socrates ... and philosophy has not yet gripped you as, in my opinion, it will in the future" (130e).

Is this exchange consonant with the view that the character Socrates personifies the previous presentation of Forms? Very much so. For reflect that the concentration of the *Symposium* on the case of Beauty meant that the general issue did not even come up. The *Phaedo* clearly envisioned a whole population of Forms, but still did not tell us how extensive the population was—or what the criterion for positing its members might be. We typically heard of a few examples together with some generalizing phrase(s). So, at 65d, we hear of the Just, the Beautiful, the Good; and "all things such as" the Large, Health, and Strength. (Cf. 75c–d, with its reference to "when we are putting [Socratic what-is-it] questions and answering them," and 100b.)

The *Phaedo* contrast between ordinary objects and Forms was made in cases, like the equal sticks vs. Equality itself, where ordinary objects clearly mix being and not-being, so that a reader could be unsure whether the pattern was meant to generalize to all predicates. Consider the claim that Simmias (who is larger than Socrates but smaller than Phaedo), is not larger than Socrates "by being Simmias" (102b–c, translated literally). Some have read this as having in its implicature that there is something he is by being Simmias, with no countervailing not-being: the popular candidate was at one time man or I suppose in the age of less sexist diction human. Note though that the original assertion really only has the force: it is not the case that he is larger by being Simmias. This is equally compatible with there being *nothing* that he is by being Simmias. Moreover, there is the question whether cases in which sensibles Fs are and are not should be taken to be the only ones in which there are Forms. Possibly, once we posit some Forms, we should treat all legitimate general terms in the same way.

In the *Republic*, different passages have seemed to scholars actually to pull in different directions. The distinction at 523a–524d between properties on which the deliverances of the senses are confusing so that we are prompted to "what is it" questions vs. those which are not provocative in this way was at one time thought to suggest that there are Forms only for these special properties. Yet the "one over many" premise used at 596a in discussing literature (we are accustomed to posit a single Form in each case in which we find ourselves applying the same designation to a many) has seemed to yield a much larger population.[3] An approach is gaining ground among scholars on which Plato did not mean in these passages to present a dogmatic and official view concerning either the extent of Forms or the criteria for positing them. The first text—after all, part of the discussion of the educational curriculum—is properly about cases where *we most easily are led* to Forms; there need be no implication that these are all there are. The second gives a consideration in favor of way more, without ruling out that some of the terms we originally work from may prove ultimately to be ambiguous or, indeed, specious.

For the purposes of the *Republic*, determining the extent of Forms was not pressing: Justice and The Good clearly figure in even the smallest population. More generally we may suppose that in works preceding the *Parmenides*, Plato was content to leave this issue unilluminated. In making Forms his topic in the *Parmenides*, he wants us to realize that there is a question here that has not been settled. Because the venerable Eleatic is the guiding philosophical presence in this work, his counseling Socrates to accept more Forms than the youth is presently certain of seems to indicate that this is the direction Plato recommends. And later works confirm this. The *Timaeus* has Fire (51b) and Living Thing (39e) among its Forms; in the *Philebus* Socrates gives Man and Ox as examples (15a). Indeed, a fragment of a comedy of Epicrates shows awareness among the general public in Plato's time of attempts in the Academy to give accounts of biological Forms. In the play, Plato is encouraging some students who are having trouble with the Pumpkin (fragment translated in Dillon 2003: 7–8).

Problems of participation

The first actual argument with which Parmenides presents Socrates is a dilemma growing from the question whether participants get the whole or a part of a Form in which they share (131a–e). Socrates gets into trouble with each of these two branches. Parmenides initially suggests that the option of the whole Form's being present in each of several participants that are separate from each other would have it literally beside itself, a threat to its unity. Socrates tries to counter that the Form could be like a day, which is present as a whole in different places. While many readers over the centuries have thought that Socrates is onto something promising here, he is only groping towards it. Far from being able to recognize clearly and exploit effectively the relevant features of his analogy, he lets Parmenides assimilate a day to a sail. But he cannot deny that when a sail is spread over a plurality of people, strictly speaking only a portion of the sail is over each individual—and so there has been a segue to the other option, on which each of the many participants gets a part of the Form. But with a part of it in each of many dispersed participants, the Form itself now seems to be dispersed so that its unity is again threatened.

Moreover, on this branch we have special problems with certain examples. Remember that, on an Anaxagorean interpretation of participation (which Socrates seems to be falling into here), shares of the fundamental entities themselves have the very properties they are accounting for, and bring them to the composites. As we saw in Chapter Eight, this works well for cases in which things around us are gold, or hot, or wet; not so much with some of the other ones Plato is interested in. Our present text problematizes the application of Anaxagorean thinking to sensible particulars that are large, or equal, or small; here's how I would fill out the thinking in one such case. On the Anaxagorean scheme, what makes our planet large must be that it has a share of the large that brings its largeness with it. But considering the many billions and billions of stars (not to mention other large things), our planet's share of the large would have to be quite a small one. Being a small thing prevents it, in Socrates' eyes, from having the requisite largeness to bring to our earth, so that he can no longer see how it could make our planet large.

This problem is a variant of one we saw in the *Phaedo* in the section about how study of Anaxagoras and other philosophers of nature disappointed and confused Socrates: the puzzle of being taller by a head. Plato in the present portrayal of Socrates falling into the trap is showing him not to be in command of a clear alternative to the Anaxagorean way of understanding getting a share. And remember the virtual admission of this in the *Phaedo* when Socrates stated the simple and safe way of explaining that a thing is beautiful by declaring:

> I think that, if there is anything beautiful besides the Beautiful itself, it is beautiful for no other reason than that it has a share of/participates in [*metechei*] that Beautiful, and I say so with everything … I simply, naively and perhaps foolishly cling to this, that nothing else makes it beautiful other than the presence of, or the communion with [*koinōnia*], or however you may describe its relationship to that Beautiful we mentioned, for I will not insist on the precise nature of the relationship, but that all beautiful things are beautiful by the Beautiful.
>
> (100c–d, my translation, based on Grube in Cooper, ed., 1997)

Remember how, in the Anaxagorean precursor of Plato's theory, pure gold accounted for gold objects: each of the many gold things had a share of gold as an ingredient. The situation for the wet and the hot (thought of as a stuff, like caloric) was analogous. It was easy to see how such Anaxagorean elements were able to endow composites with their own properties: pure gold actually is gold in the same way as composites except without the admixture of any competing elements, so the portion of gold that is a constituent of my earring straightforwardly makes the piece golden. We also traced Plato's realization that the Anaxagorean interpretation of what having a share amounts to did not work for the full range of properties he himself was interested in. In fact, cases of things' being tall/large, or thin, or beautiful, or one all resist the Anaxagorean understanding. Did Plato make the minimal change of still positing fundamental items that were pure instances, and simply denying that physical parts of them were ingredients in mixtures (so that

Forms were, perhaps, "laid up in heaven" there to be approximated or imitated by sensibles?) Or did he contemplate a more radical change in the way in which the F itself was F?

The third man

From considering participation we have now arrived naturally at the primary issue of the pure being of Forms: the realm of Forms is the domain of the single intelligible Beauty that is purely beautiful, the single intelligible Justice that is purely just, the single intelligible Goodness that is purely good, and so on. Is Plato committed to thinking that each Form does its job by being some sort of superb and unqualified instance of itself? This would be highly problematic. To remind ourselves of the problem involved: Many-ness cannot be plural without alloy, or how could it sustain the characteristic unity of a Form? No perfect specimens of Hedgehoggery or Foxhood could qualify as the Hedgehog or the Fox itself; the birth and inevitable death of any such specimens would be incompatible with the stability and eternality of the Forms. The threat generally called "the third man" after the bogey in view in Aristotle's formulation involves self-predication as well.

The argument in question is actually a closely related family of arguments—both the illustrative subject and the exact formulation of the premises are different in different authors. Nevertheless, it has been recognized since antiquity that essential parts are played by (some version of) claims called in the secondary literature "one over many," "non-identity"/"non-self-explanation," and "self-predication" (often referred to by the acronyms "OM," "NI" or "NSE," and "SP").[4] In our text, the exact formulations these should receive are underdetermined and the key moves flash by at 132a1–b2. This is one manifestation of the immaturity of the character Socrates. Because he lets his questioner proceed without clarity and explicitness, he doesn't even have a chance to fend off problematic interpretations of and illicit inferences from his initial claims.

Parmenides starts Socrates off with the many large things he sees and suggests Socrates believes in one Form that is over them all, the Large (he posits a one over many). Parmenides goes on to speak of the Large itself "and the other large things," a formulation that we can unpack as involving many assumptions: the non-identity of the Large with the sensibles, the self-predication: "The Large is large," and the self-instantiation reading of that. What he says explicitly about the Large and the other large things is that they now require *another* Form by which all of them will be large (presumably because the new group prompts a new application of the one over many and non-identity/non-self-explanation principles). Evidently there will be no end to the threatened regress: this new Form will also be large, occasion recognition of a new group of large things, which require *yet another* Form by which they are all large, and so on without end.

This argument is widely considered out of context and taken as fatal for Plato's theory of Forms. But our reading of Plato's text has led us to expect that he was offering this difficulty—like the others—precisely in the expectation that he was about to give us the resources to deal with it. So before we make up our minds on these issues, we should consider the application of those resources. To do this, we need to harvest (some of) the results of the second part of the dialogue—the exercise offered to help with the problems of the first part.

The key development

This chapter does not afford scope to go through all the evidence on which I base my reading of the main innovation in question—the exercise constituting the second part of the *Parmenides* is thirty pages of unbroken argument, and detailed consideration of the Greek text of both the exercise and Plato's descriptions of it is required in this connection. For present purposes, I will base myself on what I have argued for elsewhere (Meinwald 1991, 1992, 2014[5]).

The most obvious feature of this awesome and tremendous exercise is that the conclusions of its first section seem systematically to contradict those of its second, and so on. Yet at the end of the entire exercise neither questioner nor interlocutor displays any distress, and the interlocutor goes to an extreme in accepting the summary of the total results with the superlative form, which we could translate literally as "Most true" (166c). This should prompt us to wonder whether the contradictions could be merely apparent.

And Plato has provided indications that that is so. He uses an opaque pair of qualifications pervasively in venerable Parmenides' methodological advice describing the sections of argument constituting his exercise, and these appear again in his compressed summaries of both the first half of the exercise and of the exercise as a whole. These qualifications stress an unexplained distinction between sections that investigate what follows for something "in relation to itself" versus those that do so "in relation to the others." If, for example, the first section is generating results for the One (in relation to itself) and the second doing so for the One (in relation to the others), we can see that there need be no real tension between the sections. But the idea so put is too abstract to leave at that.

Thus, I see Plato as in effect assigning us homework. We must work out for ourselves how these mysterious qualifications govern the sections of the exercise Parmenides demonstrates and which he has described using them. To assign such a task to us is characteristic of Plato in his advanced works (Burnyeat 1990). And it's an understandable way for him to proceed given his view about the naïveté of thinking that one can transmit wisdom to others by giving them written formulae (Chapter Two).

Since Plato leads us to expect that each section of argument in the exercise as demonstrated is governed by one or the other of this pair of qualifications, I guide myself in interpreting the qualifications by the contents of those sections. I tailor my interpretation of these key phrases so that the conclusions each implicitly qualifies are supported by the arguments for them. Thus my interpretation of this language is guided maximally by the totality of the text. Each of the pair turns out to mark a distinct kind of statement of importance in Plato's theory. In fact, the distinction in question is one between two very different kinds of predication, grounded in two very different kinds of facts.[6]

One of Plato's kinds of predication contains all the ones we ordinarily make. These are about what I call non-technically subjects' displays of features.[7] We today are inclined to describe such states of affairs in terms of the subjects' instantiating or exemplifying something associated with the predicate terms. Such ordinary predications include: "Socrates is pale," "Socrates is a man," "Beauty is eternal," and "The Good is at rest." This grouping is indifferent to further distinctions some would like to make within this class based on taking the facts in question to be essential or accidental, necessary or contingent. Sensibles and Forms alike can have this kind of truths about them.

Ordinary predication is what we are employing when we assert truths about displays of features, as it might be that Chloe (a pet rabbit), or an orchid, or a math proof, or for that matter a Form is beautiful. Now remember, as we have seen in earlier chapters, that it is central to Plato's program to hold that none of the states of affairs just mentioned can obtain without the Form, Beauty, having something to do with it. Indeed, he has made us familiar with his characteristic claim that it is the Form, Beauty, that makes things beautiful. The *Parmenides* in effect offers a linguistic regime that we can use to make the metaphysical situation fully clear by noting explicitly that Chloe for example is beautiful *in relation to Beauty*. What is that relation? To be as conservative as possible, we might say that Beauty is the nature to which Chloe's display is conforming. Or we could say that she is satisfying the account of what beauty is, an account that articulates what it is to be beautiful.

A note on Plato's phraseology. This is an instance of being F "in relation to the others"—Beauty is the relevant "other" in this case. Beauty is obviously distinct from Chloe, as it is also distinct from the orchid, the proof, and from Justice. Since a nature so invoked will typically be distinct from the individuals whose displays of features it explains, we can see why Plato would attach the tag "in relation to the others" to this category of results. (In fact, the subject and the nature explaining its display need not always be distinct: Beauty is a beautiful thing, and the One is a unified object. Plato's scheme categorizes even these results as "in relation to the others"—I suppose because the relation that grounds them is one that the subjects *may and typically do* have to what are literally "others.")

I mentioned that both Forms and sensibles can be the subjects of assertions of this type. Notice that each individual will be the subject of a huge variety of such ordinary assertions. Chloe is not only beautiful (in relation to Beauty), but (assuming that she is a beautiful, wiggly, friendly rabbit), she stands in the same relation to Unity, Rabbithood, Wiggliness, Friendliness, and so on. Indeed, we can also consider Rabbithood itself as a subject: it will have its own assortment of features. In addition to being beautiful in relation to Beauty (assuming that every animal Form is beautiful), the Rabbit stands in the same relation to Unity, Eternality, Stability, Intelligibility and so on. Each of these natures is something (part of) this Form's display of features conforms to.

At this point readers may be wondering what other kind of predication there can be. While sensible individuals are the subjects of ordinary predication only, Plato develops a more fundamental type of assertion we can make concerning Forms. Plato's predication of a Form "in relation to itself" is not about the subject's display of a feature; it is not about the subject's instantiating or exemplifying something associated with the predicate term. Rather, this kind of predication is grounded in a much more internal matter: it allows us to articulate accounts of the subjects' natures. That is, it is a vehicle for expressing the very accounts whose explanatory bearing on the displays of individuals we recently invoked.

The program of Platonic division aims to map fundamental relations among natures and so to provide many such accounts. This approach is widely familiar today through its descendants in the biological classification of living things. Plato's basic idea is that of dividing a kind into its sub-kinds by the use of differentiae, and so on down. Laying this out in a diagram that uses branching to represent division at each level results in a structure often called a "tree." Such a tree shows the variety of sub-kinds (and sub-sub-kinds, etc.) each higher kind comprehends. It also allows us to read off (entire or partial) accounts of each of the lower kinds, in terms of what the tree reveals goes toward specifying it. One might be the familiar characterization of our own kind as Rational Animal. Of course, entities at the tops of their trees (or on no tree) will not have this type of account—though they may have accounts of a different sort. (For useful discussion of the general point, see Gill 2012: 2, 101; Meinwald 1991 treated the special case of the One.)

We will look in detail at a variety of texts on the evolving division program in Chapter Ten; in this chapter we will use the present, basic characterization of it to see how the program goes with Plato's predication of a subject "in relation to itself." It is important to realize that "X is Y" holds as a predication of this type if and only if the nature associated with "Y" is involved in the nature associated with "X," as either part of it or the whole. That is the whole force of the assertion—there is no commitment to X's instantiating Y-ness. I sometimes use the tag "tree predication" for this class of assertions, as a way of gesturing towards their special truth conditions.

Tree predication is grounded in the structure of the nature in question. Let's take some examples. "Angling is fishing" is true when made as a predication of this type. For, as the *Sophist* lays out, Fishing is part of what Angling is: a sub-sub-kind of Fishing is Hooking, and Angling is the sub-kind of Hooking that involves a blow drawing a thing upward from underneath. (For the larger structure from which I take these bits, see the summary at *Sophist* 221a–c.) "The Even is divisible by two" also holds as a tree predication if being divisible by two is part of what it is to be even (following the suggestion of *Euthyphro* 12d, to produce the idea that the Even is the kind of Number that has this differentia).

In general, the nature associated with a Form, A, *is* what is specified in the account of what it is to be (an) A, and it is in virtue of this that the predications hold. For when made as a tree predication, "A is B" has the force that the nature associated with "B" is involved in that associated with "A."[8] Either the former is a proper part (i.e. less than the whole) of the latter or they may be identical. If A is a sub-kind on a tree, then terms associated with the natures of any kind or differentia that is at or above A's position on the branch leading to A itself will hold of A in a tree predication. If A is not a sub-kind but it still has an account, "tree predications" that express the account in its entirety will hold. That account specifies A's nature as a whole—thus what the account specifies is in my sense "involved in" A's nature.

Because these trees represent what reality *really is*, many tree truths will be significant and hard-won discoveries, such as that the Whale is a mammal. By contrast, consider the following self-predication sentence:

The Rabbit is a rabbit.

We can appreciate that this sentence is safe if unexciting when used to make a tree predication, since being a rabbit is involved in being a rabbit. Here we are at the limit case. We may however see this self-predication as containing in kernel the fully expanded informative account. If the nature of Rabbithood is being an animal with XYZ, we can go beyond gesturing at the nature twice under the same designation, and can expand one occurrence to assert as a tree predication:

The Rabbit is an animal with XYZ.

To sum up, Plato's key qualifications turn out to mark two distinct and philosophically significant relations, each of which grounds a distinct kind of predication. The different force of the tree predication:

A is B (in relation to itself)

and the ordinary predication:

A is B (in relation to the others)

is ultimately due to the different relations grounding the two types of assertion and so to the different ways in which B is predicated of A.

In fact, when the subject is a Form, the single form of words "A is B" can be used on different occasions to make two distinct assertions, one of each type. These always have different truth conditions, and often have different truth values as well. "Bravery is brave" when used to make an ordinary predication is false, though when used to make a tree predication the same sentence comes out true. The tree predication "Intelligibility is intelligible" and the ordinary predication that could be made by the same sentence are both true, but still have different force and different truth conditions. The tree truth holds in virtue of the tautology that being intelligible is being intelligible, while the ordinary one tells us that the Form in question is an intelligible thing.

The fact that, when made as a tree predication, "A is B" has different truth conditions and different force from the very same form of words when that is used to make an ordinary predication is of great moment for eluding the famous problems. It puts us in a position to see that the self-predications and other truths about a

Form which are most fundamental are tree truths and as such not about displaying. Thus we have a principled reason from within the text for saying that Forms do not do their job by self-exemplification. Plato need not regard each as a perfect instance of itself.

The exercise constituting the second part of the *Parmenides* was introduced to help after Socrates fell into difficulties in the first part of the dialogue, so there is a presumption that what we learn from it will apply to those famous problems. Plato does not spell out the applications though; he is leaving that for each of us to do. Greekless readers: whenever any scholar offers a reading of the second part of the dialogue, you can consider on your own how it helps with the problems of the first part. You are certainly welcome to try that using the reading I have offered! Don't read the next three sections immediately if you prefer to do this yourself first. I'll record there how I think the exercise helps with the problems we had in view at the beginning of this chapter.

Application to the extent of Forms

Our first issue was Socrates' uncertainty concerning the extent of Forms. Here since no actual argument was in play, there is no exact problem to solve. However, we can see how the way of thinking about Forms we've been developing bears on the issue. It now seems possible that Socrates' reluctance to countenance Forms for living things like man and undignified things like mud was at least partly due to his not having a clear alternative to the super-exemplifier picture. Being muddy, even supremely and without qualification, is inappropriate to the kind of eternal and glorious entities Forms are supposed to be; likewise with being mortal. On the other hand, *what it is to be mud* may be something perfectly specifiable and not at all messy, while what it is to be a man is (in Plato's view anyway) eternal.

Application to problems of participation

The dilemma for Socrates on this score was whether to say that each participant gets the whole or only a part of a Form in which it participates: whether, for example. to assign to each beautiful thing the whole or only a part of Beauty. Each of these choices has some motivation in its favor; in our text Socrates also fell into problems associated with each. We can now see how to sustain the motivations without the problems.

What is the initial appeal in choosing the "whole" option? A core motivation of the program is to carry out the idea that we are seeking some one thing common to all the cases that makes them what they are. The worrying problem with taking the "whole" option that threatened Socrates in the first part of the dialogue may have been due to his staying too close to the model of Anaxagoras. An Anaxagorean stuff can obviously not be wholly contained simultaneously in Thing One over here and also in Thing Two over there without being problematically beside itself.

The newly articulated scheme has no such worries. We still achieve the goal of relating all the participants to a single whole. Whatever it is to be energetic, this whole nature is involved in all displays of energeticness; this is what they are conforming to. Explanatory oomph is ultimately provided by the articulation of the nature, as specified in the truth about the Energetic "in relation to itself." Since it is the whole of the nature that makes energetic individuals what they are, that is what we should identify as explanatory of them. This is just as able to unify them as any super-exemplifier could have done—though its way of doing that is of course neither by physical ingredienthood nor by resemblance as we ordinarily conceive of that. Rather we are now clear that the Form is what the many sensibles have in common because the nature of the Energetic is the single structure that causes and explains all the relevant displays; the account of that one nature (whatever it turns out to be) is what they are all satisfying.

Since the relation of conforming to a nature now in question clearly has no tendency to make the whole Form be in each individual in the problematic physical sense, there is now no threat of the Form's being "beside itself" in virtue of its participants' separation from each other.

Notice that the way we are now thinking of a participant as having its display conform to the nature associated with the Form isn't one that "uses up" the nature in question in such a way that nothing else can stand in the same relation. Chloe's conforming to what

Beauty is has no tendency to prevent an orchid from doing so as well. A given participant, in conforming to the whole of a Form's nature, still may account for only part of that Form's manifestation in the world. The idea of ordinary objects "getting shares" of Forms was to make clear that a "participant" need not use up the whole Form. On the present scheme too, we are perfectly able to accept that different participants can be different parts of a given Form's manifestation in the world.

Let's see how the present way of thinking avoids the problems formerly associated with the "part" option. The first was that, in giving distinct participants distinct parts of the Form, we divide the Form and destroy its unity. But as we just saw, the unity of the Form on the present scheme is provided by the single whole nature— which is not divided by having physically dispersed sensibles conforming to it.

We also considered difficulties with each participant getting only a part of a Form as its share for certain special cases. When Socrates thought of the situation in a way close to that of Anaxagoras, he was thinking that when something acquires a property, that property is transferred to the participant by coming along with the participant's share of a Form—where the share and the Form both have the property. Remember the problem for Largeness: an individual participant (such as our planet, which is after all only one of billions and billions of large objects) can receive only a miniscule share of the Large. And as a small item the share seemed not to be able to endow the planet with Largeness. But Plato has now helped us to make the gestalt shift away from thinking of the Form as functioning by being a pure instance—thus there is no longer any question of the share an individual gets needing to have the property so as to ferry it along to the individual. A share is no longer a portion of stuff that figures as an ingredient in a composite.

We have seen that a given participant, in conforming to the whole of a Form's nature, still may account for only part of that Form's manifestation in the world. So if there is a tremendous number of large things and our planet accounts for only a tiny portion of the being of Largeness, we can say for that reason that it has a small share of the Large. However the smallness of this share does not threaten the explanatory ability of Largeness. It does nothing to undermine the fundamental fact that what the planet is related to by the conforming relation is the nature of Largeness itself, *what it is to be large*, the specification of which the planet satisfies.

Application to the third man

We have seen that some Forms (like the Brave and the Hedgehog) don't instantiate themselves, while others (like Beauty and Intelligibility) do. But in neither case is this relevant to how they perform their key function. *Forms do not do their jobs by being perfect instances of themselves*; the deepest and most fundamental truths are the results about a Form "in relation to itself," not those "in relation to the others." (More on this in Chapter Ten.) Being clear that Forms don't perform their fundamental role by instantiating the very property they are is key for avoiding the Third Man. The basic gestalt shift we have made allows us to accommodate both self-exemplifying and non-self-exemplifying cases (though with slightly more elaboration in the self-exemplifying case). The crucial thing is that, even when Forms do exemplify themselves, that fact is rather incidental. Since the Large (Plato's example in the text) elicits diverging intuitions on the matter of which type of case it belongs to, it may be useful now to take an uncontroversial sample of each.

Let's start with the most notorious case. Looking at the many men around us, some version of the one over many principle prompts us to posit the Form, Man itself. This is perfectly in order: there is no problem so far if we wish to posit, according to the core commitments of the theory Plato is developing, that there is some one nature conforming to which makes all the sensibles in question men, and whose real account (rational animal or whatever) we use in explaining the relevant displays.

On to the next step. We saw in our preliminary look at the problem that Parmenides snuck in not just self-predication, but the self-instantiation reading of that. Is the Man itself (a) man? We now clearly see that, *as a tree truth*, the self-predication "The Man is (a) man" is safe though uninformative: being a man is involved in being a man. *In relation to itself* Man is a man. But since this tree truth is not about the Form's display, there is no pressure to accept any claim about self-instantiation on the part of the Form. Thus the distinction between the two kinds of predication allows us to preserve the needed self-predication while still being perfectly able to deny that the Form is an additional member of our species. With no new group there is no need for further explanation, and so no third man.

Really understanding how the Form plays its explanatory role in this, typical, case—while remaining free from any self-instantiation—should help us with the special case in which a Form does, incidentally, instantiate itself. Let's consider how the argument would go in the case of Beauty. We start off with the base group of ordinary beauties. To account for what they have in common we introduce the form, the Beautiful itself: in parallel with our previous case of Man, there is no problem if we wish to suppose that there is some one nature conforming to which makes all the sensibles beauties and whose real account we use in explaining the relevant displays. And again in parallel, we preserve the self-predication concerning the Form's pure being by maintaining the tree truth "Beauty is beautiful." Since the tree truth is making no commitment about Beauty's self-instantiation, we have in this case too taken care of the Form's fundamental grounding work without for that purpose invoking an additional display and so producing a new "many" that requires an additional "one."

But in our present case, the Form does in fact make such a display—even though that is not how it performs its explanatory function. Beauty (like all Forms) is a beautiful thing. Thus the deep truth (in relation to itself) is not the only self-predication that holds; it is also correct to make the ordinary assertion: Beauty is beautiful. This extra display does create a new group (the original beauties plus the Beautiful itself) of things that are beautiful in the same way. Will we need another Form to explain that, and so be faced with a problematic third beauty and so on forever?

Of course not. Instead of mechanically applying one of the formulations of "NI"/"NSE," let's think for a minute about the motivation for something in that area at the base step, when we posited the Form, Beauty, to explain the displays of the sensibles. None of the sensibles could sustain the role of being the explanatory factor; that is why we needed to invoke something besides them. So the appeal of "non-identity" of sensibles with the Form which explains their displays derives from the explanatory inadequacy of the sensibles. Put otherwise, "non-self-explanation" at the base step derives from the circumstance that a sensible's display is inadequate to explain the displays of the group among which it itself figures. Yet this is not enough to license a claim that nothing can ever explain anything about itself.

We are now in a position to see why Beauty itself is capable of explaining its own display of beauty when a vase for example is not. We will use the insight we have been developing that, on the new picture of Forms, there are two different kinds of facts about them. Forms differ from sensibles in that their repertoire is not restricted to their displays of features. Indeed, in the way of thinking we've been developing, displaying is never explained by reference to any display—however distinct and superior. When we brought in the Form to explain the displays of our original group of sensibles, we were appealing to a different sort of fact, about the articulation of the nature in question, what that nature really amounts to. (This is true throughout Plato's exercise as well as in our recent case of sensible men and in the base step of the present case, of sensible beauties.)

Nothing prevents the same nature that explains the base group from explaining the new group formed by recognizing that Beauty is a beautiful object. What is explanatory and metaphysically grounding of all the displays in question is the account of the nature: what it is to be beautiful. We are appealing to an explanatory fact distinct from those about any displays, but to do this there is no need to produce a Form distinct from the original one. There is something about our original Form way more fundamental than its displaying: this explanatory factor grounds all the displays in question (including, but only incidentally, its own). To sum up my approach in terms of the jargon, I believe that the gestalt shift I have been exploring is not restricted to a more nuanced understanding of SP—this leads on to a better understanding of NI/NSE as well.

Conclusion

On one way of thinking of Plato, his flagship theory was committed to Forms as super-exemplifiers (to cite just a sampling: Vlastos

1954; Annas 1981: chs 8 and 9; Bostock 1986; Dancy 2004; Rickless 2007; Gill 2012). This is the view that we saw has been expressed by saying that Plato takes Equality to be something equal—"never mind to what" (Penner 1987: 48–9 reporting the interpretation of Owen 1957). Aristotle in fact had taken the lead in reading the central sentences as assertions of the unqualified displays made by perfect exemplars.

We do not need automatically to endorse Aristotle's interpretation. He will be within his rights as a working rival philosopher if, when thinking about the *Symposium*, *Phaedo*, and *Republic*, he employs a natural reading from which Plato has not clearly distanced himself of this characteristic claim (Fine 1993). Perhaps this was the activity in recognition of which Plato is reported to have called Aristotle "The Reader" (*Vita Aristotelis Marciana* §6, cited by Irwin 2008: 67). But Aristotle would be cheating outright if he foisted on Plato a reading of this central commitment that was clearly and from the start not the intended one. Thus Aristotle's reading and the similar construal of so many throughout history do show that Plato's language naturally suggests the perfect-exemplar interpretation of Forms.

The belief that Plato was committed to a super-exemplifier theory that was hopeless from the start goes with a rather sad developmental story: that the famous problems of the first part of the *Parmenides* show that Plato saw the unviability of his most exuberant creation. The dialogue on this view is flying with some panache the tattered banner of philosophical integrity. It is at least a drawback of the pessimistic interpretation that it commits the *Symposium*, *Phaedo*, and *Republic* to a theory proposed as foundational to everything else, but which is manifestly unviable. Not only reverence for Plato makes this developmental story unattractive; it is in tension with how easily and quickly he himself showed the unviability of the super-exemplifier picture (remember that the *Parmenides* is stylistically and so quite likely chronologically in the *Republic* cluster.) Moreover, purveyors of the negative story often ignore Plato's indications that the second part of the *Parmenides* provides the resources to handle the problems broached in the first part.[9]

There is an opposite, determinedly charitable family of readings. These give an unproblematic interpretation of self-predication claims along the lines of: Justice is what it is to be just; Largeness is what it is to be large, etc.; and insist that Plato's works from the start called for that (Nehamas 1975, 1979; Patterson 1985; Penner 1987). Yet to the extent we recognize that the basic unit for interpretation is the text of each of Plato's individual works, this interpretative option for the Socratic dialogues and for the *Symposium, Phaedo,* and *Republic* will decrease in credibility: the determinedly charitable proposal concerning Forms in those works has always depended on what its proponents brought to the relevant passages. A version of confirmation bias can lead interpreters who come to a text with a preferred reading in mind to see that text as establishing that reading when it perhaps only does not rule it out.

These determinedly charitable readings at least show that the interpretation in question is not incompatible with these texts—but cannot show that it is at all plausible as what Plato could have expected readers to think. Moreover, in a completely different way from the natural reading we first considered, this line of interpretation also makes nonsense of the *Parmenides.* The first part of the dialogue clearly shows Socrates—representing the presentation of the *Phaedo* and *Republic*—being at a loss when questioned. This makes no sense if these works had unambiguously contained unproblematic self-predication claims.

I have thus been arguing that in texts preceding the *Parmenides,* we should let the force of self-predication sentences be less than fully interpreted. It is undesirable either to commit Plato dogmatically to nonsense, or to avoid that by stipulating a view one is bringing to those texts from works that their original readers could not have known.[10] The *Parmenides* is the first dialogue in which we can securely ground an unproblematic interpretation of self-predication in Plato's text: this dialogue thematizes its distinction between two different readings of sentences of the grammatical "S is P" type.[11]

This is the point of juxtaposing massive paired sections of argument, where each section's results are apparently in systematic contradiction with those of the section it is paired with. In this text for the first time, Plato is showing over and over that sentences of the grammatical form "S is P" have two systematically different readings—the very thing that is a precondition of charitable interpretations that seek to choose the less obvious one as the kind of self-predication that will be central to the theory. Thus with the charitable interpreters, I too attribute to Plato the realization that Forms are not, in the general case, super-exemplifiers: Platonic Forms do not play their central metaphysical and epistemological role by being unalloyed instances of themselves. Yet I claim that only with the *Parmenides* (and the related *Sophist*) do we have texts that it is appropriate to read as making this point. Nevertheless, the existence of the charitable interpretations of the preceding dialogues, however much bending over backwards they may require, is extremely important for my overall picture of Plato's work. From my point of view, the scholars in question have shown that the central claims about Forms in those earlier works (which for me are under-determined in their actual environment) do not become false if we now go back and read them according to our (lately won) way of understanding self-predication and the true being of the Forms.

So on this view, the theory is still alive in the *Parmenides* and beyond. In this chapter we have seen how the new innovation lets us deal with some famous problems from the first part of that dialogue. In Chapter Ten we will trace other aspects of the development of the theory.

Further reading

See Bibliography for full details of the works listed below.
D. Bailey (2009) "The Third Man Argument."
F. Cornford (1939) *Plato and Parmenides.*
G. Morrow and J. Dillon (trs) (1987) *Proclus' Commentary on Plato's "Parmenides."* Ancient Greek commentary now accessible in English.
S. Peterson (1973) "A Reasonable Self-Predication Premise for the Third Man Argument."
K. Sayre (1978) "Plato's *Parmenides*: Why the Eight Hypotheses Are Not Contradictory."
G. Vlastos (1954) The Third Man Argument in the *Parmenides.*"

Notes

1 There is much else of huge importance in the dialogue, such as the emergence of the One as a principle (Meinwald 1991).

2   Modifying Michael Frede's original way of putting this with help from Walter Edelberg and Mahrad Almotahari.

3   And may not the examples of animals and plants and artifacts which the Divided Line specified for objects of *pistis* with images of them in *eikasia* at least suggest that there are Forms of these things in the intelligible domain?

4   For discussion, see Fine (1993: chs 15, 16).

5   From which some formulations in the balance of this chapter are taken.

6   The distinction, given so much fanfare at its debut, will thus be available to be used later—figuring as the two uses of "is" in the *Sophist* (see the ground-breaking work of Frede 1967, 1992).

7   Since this is meant to be non-technical, there is no commitment on such issues as whether or not features are private to individuals.

8   Predications made without the word "is" or another copula are treated as equivalent to those with it. Thus, "Motion moves" and "Dancing moves" will be true tree predications, just as "The First Lady moves" will be a true ordinary one.

9   Gill (2012) and Rickless (2007) each undertakes to show that the second part of the dialogue leads to amendment of Plato's theory–how successfully they do this is of course for each reader to consider.

10   Thus Nehamas (1975) in claiming his is a normal reading of the "S is P" sentence-form can come up with parallels only from poetry and not ones that are numerous and clear-cut at that, and Silverman (2002) seems to bring to his reading of Plato's texts from the start a logic of Being and Having taken from work on Aristotle.

11   It would be perfectly open to Plato to introduce different linguistic forms for these (thanks to Mahrad Almotahari for remarking this spontaneously). In fact, Plato in the *Timaeus* makes use of the fact that Greek has two different verbs that can function as the copula (*einai*, generally "to be" in English, and *gignesthai*, sometimes rendered "to be" and sometimes "to become"); this move is antic-ipated as early as the famous discussion of the poem of Simonides in the *Protagoras* (Frede 1988; Mann 2000). But, true to his style of minimizing reliance on dedicated and rigidly used technical terms, Plato himself does not consistently follow that regime.

Ten

Forms II

The continuing program

We have seen how the *Parmenides* leads readers into Plato's late dialogues with an exercise that helps us come to understand some of the most crucial matters about Forms. In this (open-ended) chapter, we will see how that approach allows Plato to continue his investigations into Forms with new attention to their complexity. We will also get a glimpse of how Plato often intertwines these investigations in the familiar way with study of other topics for which they are foundational.

We had seen in Chapter Eight that Plato set great store by the contrast between the pure being of Forms and what Socrates in the *Republic* so pungently put as "being tumbled about" between being and not-being (479d4–5, tr. Shorey 1930)—where the latter was associated with sensibles. Yet, as we will see in this chapter, the *Parmenides* and later works draw attention to the fact that Forms themselves mix being and not-being! We will want to ask how this is compatible with their possessing the pure being that is the Forms' *raison d'être*. Another issue of a similar cast: Plato had made it characteristic of Forms to be literally "uniform" (*monoeides*; *Symposium* 211b, e; *Phaedo* 78d). This can seem to suggest that each can have at most one property—yet no such individuals are possible. How can Plato get what he was driving at with this language? How can Forms have properties (like unity, sameness, eternality, purity) that Plato clearly attributed to them all, while there is also a special something in virtue of which each one deserves its own special name and role?

We will start this chapter by considering complexity in the truths concerning each Form's display of features. We will first take up the varied issues involved in understanding their being tumbled about. We will see why it can be perfectly fine that a Form both is and is not F. Many cases actually concern opposites, sometimes represented by writing that the entity in question is "both F and not-F." The work we do with regard to these issues will then make it easy for us to see how Plato was able to accommodate the intuition behind the word *monoeides* without having to deprive Forms problematically of properties they need to have.

Then, in the second half of the chapter, we will turn to another way in which Forms are not utterly simple. We will now have scope to look in some detail at important passages on Plato's method of collection and division. We previewed this method briefly in Chapter Nine in connection with what I there called "tree predication." The scheme seems to us reminiscent of a familiar approach to classification of living things. But of course, it is the other way around. Plato's project—together with its immediate descendant, the version produced by Aristotle—is the ancestor of a way of thinking that is still in use today. We all probably remember that the kingdom, Animalia, has several divisions. Further divisions of these produce such kinds as Vertebrata, Cephalochordata, etc., and Vertebrata itself has Mammalia as a sub-kind. Well below that, we find Leporidae, and so on down to species like the broom hare (*Lepus castroviejoi*) and the mountain hare (*Lepus timidus*). In this chapter, we will have scope to look at a variety of texts in which Plato discusses, demonstrates, and develops the ancestral classificatory procedure of collection and division. We will see both how the idea relates to the program Plato had had from the start, and how it received considerable development from the *Phaedrus* on.

Before we do any of this, we should come to grips with an understandable—but potentially confusing—translational practice. In English translations of texts on Platonic division, we often find the vocabulary of "kinds," "genera," and "species." This can make it look as if Plato has turned from his previous study of Forms to different objects. Yet the story I am offering is that classificatory division, thematized for the first time in our tradition by Plato, is for him a way of mapping relations among Forms. Why then, the English-speaking reader may ask, the change in terminology?

There is no such change. In fact *eidos*, usually translated as "Form" in the middle dialogues, can also be translated as "kind" or as "species"—and in the passages we will be considering, it often is. So there is important continuity of vocabulary with the previous passages on Forms. This at the very least opens up the possibility that Plato thought of these texts as carrying on his continuing study of Forms. On this scenario, we can combine the unproblematic, technical, and sober way of thinking of the kinds of the late dialogues with the motivating excitement of the preceding mentions of Forms.

Of course the appearance of the word *eidos* is not enough to justify this. When we turn to passages directly about the method of collection and division, we will note organic connections the method has to Plato's work from the Socratic dialogues through the *Republic*. We will see in detail that the collection and division project is a natural way of setting about the work Plato had advocated from the very beginning: to find the accounts of natures that specify what each thing is. The vocabulary of "genus-species definition" is often used by scholars of ancient philosophy as a way of getting at the particular program we will be considering in this chapter for mapping how natures are related to other natures. It is important to realize that in this usage, the pair "genus" and "species" (when used together) simply denote that the latter is a sub-kind of the former—no fixed level of the classification tree is picked out automatically.

Tumbling about, contradiction, and impurity

Our first topic is the striking news that Forms actually are "tumbled about." Discussion of this will continue from our work in the two previous chapters. The new point we will now address is that, as many scholars read Plato's works from the *Parmenides* on, these works are committed to results showing that Platonic Forms themselves "both are and are not" F. (Again, the particular cases often concern opposites.) And they can even concern the property that the Form itself is. Thus, in the most extreme kind of case, The F itself can be F and not-F! Are these truly acceptable results?[1]

Some have thought they are not. And this in fact could be for two different reasons. Let's preview them before going on to discuss. The tumbling-about results of some texts can seem to be logically impossible conjuctions (Gill 2012: 50 reporting Ryle on the *Parmenides*) or to involve the attribution of properties that are *incompatible* (the preferred formulation of Gill herself concerning the same dialogue.)[2] But to assess whether the situation is problematic, we have to observe not just the surface grammar of the claims in question, but consider what inferences to and from these formulations Plato accepts. It will turn out that there is no incompatibility or inconsistency in these results about Forms, any more than there is with the parallel results about sensible particulars. In fact, any entity at all will have to show this kind of complexity in its display of features.

But the second worry then arises. It may seem to defeat the whole purpose of having Forms if they are as like sensible particulars as that. After all, if being tumbled about in the case of sensible particulars was why they couldn't be fundamental, how can Forms be subject to it and still do their jobs? In answering this question, it will be important to appreciate how the more developed way of thinking of Forms we have been considering affords Plato a domain of pure being as required for his theory.

Now we are ready to consider in depth the first worry. Let's start by reflecting a bit on our own practice. Consider the famous truth, held to be self-evident, that all men are created equal. Why is someone who remarks "All men are not created equal!" (having in mind differences in strength, or cleverness, or advantages of geographic and social location) not defeating the original claim? Here it is obvious why there is no logical tension between the evident fact that individuals are born unequal with respect to their strength, weight, etc. and the famous claim from the Declaration of Independence. It is jejune to take the Founders to be committed to the claim that all "men" are created equal *in all respects*. Thus, when we want to check whether or not there is contradiction here, we articulate that we can be unequal *with respect to* weight and strength, and still be equal *with respect to* something like human dignity or value or rights. But we don't have to put all that in all the time. In fact Jefferson's ringing formulation is heard constantly and I at least have never come across the fully specified one.

Similarly, consider that it is obvious and logically unproblematic that Stephen Hawking is extremely powerful (mentally) and the very opposite of powerful (physically). Is it appropriate for us to say, "Hawking is and is not powerful"? It *is and it isn't!* It is easy to imagine a context in which the *very contrast* is of interest, so that the streamlined formulation is worth asserting—given, naturally, that the fully specified analogue has shown us that there is no violation of logic. So to sum up: even for us, some but not all contexts invite the streamlined forms.

Plato's practice when discussing sensibles parallels ours. As his argument for the soul's division in the *Republic* shows, he makes the test of the impossibility of streamlined results along the lines of "a is F and a is the opposite of F" depend on the most fully specified descriptions of the states of affairs in question. As I rendered 436b: the same thing cannot do or undergo opposites "in the same respect, in relation to the same thing, simultaneously." (While translations vary, Plato's clear purpose here is to accommodate any relevant qualifications or specifications.)

We are now ready to review some tumbling-about passages from different parts of the Platonic corpus. Consider the beautiful girl of the *Hippias Major*. However lowering it is for her to be both beautiful and ugly (289a8–d2), this is perfectly possible. Plato indicates explicitly the more fully specified formulations that vindicate the claim in question: the *most beautiful girl* (i.e. one who is beautiful compared to all other girls) is ugly *in comparison with gods* (289a8–b7). These fully specified formulations make clear why there is no incompatibility within the tumbling-about claim.

To get to the tumbling-about result here, Plato has assimilated positive and comparative terms. Someone might think this is a mistake: maybe you can be more beautiful than all other girls without being beautiful, or less beautiful than the gods without being ugly. But let me suggest how we can understand what Plato is doing: he is using these comparative claims to draw our attention to the fact that displays of beauty are context-dependent. Thus we could put essentially the same point by saying that a girl who is beautiful when appearing at the Miss Universe pageant would be drab on Mount Olympus. For context-dependency with no suggestion of comparison, consider other examples: a black outfit that is beautiful in the city is ugly out in the fresh air and daylight of the country; sweaters that are beautiful in the country can be ugly in the city.

The *Symposium* ascent passage indicates many types of qualifications that can be relevant (211a). Gregory Vlastos catalogued and discussed them in a way whose clarity and explicitness makes it useful (formulations here put together from material in his gloss, discussion and footnotes in Vlastos 1965: §2). A thing can be:

1   beautiful in one of its features or parts but ugly in another;
2   beautiful at one time but not at another;
3   beautiful by comparison with one thing but ugly by comparison with another; and
4   beautiful in one location/observed from one position but ugly in/from another (where this is not limited to visual perspective).

Since the original passage is clearly meant to be as comprehensive as possible and Vlastos' precision in formulation may leave out some cases Plato's original text admits of, I supply two additions (using asterisked numerals to indicate cases supported by the underlying Greek that Vlastos' clauses derive from):

1*   beautiful in one way but ugly in another; and
3*   beautiful by one standard but ugly by another.[3]

Vlastos shows that (3) does not involve a logical contradiction, and the same clearly goes for (1), (2), and (4), and for (1*) and (3*) as well. He also agrees that cases along the lines of his (1), (2), and (4) justify Plato's streamlined assessment, which Vlastos represents schematically by writing that such a subject is "F and not-F."

Yet he says that for cases of his type (3) "it should be evident ... that Plato suffers from ... confusion" (Vlastos 1965: 13). The *Hippias Major* case falls under this head. Working off of *Phaedo* 102, Vlastos writes:

> Anyone who knew that Simmias was 6 feet 5 inches, but still declared that he was short, and then explained, when challenged, that he only meant that Simmias was short by

comparison with Phaedo, would be thought a liar, unless he
could be let off as a practical joker.

(Vlastos 1965: 14)

Is this really so? Only consider the case of the NBA star Steve Nash
who in high school was scorned by coaches as a "short, white,
Canadian." He was over six feet tall.

Obviously in some context other than basketball—say a class
photo—it would equally have been correct to assert that Nash *was*
tall: surely he would have been placed in the back row of such a
grouping.[4] Yet far from someone's being (then or now) thought a
liar or practical joker for saying that Steve Nash is short, the phrase
"short, white, Canadian" is in widespread use.[5] It would be bizarrely
pedantic to insist that everyone has to say that Nash is *shorter than the
average professional basketball player* (or perhaps *shorter than typical players at his
position*). Plato's policy—to use some such specification (and correspondingly perhaps that Nash was tall for an American high school
student) when checking that there is nothing impossible in the situation and, given that, to allow that it is appropriate in many normal
situations to make the streamlined assertions—seems reasonable.

In the *Phaedo* as in the *Hippias Major*, we see Plato going back and
forth between positive and comparative forms. And here again, it
need not be a mistake. Consider that Plato might cash out being
large as a capacity to exceed (Sedley 2007: 70–71; 1998: 127–8).
Or perhaps, to adapt this a bit, Plato might have thought that being
large is exceeding salient competitors in magnitude; English tallness
then could amount to exceeding salient competitors in height. With
this kind of approach, being large/tall already builds in a contextual
component: it is the context that lets us know which competitors
are salient. On this way of looking at it, the explicitly comparative
"larger than" simply allows us to specify the particular comparison
that is relevant in a given case.[6]

In fact, I think Vlastos makes his anathematized type (3) seem a
more isolated kind of case than it is. Nash's being shorter than
typical NBA players (type (3)) can surely also be expressed by
saying that he is short by NBA standards (type (3*)). This in turn
makes clear how closely linked the case is to his being short *as an
NBA player* (1*). Again, this connects directly with Nash's being short

on the floor of a play-off game (type (4)). Indeed this case makes natural and unproblematic the mention in the *Symposium* of "in some people's eyes" (211a, tr. Griffith 1986) since being short on the floor of a play-off game goes with being short in the eyes of fans.[7] So one can make a case that category (3) should not be set apart from the others. They are actually intertwined, and all perfectly plausible. Steve Nash is short. Only in some contexts, of course, but after all everything about sensibles is in some context. Again, there is no logical problem here.

What about the sticks of the *Phaedo*? The description of them as appearing equal "to one" and unequal "to another" (74b) is rather schematic, and so has led to the spilling of a lot of interpretative ink. Scholars discuss whether we are supposed to take this as a matter of a pair of sticks' being equal in someone's view but unequal in someone else's, or in some respect or dimension but not in another, or rather as a matter of each individual stick's having some object it is equal to and some other object to which it is unequal, and so on. Or, if we adopt the alternative manuscript reading, the contrast could be between one time and another. But for present purposes these are all alike, for the key thing is built into even the schematic language of the original text. That contains a placeholder for further specification that the different commentators are precisifying: the sticks appear/are equal to *one*, and unequal to *another*. Obviously, this is no more impossible than it is to be helpful to friends and hostile to enemies, or younger than your parents and older than your children.

We saw in Chapter Eight how such claims fit the schema of the imaginary discussion with the lover of sights and sounds concerning the status of sensibles as things that are between being and not-being (*Republic* 478d ff). Certainly Plato both in the *Republic* and in all the other works that draw attention to this phenomenon for sensibles connected it with their not being fundamental either metaphysically or epistemically. But I'd like to emphasize that the results themselves must be correct to establish that—and they could hardly be correct if they were logically contradictory. In that case, Plato (or the characters in the dialogues) would have made a mistake in characterizing sensibles, not shown them to fall short.

So our question now becomes: are the members of the family of results for Forms we are considering (that a Form both is and is not F; in many cases, that a Form is both F and the opposite of F) as logically acceptable as these familiar assertions? Absolutely. Consider the second section of arguments within the second part of the *Parmenides*, which explores ordinary predications concerning our subject (142b–155e). We learn that the One is one because it is one whole, or a single Form. It is also many in several different ways, resulting from its possession of features and of participants. All the results of this section, thirteen Stephanus pages in length, are in tumbling-about pairs! Such results are no more impossible than it is for a girl in the sort of example we discussed to be beautiful and ugly. In some passages, Plato actually puts in explicitly phrases along the very sort of lines we have been considering (as at *Parmenides* 154c3–6 and 155b4–c4).[8]

If these tumbling-about results for Forms aren't internally incompatible, they may still seem to be incompatible with Platonism, which claims centrally that Forms are very different from sensible particulars. The way Forms are contrasted with sensibles in the very passages I have been relying on can seem to rule out any tumbling about for Forms. After all, what disqualifies sensible particulars from being metaphysically and epistemically fundamental is the fact that their displays of features are qualified, confused, or impure. The point of demonstrating that sensibles mix being and not-being is to show that it's no good looking to them if one wants to answer the "What is it?" question, i.e. to say of Justice, Beauty (or whatever one hopes to understand) what it is. To have knowledge concerning any such matter, one has to grasp pure being. That is the domain of Forms.

But here is a more nuanced way of describing the situation: the confused and impure displays of sensible particulars disqualify them from being fundamental *because displaying is all they can do*. Problematic versions of the theory of Forms result if we assimilate Forms to them, and assume that their repertoire is likewise limited to displaying—then we have to suppose that for some mystical reason they are able to do it much better. This picture has well-known difficulties. As we saw in Chapter Nine, some Forms (for example: Bravery, Fire, and Animality) cannot be instances of themselves. And we can now see why some should have the eponymous display but in a manner just as confused as that of a sensible: surely Sameness itself should be different (from everything else) as well as the same (as itself). How then can Forms possibly do their job and provide the pure being we needed them for in the first place?

In Chapter Nine we saw that developing an understanding of the key innovation introduced in the *Parmenides* and used in the *Sophist* involves coming to see that what is fundamental about a Form is not a matter of its making a mystically pure display, but is rather articulated in the "tree truths" about it. Here's why we can regard what these map as pure being. We can readily see that, given any two natures, the first is either involved in the other as a part or the whole of it, or it is not. We won't get a tree conjunction that the Rabbit is and is not a lagomorph. And since Plato's picture is that each genuine nature has a unique position on its single correct tree, we will certainly not find any such conjunction of tree truths as that The Rabbit is both animate and inanimate!

Once this domain of pure being is secured, it is perfectly all right to embrace some mixture by Forms of being and not-being. There is no threat in accepting that this tumbling-about conjunction of *ordinary* predications holds:

Sameness is the same and different.

Also we can see now that two types of "mixed" results hold. We already noted that some Forms are not instances of themselves. Like Man and Hedgehog (our previous examples), Rabbithood doesn't instantiate itself. But if we turn from these matters of display and instantiation to consider the nature by itself, it is absolutely true that being a rabbit is involved in being a rabbit. The mixed, superficially paradoxical conjunction below registers that the Form in question does its job without instantiating itself:

The Rabbit is a rabbit and not a rabbit.

For this mixed conjunction is true when we take the positive assertion as a tree truth and the negated one to be concerning a display.

Forms also can *have* properties that are no part of what their natures *are*. For example, the Rabbit (like every other entity) displays

Sameness. Yet the nature Same is not part of the nature Rabbit. Thus the mixed conjunction:

The Rabbit is the same and not the same

holds where the positive assertion is the ordinary predication and the negated one the tree truth. This true mixed conjunction is the other way around from the previous one.

All the sorts of tumbling about for Forms we've just been considering (the type with both conjuncts ordinary assertions and the two mixed types) are fine to accept now, since we have a principled way of marking off the pure being that Forms enjoy, and which it is necessary to grasp to have knowledge. The class of fundamental truths isn't marked off only by being about a special population (Forms); it's a special kind of truths about them (cf. M. Frede 1967: B.III.5). The realm of tree truths is free from any tumbling about between being and not-being and is in Plato's sense fundamentally real: it constitutes the most basic structure of reality, and is most explanatory. Once we have this pure domain, once we see that the unqualified nature of the accounts that articulate relations between natures is unaffected by whatever pattern of displaying the Forms may exhibit, we are free to accept—in the case of any given Form— all (and only) the displays that are in fact desirable to acknowledge. Thus Plato seems actually to revel in tumbling about of a perfectly acceptable and indeed welcome sort when he generates the superficially paradoxical results of the second part of the *Parmenides* and of *Sophist* 254b–259d.

We can also use this basic approach for an even more extreme issue of a related type. On the conception both the word *monoeides* (literally "uniform"; *Symposium* 211b, e; *Phaedo* 78d) and the repeated claim that each Form is one suggests to some readers, a Form shouldn't instantiate any properties at all besides itself. Additional properties would be impurities, and cause forbidden complexity. Notice that the very claim that any Form other than the One itself is one becomes inexplicable if we press this line of thought. For to be one, each Form must have the property, Unity. So if having any property besides itself is intolerably pluralizing for any Form, then the very possession of the property, Unity, contributes intolerably to pluralize all Forms (other than Unity) by this criterion! We have also seen that Plato stressed as key for the roles Forms play that each be eternal, and unchanging as well—two more properties to pluralize them.

Of course, I don't accept that Plato ever wanted to commit himself to the claim that each Form does its job by possessing the very property that it is—let alone to the exclusion of all other properties. But the language that suggested this to some was getting at something—which we are now in a position to spell out unproblematically. Each Form is indeed associated with a single nature. But on the way of thinking now under consideration, we can see that the uniqueness of the property it is is not at all compromised by a Form's *having* multiple properties. We have a clear and principled way of marking off the special articulation of what the nature *is* from facts about the Form's displays. Coming to recognize that allows us generally to attribute to each Form whatever pattern of displaying is appropriate to it.

"Collection and division" and Forms

We have been seeing how the picture we are exploring can accept complexity in the facts associated with each Form's display of features because it is able to mark those off from truths expressing the Form's pure being. We now turn to look in greater detail at the developing program for fundamental exploration of that privileged domain, a program often referred to as Platonic "collection and division." This is described with different details and different emphasis in different works—and Plato experiments with different ways of carrying out the divisions. To start with what we need in order to justify giving this procedure the role I indicated in Plato's ongoing investigations, let us first trace the organic connections these texts have with Plato's works from the Socratic dialogues through the *Republic*. In order to do this, we will need to have in hand an initial sense of the procedure; let's start from what may well be the first official description of collection and division, in the *Phaedrus*.

Earlier in the dialogue, Socrates had made a speech on the same counter-intuitive theme as one of Lysias, admired by his younger friend (who here as in the *Symposium* shows a characteristic interest in speeches and in *erōs*). The discussion on method is prompted by Socrates' wish to recant his own earlier speech. He explains to Phaedrus that the key mistake was a one-sided understanding of the nature of Madness. Socrates had attributed drawbacks of some kinds of Madness to all (244a).

The general method that Socrates recommends heads off this mistake by requiring a comprehensive view of one's subject in all its variety. Within the *Phaedrus*, two applications of the method are relevant, since both knowing the underlying subject matter of a speech and knowing about the kinds of souls of potential listeners turn out to be required if one is to be able to pitch a speech to its audience in accordance with art. But the method's description as well as its naming as "dialectic" hint that its use is even wider than that. Socrates advocates in connection with understanding any subject not only:

> seeing together things that are scattered about everywhere and collecting them into one kind, so that by defining each thing we can make clear the subject of any instruction we wish to give.
>
> (265d)

In addition, he articulates a further requirement:

> to be able to cut up each kind according to its species along its natural joints, and to try not to splinter any part, as a bad butcher might do ... I am myself a lover of these divisions and collections ... and if I believe that someone else is capable of discerning a single thing that is also by nature capable of encompassing many, I follow "straight behind, in his tracks, as if he were a god." God knows whether this is the right name for those who can do this correctly or not, but so far I have always called them "dialecticians."
>
> (265e–266c)

This passage connects the newly *described* method with other work of Plato's, both by the claim that Socrates is a lover of collections and divisions and by naming the method "dialectic." Let's consider how the method as described can support these claims.

How can we understand Socrates' claim in the *Phaedrus* about himself as a lover of collections and divisions? The character Socrates in previous works never laid things out like this exactly, but if we look back at them from the point of view of this passage we can indeed see what was going on there in these terms. From the start, the Socratic dialogues frequently and characteristically made the demand that someone with knowledge of a subject ought to comprehend its full variety in his account of it. For example, as we saw, in the *Laches* any approach to bravery that applied only to hoplites or indeed took in only military bravery was rejected: Socrates pointed out (191d–e) that people can show bravery at sea, in illness, in poverty, and so on.

So Plato's works from the start featured a preliminary version of the interest that in the *Phaedrus* will be put in terms of collection. In the earliest dialogues, interlocutors (who were being tested on their understanding of F-ness) needed to be taught to isolate, when giving their candidate accounts, the one thing common to *all* cases that are F. For this purpose, we need to include all the variety of F things to ensure that our candidate for the F itself explains them all. But we don't need to decide whether the additional features in terms of which we conceive the variety (e.g. bravery in sickness and in poverty) are parts of the natures of scientifically significant kinds of F, or merely coextensive with such sub-kinds, or perhaps cut across sub-kinds—or even whether genuine sub-kinds exist.

Plato in the later works will draw explicit attention to cases in which some Form truly does have genuine sub-kinds. Indeed, the early *Euthyphro* had already contained an anticipation of this scheme, and showed how it is relevant to giving accounts. After repeated failures on the part of the interlocutor to give an account of piety, Socrates offered some help. Pointing out that one can specify the even as that part of number which is divisible into two equal parts, he suggested that Euthyphro try to specify piety by saying what part of justice it is (11e–12e). While Socrates did not tag the elements in this type of account, we can say that in his paradigm, he is giving the basic roles of genus, differentia, and species respectively to number, divisible into two equal parts, and even. For number is a kind and he proposes to treat even as its sub-kind. What he adds to the genus to get the account of the species is what serves as the differentia: divisible into two equal parts.[9]

Euthyphro tried to follow the pattern in giving the answer that the pious is the part of the just that is concerned with service/assistance (*therapeia*) to the gods, while that concerned with service/assistance to men is the other part (12e). Quite possibly his idea was that justice as a whole is something like rendering due service/assistance. Then we could specify the differentiae of the sub-kinds using the phrases "to gods" and "to men." Euthyphro failed to maintain this proposal as a result of his inability to uphold any viable interpretation of the service/assistance we render to the gods. But scholars have thought that the introduction by Socrates of this schema for an answer, especially given its final position in the dialogue, suggests Plato means to offer this model for giving accounts as promising. While we then lose sight of this pattern for a time, from the point of view of the *Phaedrus*, the *Euthyphro* passage can be recognized as the tip of the iceberg of a way of giving accounts that the method of division develops explicitly.

Before we go on, let's appreciate the significance of Plato's giving the name "dialectic" to collection and division in the *Phaedrus* quote. It is important not to think of this as the proper name of a single and wholly negative practice—elenctic dialectic. Plato can use *dialektikē* and *dialegesthai* for whatever method of philosophical interchange he at the time of writing regards as promising. Socratic *elenchos* naturally deserved the name, since *dialegesthai* can just mean "to converse" and correspondingly *dialektikē* has by word formation the broad and somewhat indefinite sense "conversational [method]." Remember also that, even if the victims of Socratic *elenchos* kept failing, the conversation as we saw in Chapter Three was designed as a search for accounts.

In the *Republic*, the character Socrates gave what he there called "dialectic" a very lofty brief in his presentation of the upper, intelligible, segments of the Divided Line. We saw before that the lesser manner (*dianoia*) of proceeding in the intelligible realm had been characterized as that in which the soul (using sensible images i.e. diagrams, but only as a heuristic device) *investigates from hypotheses*, "proceeding not to a first principle but to a conclusion." Socrates helped Glaucon catch on by pointing out that this is familiar to us as the usual procedure of mathematicians (510b–e). The *Republic* assigned to dialectic the super-honorific task of helping us to do even better than that. The highest subsection (representing *noēsis*) of the Divided Line had initially been described as that in which the soul "makes its way to a first principle that is not a hypothesis, proceeding from a hypothesis but without the images used in the previous subsection, using forms themselves and making its investigation through them" (510b). A bit later in the passage we read of this:

> Then also understand that, by the other subsection of the intelligible [i.e. the higher section, *noēsis*], I mean that which reason itself grasps by the power of dialectic. It does not consider these hypotheses as first principles but truly as hypotheses ... enabling it to reach the unhypothetical first principle of everything. Having grasped this principle, it reverses itself and, keeping hold of what follows from it, comes down to a conclusion without making use of anything visible at all, but only of forms themselves ...
>
> (511b–c; emphasis added)

Exactly how dialectic achieves all this was not transparent in these texts.

In the secondary education projected for developing guardians (in *Republic* Book 7), mathematics bulked very large and again had a penultimate position. Socrates laid out (522b–531d) an elaborate sequence of advanced mathematical studies culminating in mathematical harmonics. This is the study of ratios, said in our text to include study of the question which numbers are concordant with each other and why (531c). Socrates justified this difficult study by saying that it is useful for coming to understand the Beautiful (*kalon*) and the Good, but useless otherwise (531c). He then said that dialectic will ultimately give accounts of the *ousia* (being/reality/nature) of each thing, that is, say of each thing what it is (532a6–7, 533b1–3, 534b3–4).

In the late period, dialectic is explicitly associated with giving accounts through the method of collection and division. The method is used pervasively in the *Sophist* and *Statesman*, and discussed directly in important passages in the *Sophist* and *Philebus* (a late return to examination of the roles of pleasure and a cluster containing intelligence, wisdom, and right opinion in connection with the good human life). The Eleatic Visitor in the *Sophist* indicates how he suggests coming to an understanding of the titular subject through a paradigm: he shows how one can provide an account of the Angler through a series of divisions. At each stage a kind is divided in two, starting with a division of Expertise into Productive and Acquisitive sub-kinds, and continuing until we get the sub-kind that is Angling. He sums up as follows (and as always, one has to put up with varying practices concerning capitalization):

> So now we're in agreement about the angler's expertise ... Within expertise as a whole one half was acquisitive; half of the acquisitive was taking possession; half of possession-taking was hunting; half of hunting was animal-hunting; half of animal-hunting was aquatic hunting; all of the lower portion of aquatic hunting was fishing; half of fishing was hunting by striking; and half of striking was hooking. And the part of hooking that involves a blow drawing a thing upward from underneath is called ... angling—which is what we've been searching for.
>
> (221a-c)

The dialogue offers a series of attempts at following this model for the project of finding the account of the Sophist. The account of the Angler (who has an Acquisitive Expertise that ... goes to water ... and hooks fish from below) is a set-up for an early suggestion that the Sophist is a hunter on land of rich young men! The way this works as a joke may encourage the idea that of all these attempts, at most one can actually be correct. The last word of the dialogue is Theaetetus' agreement to the Eleatic Visitor's having summarized their final account as follows:

> Imitation of the contrary-speech-producing, insincere and unknowing sort, of the appearance-making kind of copy-making, the word-juggling part of production that's marked off as human and not divine. Anyone who says the sophist is of this "blood and family" will be saying, it seems, the complete truth.
>
> (268c-d)

We may note now (though it goes beyond the present point of illustrating division) that the discussion in the *Sophist* of there being false speech and misleading appearances, both cases in Greek idiom of "what is not," leads to treatment of Not-Being as well as Being. Not-Being is now explicated as unproblematic, at least in many important kinds of case, for the first time since Parmenides of Elea problematized it! The discussion leads to treatment of the association of kinds, where two kinds are counted as associating—and a huge variety of vocabulary is used for this—if one is predicated correctly of the other. In this dialogue, Plato offers a ground-breaking study of the nature of statement; the dialogue's examinations of many of the points we considered in Chapter Nine come in here.

We can't go into all this now, but for our present theme we should note that the Eleatic Visitor explicitly suggests (and Theaetetus endorses the suggestion) that it is expertise in dialectic that allows us "to divide things by kinds" (253d). This is the characteristic Knowledge of the Philosopher (253b–c). It enables us "not to think that the same form is a different one or that a different form is the same" (253d), and is necessary if one is going to show "correctly which kinds harmonize with which and which kinds exclude each other" (253b–c). So here classificatory knowledge is identified with dialectic, and explicitly said to go with an ability to identify (and not mistake) the thing in question, as well as with a grasp on the possibilities for combination and separation. Forms are said to be like letters, where some combinations are viable and others are not, and where it belongs to an expertise to know which sort are able to associate with which (252e–253a).

In the *Philebus* too letters are prominent, but not as a simile. Rather, kinds of Letter/Phoneme are the star *examples* illustrating the use of the method. In this dialogue too, as we will see, combination is mentioned (though the combination in question ends up being of a slightly different sort). First let's start with the abstract description of what Socrates this time introduces by saying "there is not, nor could there be, any way that is finer than the one I have always admired, although it has often escaped me and left me behind, alone and helpless" (16b). Note, as in the *Phaedrus*, the claim on the part of the character Socrates that he has had long engagement with the method he is advocating (he also at 17a associates it with proceeding dialectically). His description starts:

> we have to assume that there is in each case [of something said to be] always one form [*idea*] for every one of them, and we must search for it, as we will indeed find it there. And once we have grasped it, we must look for two, as the case would have it, or if not, for three or some other number. And we must treat every one of those further unities in the same way, until it is not only established of the original unit that it is one, many, and unlimited, but also how many kinds it is.
>
> (16c–d)

Protarchus' need for further clarification leads Socrates to give the example of Letters (or Phonemes):

> The sound that comes out of the mouth is one for each and every one of us, but then it is also unlimited in number ... Neither of these two facts alone yet makes us knowledgeable ... But if we know how many kinds of vocal sounds there are and what their nature is, that makes every one of us literate.
>
> (17b)

Socrates explicitly discusses proceeding in both directions:

> Just as someone who has got hold of some unity or other should not, as we were saying, immediately look for the unlimited kind but first look for some number, so the same holds for the reverse case. For if he is forced to start out with the unlimited, then he should not head straight for the one, but should in each case grasp some number that determines every plurality whatever, and from all of those finally reach the one.
>
> (18a–b)

The example of Letters makes apposite the legendary achievement of our old friend, the Egyptian god Theuth:

> He was the first to discover that the vowels in that unlimited variety are not one but several, and again that there are others

that are not voiced, but make some kind of noise, and that they, too, have a number. As a third kind of letters he established the ones we now call mute. After this he further subdivided the ones without sound or mutes down to every single unit. In the same fashion he also dealt with the vowels and the intermediates, until he had found out the number for each one of them, and then he gave all of them together the name "letter." And as he realized that none of us could gain any knowledge of a single one of them, taken by itself without understanding them all, he considered that the one link that somehow unifies them all and called it the art of literacy.

(18b–e)

So when it comes to its description of the method, the *Philebus* seems broadly consistent with the *Phaedrus* and *Sophist*. In whatever exact way we allocate different portions of text to division as opposed to collection, the basic idea is clearly that once all this is finished we should have a classification tree mapping genus-species relationships among the kinds in question. Thus Letter or Phoneme will be divided into Vowel, Mute, and a third kind; and these will be further divided into individual Letters such as (the universal) "A." This text says directly that we can't know a single Letter on its own—one has to have expert understanding of the entire field.

The *Philebus* does not explicitly make the claim we saw in the *Sophist* that being literate involves knowing which combinations of letters are and are not viable. It does however make a parallel point with its example of music, which comes in between the last two passages quoted. The opening bit is controversial but we may omit it for now, skipping to what we are concerned with:

you will be competent, my friend, once you have learned how many intervals there are related to high and low pitch of sound, what character they have, by what the intervals are defined, and *the kinds of combinations* [or systems: *sustēmata*] they form—all of which our forebears have discovered and left to us, their successors, together with the names of these modes of harmony.

(17c–d, my translation, based on D. Frede in Cooper, ed., 1997; emphasis added)

This goes beyond specifying the classification of elements (intervals, I believe, but some think notes). It tells us that someone with the art in question knows how the elements can and cannot combine to make up modes. As is widely noted, this seems a little different from the combinations in view in the *Sophist*, where Plato's point concerned one Form's being (truly) predicated of another as the relevant analogue of the letters "B" and "A" being capable of combination. We can regard each text as bringing out an interesting kind of combination of Forms—or perhaps there is some way to subsume all this into one! At any rate, the suggestion the *Philebus* is making here is plausible: that a grasp of each element's possible and impossible combinations with other elements to form the complexes the art is concerned with is part and parcel of the understanding of the individual elements itself. And all of this indeed contributes to the explanatory power and usefulness of the *technē*.

The *Philebus* also experiments with a particular and highly technical way of carrying out the division program. This emerges from the way the program's initial description works together with a foundational passage at 23b ff (Meinwald 1998, 2002). The *Philebus* is proposing to mathematize genus-species trees in a veritable masterstroke of hedgehoggery. While the *Republic* had called for a tremendous amount of study of mathematics, and for the study of Forms (and for accounts saying of each thing what it is), the *Philebus* makes evident how all these fit together: it offers a way to understand Forms by giving accounts of their natures that are mathematized. While this would have been familiar to everyone for Plato's example of musical intervals, he here proposes parallel treatment in all other domains. And indeed, the *Philebus*' use of a mathematical approach to distinguishing kinds has had a significant legacy in the history of biology from antiquity through at least the twentieth century.[10]

Even more particularly, the *Philebus* is proposing that the accounts marking off sub-kinds at each level of a tree be given by specifying certain desirable ratios governing an underlying indefinite dyad (Meinwald 1998). Below the lowest scientifically distinguishable sub-kinds on a given genus-species tree is a blurred continuum of types representing other combinations of the elements in the dyad.

This relies on the work of Greek mathematicians who had a

criterion from within mathematics for identifying some ratios as better than others. In this value-laden mathematical harmonics, the better ratios were responsible for and explanatory of the finer (i.e. concordant) musical intervals (Barker 1994). In Plato we find "systematic exploitation of the fact that Greek value-concepts like concord, proportion, and order are also central to contemporary mathematics ... so that to study mathematics is simultaneously to study, at a very abstract level, the principles of value" (Burnyeat 2000: 76). We can also bring in the fact that concord was thought of by the Greeks as a matter of unification: the notes in a concord form a unity in a way that discordant ones do not (Barker 1994). Here it is relevant that there is independent evidence that the One is for Plato the technical version of the Good, and that the *Republic* pervasively drew attention to the importance of unification in its treatments of psychology, ethics, and politics (Burnyeat 2000). This complex of ideas fits well with the cryptic claim we noted before in the dialogue that the study of mathematical harmonics is useful for inquiry into the Beautiful and the Good, but useless if pursued in any other way.

The *Philebus* scheme understood as I have indicated shows immediately why mathematical harmonics—if only it would ask which numbers are concordant with each other and why—is the final prerequisite for dialectic (as the *Republic* had made it). For the *Philebus* actually builds the ratios identified as better by mathematical harmonics into its program for giving the accounts dialectic seeks. Thus the scheme expresses within Platonism the perennially attractive view that serious understanding is fundamentally mathematical.[11]

Bracketing for now the specific possibility of mathematizing the trees, what would we have if we succeeded in carrying out Plato's program of collection and division? To show the Virtues, we'd have to know whether or not Piety is part of Justice, and whether Wisdom is coordinate with the others, or is rather the genus to which they belong. Trees would go down to lowest kinds. Each real thing has a correct place on exactly one tree. However, when it comes to instantiating the universals so articulated, individuals participate in a large and sometimes shifting array from an assortment of trees. A strong relation (involved in what I've called "tree predication") holds between items on the trees and items above them on their branch; a weak relation (involved in what I've called "ordinary predication") holds between any individual at all (whether or not it is one of Plato's "real things" on the trees) and the realities whose natures are explanatory of the individual's displays.[12] The trees, in showing the articulations of the fundamental natures, show the content of what we might call pure knowledge. And since the accounts we can read off from them are what individuals are conforming to or satisfying in their displays of features, there will be a variety of applications of this knowledge to the domain of sensible particulars as well.

Is this overall way of thinking confined to dogmatic Platonists? The utility of the kind of understanding Plato is advocating here is by now recognized well beyond any such circle. For example, cooks have been realizing recently that understanding how vegetables are and are not related to each other in the botanical classification scheme pays off in actual, physical gardening and in cookery. It helps in producing delicious food![13]

Throughout this book, we have seen elements from Plato's thought that have proved seminal from antiquity to the present. Some later thinkers have adopted and developed suggestions from the dialogues; some have addressed problems posed there; some have been moved to argue against what they have found in Plato's text. I have suggested that the purpose of these works was largely to prompt philosophical activity in us—I hope readers will continue thinking with Plato in future.

Further reading

See Bibliography for full details of the works listed below.

A. Barker (1994) "Ptolemy's Pythagoreans, Archytas, and Plato's Conception of Mathematics."

A. Barker (1996) "Plato's Philebus: The Numbering of a Unity."

M. Burnyeat (2000) "Plato on Why Mathematics is Good for the Soul."

M. Gill (2012) Philosophos: Plato's Missing Dialogue.

M. McCabe (1994) Plato's Individuals.

W. Mann (2000) The Discovery of Things. How Plato's work leads into Aristotle's Categories.

Notes

1   A few formulations in this section are taken from Meinwald (2014: 485–8).

2   Gill (1996: 72, 79; 2012: 50, 54, 62–3). In her view Plato wants us to see that these consequences are unacceptable. One woman's *modus ponens* is another's *modus tollens*.

3   (1*) is to make sure we take into account the circumstance that the Greek—on Vlastos' own translation (first list, Vlastos 1965: 9) "in one respect … in another" and his explication (Vlastos 1965: fn 37)—may not be wholly captured on a narrow reading of his gloss (second list, Vlastos 1965: 9 and fn 38); (3*) is the understanding conveyed by Dover's gloss of this bit of Greek (1980: 157).

4   A difficulty with my example that I encountered when giving a talk at the University of Utrecht actually helps make my larger point: a schoolboy who is 6 foot 1 is tall in the US, but certainly not tall in the Netherlands!

5   See for example www.success.com/articles/1384-3-things-you-don-t-know-about-steve-nash and http://deadspin.com/169805/this-guy-is-your-two+time-mvp (both accessed July 13, 2013).

6   Plato more generally treats together what some recently have distinguished as attributives and relational terms—because of which Plato scholars have developed the term of art "incomplete predicates" to cover both. To complement the case of being tall, consider the following. Being a mother is relational in the sense that every instance of it is the mother of someone. Let's say what it is to be a mother is to be someone's female parent. Plato's view would be that all mothers (Bambi's mother, Whistler's mother, James James Morrison's mother) have this in common. It seems to me correct to say that in virtue of having a child, a woman becomes a mother—not just e.g. the-mother-of-James-James-Morrison-Morrison-Weatherby-George-Dupree. For analogous reasons, Plato would think that something very important is obscured when we represent the case of Nash being tall (for an American schoolboy) and not tall (for a basketball player) as "Nash is F and not G."

7   Without any problematic kind of subjectivity or relativism.

8   Featured in Meinwald (1991: ch. 5), where I develop an approach that I believe works for the section as a whole.

9   Aristotle's scientific work in biology and other, later work led to further constraints on the scheme, which color the relevant vocabulary for some today. While it is interesting to appreciate that Plato's program eventually led to this other work, it is also crucial to avoid the confusion that can come by failing to understand how the original program and its attendant vocabulary did not include all the developments due to later thinkers.

10   Lennox (1987) gives a fascinating account of how the *Philebus* is the ancestor of a procedure illustrated by a varied group from antiquity through the twentieth century. He quotes D'Arcy Thompson *On Growth and Form*: "Our inquiry lies, in short, just within the limits which Aristotle laid down when, in defining a genus, he showed that (apart from those superficial characters, such

as color, which he called 'accidents') the essential differences between one 'species' and another are merely differences of proportion, or relative magnitude, or as he phrased it, of 'excess and defect'."

11　The *Timaeus*, which has historically been of special interest for some readers because its "likely story" tells of how a divine craftsman created the world, applies this same type of mathematical treatment to cosmology (Burnyeat 2000).

12　We can see Aristotle's procedure in the *Categories* as (in part) derived from this. He too has a strong and a weak relation, and he too maps out trees showing which items stand to which in the strong relation. But he makes crucial innovations whereby he arrives at the view for which he is most famous. Aristotle puts e.g. Socrates in the strong relation to Man and the weak one to White. That is, he claims that Man (but not White) is part of what it is to be for Socrates. Without supplying Plato's program as relevant context, it is it is hard to see why Aristotle proceeds as he does—he plunges in to all this without any motivating discussion. (Mann 2000 provides useful exposition of a picture ultimately deriving from Michael Frede).

13　This is the point of Madison (2013). For reactions, see http://deborah-madison.com/vegetable-literacy, www.thekitchn.com/vegetable-literacy-by-deborah-madison-new-cookbook-191358, and http://dinersjournal. blogs.nytimes.com/2013/04/04/cooking-asparagus-and-onions-with-deborah-madison/?_r=0 (all accessed July 18, 2015).

Appendix
The "transcendence" and "separation" of Forms

English-speakers often use two key terms to describe Platonic Forms: "separation" and "transcendence." Yet each of these terms can be used in a significant variety of ways, leading to a very problematic lack of clarity in discussion. It will be useful to spell out explicitly the associations each of these terms can have, before deciding how they apply to our texts.

The word "transcendence" diffuses, as Plato's vocabulary also can, suggestions of the mystical and sublime. Yet it can lead to great confusion. Going by the *New Shorter Oxford English Dictionary* (1993), "transcend" can mean "go beyond or exceed the limits of ... esp. be beyond the range or grasp of (human experience, reason, belief, etc.)" or "surpass, excel, or exceed, esp. in a specified quality or attribute" or the rather different "be above and independent of." In turn, "transcendental" includes among its meanings "of, pertaining to, or belonging to the divine as opp. to the natural ... world" and the Kantian usage, "presupposed in and necessary to experience." More recently it may well also have a subliminal association with transcendental meditation and Eastern mysticism.

If we think of these different glosses individually, several are clearly in order and, even if "transcendent" does not correspond to any one word in Plato's Greek, we can see how it or its relatives may reasonably be used to sum up the sense of certain passages. The culmination of the *Symposium* ascent makes it clear that Plato gives the Form of Beauty divine status, and asserts that it is not identical with or understandable by reference to everyday sensibles; the

Phaedo's affinity argument makes the corresponding claims for the general case of Forms. So they clearly qualify as transcendent under the definition "pertaining to the divine ... as opp. to the natural ... world." In addition, the recollection argument is often thought to be transcendental in the Kantian sense: turning on Forms' being presupposed in and necessary to experience. The distinct gloss of "surpass, excel, or exceed" could be in order whenever one has in mind the pure being of Forms. But notice that a certain reading of the addition "esp. in a specified quality or attribute" could take us to a more determinate assumption concerning how Forms do their jobs (by perfect instantiation) than we have found justified. Several of the other meanings are also problematic.

"Transcendent" can mean "beyond the range or grasp of human reason," and this is so far from being the message of Plato's treatment of Forms that it is actually incompatible with it. Far from being beyond our reason, Forms are what it should properly be focused on; indeed they are its true objects and the objects of its erotic longing. Reason's natural orientation to Forms was clear in both the *Phaedo* and the *Republic*. However much Plato likes to go in for the language of divinity and mystery, we cannot let our appreciation of those passages override the plain sense of the numerous texts that maintain that the best activity in life is for our reason to engage with Forms and to come to know the accounts that say of each thing what it is. Thus if "beyond the grasp of human reason" is the preferred sense of transcendence, we must reject any suggestion that Plato's Forms are transcendent. The language of divinity and mystery should be taken seriously as indicating the awesome combination of overwhelming value, fundamental character, and radical otherness from the everyday that Forms possess; none of this requires us to attribute anything like the ineffability this last sense of "transcendence" imports.

The other potentially problematic usage is "above and independent of." That the Forms are transcendent in this sense is neither clearly right nor clearly wrong, but is controversial. Of course "above" by itself is all right, assuming that it cannot be meant spatially. As a warning against taking the idea of "higher things" literally we have the charming rebuke of Socrates at *Republic* 529a–b to Glaucon, who has supposed that astronomy must obviously lead the mind "upward" (as disciplines Socrates is looking for are supposed to do). Socrates teases Plato's brother, pointing out that one may as well suppose that someone lying on his back looking at decorations on a ceiling is regarding higher things! The remaining and vexed issue is the application to Forms of "transcendent" in the sense "independent of." This is also one of the possible senses of the separation of Forms, and in fact the one that has been thematized in much discussion.

So we can now switch over to considering separation; let us start with a survey of the range of separation's senses. To say that Forms are separate can be meant in a variety of ways. Among rather ordinary meanings are merely that they are different from sensibles, or that they do not occupy the same space. There are also some rather technical senses the term can have, most notably a particular precisification of the one already mentioned: this technical sense has the force that Forms can exist independently of all sensible particulars.

On the basis just of reading the dialogues themselves, the focus in some secondary literature on separation may seem inexplicable. Plato's own text does not thematize anything called the separation of Forms (in Greek, *chōrismos*). We find only rarely any of the relevant cluster of words. On the occasions they do appear, they seem to be saying in an ordinary sense of separation that we have on the one hand sensibles, on the other hand Forms (i.e. simply that Forms are numerically distinct entities from sensibles). That claim is of course of enormous thematic importance, but it is simply the basic move of positing Platonic Forms, rather than an addition to their characterization.

How then did "separation" take off as a keyword for characterizing Platonic Forms? It is in *Aristotle's* treatment of Plato's Forms that separation bulks large, and this has brought the force he gives to separation (capacity for existence independently of any sensible participants) to the discussion. But notice that it is important in avoiding confusion not to take someone's correct observation that Plato's Forms are separate (in one of the ordinary senses) to justify the attribution of separation in this Aristotelian sense. Correspondingly, it is important not to bring to each occurrence of *chōris* and its relatives in Plato the assumption that it has the Aristotelian sense, as if it must always be referring to a commitment

Plato had made to the claim in that sense elsewhere. Rather, each occurrence should be read as having the force natural and appropriate in its own environment.

Even if we look only for the idea behind Aristotelian separation without the word, it is just not something that Plato's texts argue for or clearly commit themselves to. (*Symposium* 211b does say that Beauty is unaffected by its participants' coming into being and perishing—but this is the least developed discussion, and does not clearly have in view the existence of the form without *any* participants.) So in this case as in others, Aristotle is teasing out implications he thinks Plato's views have. He thinks that Plato's actual views—supplemented with some tenets Aristotle himself holds—lead to separation in the sense of capacity for independent existence, which (again based on some of his own tenets) he thinks is a mistake (Fine 1993).

Thus a methodological question arises concerning the place we should give Aristotelian separation in our thinking. The answer to this must depend on what we take our object of study to be. When our focus is on Aristotle, following his discussion of the notions in question almost certainly will provide illumination of his view—since his view is consciously developed as different from the one he assigns to Plato. However, when the object of our study is Plato's dialogues, then the role of Aristotle's discussion is subtly different. Plato himself did not thematize Aristotelian separation: if he thought of Forms as separate in this way at all, it certainly was not a central part of his presentation of them. So to read Plato's texts from the start through Aristotelian lenses is in this case distorting. Rather we should read and reanimate them initially independently of Aristotle; then we can if we wish proceed to compare and contrast the positions of the two philosophers.

It is possible that, though he did not thematize this, Plato's view does commit him to Aristotelian separation.[1] In this case and on reflection, we may come to agree with Aristotle that separation is a disastrous result that Plato's core motivations commit him to; at the other extreme the position in question may not seem problematic to us. A further possibility could be that Aristotle is suggesting an improvement that Plato would have no crucial and programmatic need to resist, even if he did not actually think of it himself (and even if a few of his stray remarks or examples would need to be revised in light of the improvement).

Note

1   Isolated passages on Forms of artifacts and the *Timaeus* creation story (both of which can be read to imply separation) are regarded by many interpreters as not meant to be taken literally. Perhaps the best route to separation as essential to Plato's view is through his making Forms *ousiai* (fundamental realities).

account (*logos*) In Plato, this and cognate words can have special reference to the kind of account that says of some fundamental nature what it really is.

aition See **cause**.

akrasia (adj. *akratic*) "Moral weakness" or "weakness of will." Roughly, not doing what one regards as really best for oneself because one is overcome by pleasure.

alētheia See **truth**.

aporia Lack of resource; the condition of not knowing what to think in which people found themselves after Socratic *elenchos*.

aretē See **virtue**.

cause The conventional translation of *aition*, but in Plato this has the broad sense of what is responsible for something and so figures centrally in the explanation; (*aitia* can be the account laying out the explanation).

division (Platonic) division is an approach discussed and demonstrated at length by Plato, whereby one maps the relations between fundamental realities by dividing a kind into its sub-kinds using differentiae and so on down; the ancestor of what we are familiar with from biological classification of living things.

definition In Plato, a matter of giving the sort of account that articulates what some fundamental nature really is.

dialectic Literally "conversational [method]"; Plato can use this of whichever procedure he regards as promising at the time.

Always involves two participants; formally one is questioner and one gives answers. The aim is to discover/test accounts of what is real.

dikaiosunē This and related terminology are best translated by "justice" and related terminology; the notion and its opposite are broad enough that in some contexts it is natural to use English along the lines of "right" treatment of others versus "wrongdoing."

eidōlon Shape, image, specter.

eidos Originally a look things offer to our sight; comes to mean more broadly a characteristic things can share; can also refer to the kind of things that share in such a characteristic. Plato develops a metaphysical theory of Forms according to which it is they and not everyday items that are truly real. The word *eidos* underlies many assertions translated in terms of Forms as well as many passages translated in terms of species.

elenchos (adj. elenctic) Testing or refutation.

erōs Intense desire focussed on a particular object; what is desired is usually but not necessarily sex with a person. Related vocabulary: *erastēs* lover; *erōmenos* beloved.

eudaimonia See **happiness**.

Form Each Form, F-ness or the F, is common to and explanatory of the many F things. Plato regards them as "more real" than sensibles; F-ness is the real F.

genos Genus; can refer to a Form or kind of things.

happiness Conventionally, the translation of *eudaimonia*. Not a mood or affective state. Rather, the objective condition of living a well-favored or successful life, of doing well: human flourishing.

idea Same root as *eidos*; alternative word for Form—in Plato no connotation of being mental.

kalos, kalē, kalon Inextricable fusion of beautiful/admirable/ honorable/splendid/noble/fine. While different contexts induce translators to different choices from among these English terms, Plato does not think the term is ambiguous: rather *to kalon* is some one thing common to all the cases.

logos See **account**.

mimēsis Imitation. Related vocabulary: **mimētikē** can indicate a practice *excessively* given to imitation (i.e. given to indiscriminate imitation, without proper concern for cognitive and emotional propriety).

nature Each Platonic Form is specially associated with a nature (*ousia/phusis*); whether the association is or is not less than full identity is left open. We ourselves can regard sweetness as a property shared by sweet things, as well as the nature that one analyzes when inquiring into what it is to be sweet, and which makes sweet things sweet.

ousia *Ousia, to on,* and other Greek expressions that derive from *einai* (to be) are rendered in English by a variety of terms including "what is," "being," "the real," "reality," and "real nature." In general for an ancient philosopher, what in that person's theory is fundamental; for Plato, the Forms have this role.

participation Also translatable as "having a share/portion." The relation that holds between individuals and the Forms that explain them in Plato's theory is participation. If anything is beautiful, that is because it *participates in* the Beautiful. This relation is not explicated in Plato's earliest use of it, but neither is he introducing the term on purpose to be mystical and opaque. Rather, the vocabulary of "having a share" was initially used in ordinary language, where it indicated no special theory. It does have a theoretical use in Anaxagoras: ordinary individuals *have portions of* elemental stuffs as physical ingredients. Plato's theory parallels that of Anaxagoras, but he needs to find a new way of understanding participation given his interest in explaining what makes us just, beautiful, large etc. Such facts cannot be due to our having portions of homogeneous, elemental stuffs as ingredients in our bodies.

philosophia Literally, love of wisdom. In some dialogues understood as a *desire* for wisdom (so that one could be a philosopher without actually having acquired it). In other dialogues, "philosopher" designates only those who actually *have* wisdom. In antiquity, when special disciplines had not broken off as they have by now, philosophy included a huge range of activity; it could be used of any intellectually serious thought. Plato thinks that a philosopher must come to grips with what is fundamentally real by studying the accounts articulating what each thing is, and by studying the relations among these fundamental realities.

pleonexia (adj. pleonectic) Wanting more—traditionally opposed to justice.

property Something general, which can be common to a number of things, as redness is common to red objects and cathood to particular cats. I also use the word "universal" for this. Note that my use of the vocabulary does *not* build in the understanding of these terms in the particular philosophical theories of universals developed from Aristotle to the present, or the distinction sometimes made today between universals and properties.

psychē What makes the difference between things that are alive and things that are not. What that is can be identified and developed in different ways: the "shade" in Homer; the "soul" of religious doctrine; the "psych" in "psychology."

self-predication Sentences are those that look in English like: "F-ness is F" or "The F itself is F." The term "self-predication" is a term of art from the secondary literature on Plato. Some scholars build in the interpretation that the Form is one of its own instances. Others (including the present author) do not build that in. Because self-predication claims about Forms play a central role in Plato's theory, he needs to find the interpretation of them on which they express truths.

sensible Plato often writes of what is "sensible" or "visible" in a broad sense to refer to what is patent to superficial observation, whether it is particular (like Socrates) or universal (like bright color).

sōphrosunē Translatable variously as "moderation," "soberness," "temperance" and "self-discipline" among others. By word formation, indicates sound-mindedness.

soul See **psychē**.

sumphōnia Translated as "concord" or "consonance," the desirable condition in which different notes make a unity.

symposium Literally a drinking party; typically had a component of elite socialization: ancient "networking" and recitation of poetry were common.

thumos Spirited desire.

truth To *alēthes* or *alētheia* can have an honorific sense to designate what is fundamental, what is "real and true."

universal See **property**.

virtue This translates the Greek *aretē*. In general, excellence; in the case of humans, what puts us in a position to live well.

Bibliography

Adam, J. (ed.) (1963) The "Republic" of Plato, 2nd edn, Cambridge: Cambridge University Press (first edition 1902).

Annas, J. (1981) An Introduction to Plato's "Republic", Oxford: Clarendon Press.

Annas, J. (1986) "Classical Greek Philosophy," in J. Boardman, J. Griffin, O. Murray (eds.), The Oxford History of the Classical World, Oxford: Oxford University Press.

Annas, J. (1999) Platonic Ethics, Old and New, Ithaca, NY: Cornell University Press.

Asmis, A. (1992) "Plato on Poetic Creativity," in R. Kraut (ed.), The Cambridge to Plato, Cambridge: Cambridge University Press.

Bailey, D. (2005) "Logic and Music in Plato's Phaedo," Phronesis 50: 95–115.

Bailey, D. (2009) "The Third Man Argument," Philosophy Compass 4: 666–681.

Bailey, D. (2014) "Platonic Causes Revisited," Journal of the History of Philosophy 52: 15–32.

Barker, A. (1989) Greek Musical Writings, vol. 2, Harmonic and Acoustic Theory, Cambridge: Cambridge University Press

Barker, A. (1994) "Ptolemy's Pythagoreans, Archytas, and Plato's Conception of Mathematics," Phronesis 39: 113–135.

Barker, A. (1996) "Plato's Philebus: The Numbering of a Unity," Apeiron 19: 143–64.

Barnes, J. (1982) The Presocratic Philosophers, London: Routledge & Kegan Paul.

Barnes, J. (ed.) (1984) *The Complete Works of Aristotle* (Revised Oxford Translation), Princeton, NJ: Princeton University Press.

Barney, R. (1992) "Appearances and Impressions," *Phronesis* 37: 283–313.

Barney, R., Brennan, T., and Brittain, C. (eds.) (2012) *Plato and the Divided Self*, Cambridge: Cambridge University Press.

Baudy, G. (1986) *Adonisgärten*, Frankfurt: Hain.

Belfiore, E. (1983) "Plato's Greatest Accusation Against Poetry," in F. Pelletier and J. King-Farlow (eds.), *New Essays on Plato* (*Canadian Journal of Philosophy* suppl. vol. 9), Calgary: University of Calgary Press: 39–62.

Benson, H. (ed.) (1992) *Essays in the Philosophy of Socrates*, New York: Oxford University Press.

Blondell, R. (2002) *The Play of Character in Plato's Dialogues*, Cambridge: Cambridge University Press.

Blondell, R. (2006) "Where is Socrates on the 'Ladder of Love'?," in J. Lesher, D. Nails, and F. Sheffield (eds.), *Plato's "Symposium"*, Cambridge, MA: Harvard University Press.

Bobonich, C. (2002) *Plato's Utopia Recast*, Oxford: Clarendon Press.

Bostock, D. (1986) *Plato's "Phaedo"*, Oxford: Clarendon Press.

Brentlinger, J. (1972) "Incomplete Predicates and the Two-World Theory of the *Phaedo*," *Phronesis* 17: 61–79.

Brown, E. (2012) "The Unity of the Soul in Plato's Republic," in R. Barney, T. Brennan, and C. Brittain (eds.), *Plato and the Divided Self*, Cambridge: Cambridge University Press.

Brisson, L. (2011) *Platon Parménide: Presentation et traduction*, 3rd edn, Paris: Flammarion.

Burkert, W. (1987) *Ancient Mystery Cults*, Cambridge, MA: Harvard University Press.

Burnet, J. (ed.) (1900-7) *Platonis Opera* (5 vols), Oxford: Clarendon Press.

Burnyeat, M. (1980) "Aristotle on Learning to be Good," in A. Rorty (ed.), *Essays on Aristotle's Ethics*, Berkeley, CA: University of California Press; reprinted in M. Burnyeat (2012) *Explorations in Ancient and Modern Philosophy*, vol. 2, Cambridge: Cambridge University Press.

Burnyeat, M. (1987) "Platonism and Mathematics: A Prelude to Discussion," in A. Graeser (ed.), *Mathematics and Metaphysics in Aristotle*, Bern: Paul Haupt; reprinted in M. Burnyeat (2012)

Explorations in Ancient and Modern Philosophy, vol. 2, Cambridge: Cambridge University Press.

Burnyeat, M. (1990) *The "Theaetetus" of Plato*, Indianapolis, IN: Hackett Publishing Company.

Burnyeat, M. (1999) "Culture and Society in Plato's *Republic*," *Tanner Lectures on Human Values* 20: 215–324, http://tannerlectures. utah.edu/_documents/a-to-z/b/Burnyeat99.pdf.

Burnyeat, M. (2000) "Plato on Why Mathematics is Good for the Soul," in T. Smiley (ed.), *Mathematics and Necessity*, Proceedings of the British Academy 103: 1–81.

Burnyeat, M. (2005) "The Truth of Tripartition," *Proceedings of the Aristotelian Society* 106: 23.

Cooper, J. (1984) "Plato on Human Motivation," *History of Philosophy Quarterly* 1: 3–21; reprinted in J. Cooper (1999) *Reason and Emotion*, Princeton, NJ: Princeton University Press.

Cooper, J. (ed.) (1997) *Plato: Complete Works*, Indianapolis, IN: Hackett Publishing Company.

Cornford, F. (1939) *Plato and Parmenides*, London: Routledge & Kegan Paul.

Dancy, R. (2004) *Plato's Introduction of Forms*, Cambridge: Cambridge University Press.

Denyer, N. (2007a) "Sun and Line: The Role of the Good," in G. Ferrari (ed.), *The Cambridge Companion to Plato's "Republic"*, Cambridge: Cambridge University Press.

Denyer, N. (2007b) "The *Phaedo's* Final Argument," in D. Scott (ed.), *Maieusis: Essays in Ancient Philosophy in Honour of Myles Burnyeat*, Oxford: Oxford University Press.

Dillon, J. (2003) *The Heirs of Plato*, Oxford: Clarendon Press.

Dodds, E. (1959) *Plato: "Gorgias"*, Oxford: Clarendon Press.

Dover, K. (1978) *Greek Homosexuality*, London: Duckworth.

Dover, K. (ed.) (1980) *Plato: "Symposium"*, Cambridge: Cambridge University Press.

Duke, E., Hicken, W., Nicoll, W., Robinson, D. and Strachan, J. (eds) (1995) *Platonis Opera* vol. 1, Oxford: Clarendon Press.

Eaton, A. (2012) "Robust Immoralism," *Journal of Aesthetics and Art Criticism* 70: 281–292.

Ferrari, G. (1987) *Listening to the Cicadas*, Cambridge: Cambridge University Press.

Ferrari, G. (1989) "Plato and Poetry," in G. Kennedy (ed.), The Cambridge History of Literary Criticism, Cambridge: Cambridge University Press.

Ferrari, G. (1992) "Platonic Love," in R. Kraut (ed.), The Cambridge Companion to Plato, Cambridge: Cambridge University Press.

Ferrari, G. (2007a) "The Three-Part Soul," in G. Ferrari (ed.), The Cambridge Companion to Plato's "Republic", Cambridge: Cambridge University Press.

Ferrari, G. (ed.) (2007b) The Cambridge Companion to Plato's "Republic", Cambridge: Cambridge University Press.

Ferrari, G. (2010) "Socrates in the Republic," in M. McPherran (ed.), Plato's "Republic", Cambridge: Cambridge University Press.

Ferrari, G. (ed.) and Griffith, T. (tr.) (2000) Plato: "The Republic", Cambridge: Cambridge University Press.

Fine, G. (1978) "Knowledge and Belief in Republic 5," Archiv für Geschichte der Philosophie 60:121–39.

Fine, G. (1990) "Knowledge and Belief in Republic 5–7," in S. Everson (ed.), Epistemology, Cambridge: Cambridge University Press; reprinted in G. Fine (ed.), (1999) Plato 1, Oxford: Oxford University Press; and in G. Fine (2003) Plato on Knowledge and Forms, Oxford: Clarendon Press.

Fine, G. (1993) On Ideas: Aristotle's Criticism of Plato's Theory of Forms, Oxford: Clarendon Press.

Fine, G. (ed.) (1999) Plato 1 and Plato 2. Oxford: Oxford University Press.

Fine, G. (2014) The Possibility of Inquiry: Meno's Paradox from Socrates to Sextus, Oxford: Oxford University Press.

Fodor, J. (1983) The Modularity of Mind, Cambridge, MA: MIT Press.

Frede, D. (1978) "The Final Proof for the Immortality of the Soul in Plato's Phaedo 102a–107a," Phronesis 23: 27–41.

Frede, M. (1967) Prädikation und Existenzaussage, Göttingen: Vandenhoeck & Ruprecht.

Frede, M. (1988) "Being and Becoming in Plato," Oxford Studies in Ancient Philosophy 6(suppl.): 37–52.

Frede, M. (1992) "Plato's Arguments and the Dialogue Form," in J. Klagge and N. Smith (eds.), Methods of Interpreting Plato and His Dialogues (Oxford Studies in Ancient Philosophy), Oxford: Clarendon Press.

Furley, D. (1956) "The Early History of the Concept of Soul," *Bulletin of the Institute of Classical Studies* 3: 1–18.

Furley, D. (1973) "Notes on Parmenides," in E. Lee, A. Mourelatos, and R. Rorty (eds.), *Studies in Greek Philosophy Presented to Gregory Vlastos* (*Phronesis* suppl. vol. 1), Assen: Van Gorcum: 1–15; reprinted in D. Furley (1989) *Cosmic Problems*, Cambridge: Cambridge University Press.

Furley, D. (1976) "Anaxagoras in Response to Parmenides," in R. Shiner and J. King-Farlow (eds.), *New Essays in Plato and the Pre-Socratics, Canadian Journal of Philosophy* 2 (suppl.): 61–85; reprinted in D. Furley (1989) *Cosmic Problems*, Cambridge: Cambridge University Press.

Furley, D. (1981) "Antiphon's Case Against Justice," in G Kerferd (ed.), *The Sophists and Their Legacy*; reprinted in D. Furley (1989) *Cosmic Problems*, Cambridge: Cambridge University Press.

Furley, D. (1987) *The Greek Cosmologists*, Cambridge: Cambridge University Press.

Furth, M. (1968) "Elements of Eleatic Ontology" *Journal of the History of Philosophy* 6: 112–32.

Gallop, D. (tr.) (1997) *Plato: Defence of Socrates, Euthyphro, Crito*, Oxford: Oxford University Press.

Gendler, T. (2008a) "Alief in Action (and Reaction)," *Mind and Language* 23: 552–585.

Gendler, T. (2008b) "Alief and Belief," *Journal of Philosophy* 105: 634–663.

Gendler, T. (2014) "The Third Horse: On Unendorsed Association and Human Behaviour," *Aristotelian Society* 88 (suppl.): 185–218.

Gill, M. (1996) *Plato "Parmenides,"* Indianapolis, IN: Hackett Publishing Company.

Gill, M. (2012) *Philosophos: Plato's Missing Dialogue*, Oxford: Oxford University Press.

Gosling, J. (1960) "Republic Book 5: *ta polla kala* etc.," *Phronesis* 5: 116–28.

Griffin, J. (1987) *Homer: The Odyssey*, Cambridge: Cambridge University Press.

Griffith, T. (tr.) (1986) *Symposium of Plato*, Marlborough: Libanus Press.

Griswold, C. (ed.) (1988) *Platonic Writings/Platonic Readings*, New York: Routledge.

Halperin, D. (1992) "Plato and the Erotics of Narrativity," in J. Klagge and N. Smith (eds.), *Methods of Interpreting Plato and His Dialogues* (Oxford Studies in Ancient Philosophy), Oxford: Clarendon Press.

Heubeck, A. and Hoekstra, A. (1989) *A Commentary on Homer's Odyssey* vol 2, Oxford: Clarendon Press.

Hicks, R. (tr.) (1925) *Diogenes Laertius: Lives of Eminent Philosophers*, London: William Heinemann.

Hubbard, T. (1998) "Popular Perceptions of Elite Homosexuality in Classical Athens," *Arion* (third series) 6: 48–78.

Hubbard, T. (2005) *Homosexuality in Greece and Rome*, Berkeley, CA: University of California Press.

Hunter, R. (2004) *Plato's "Symposium"*, Oxford: Oxford University Press.

Irwin, T. (1977a) *Plato's Moral Theory*, Oxford: Clarendon Press.

Irwin, T. (1977b) "Plato's Heracleiteanism," *Philosophical Quarterly* 27: 1–13.

Irwin, T. (1995) *Plato's Ethics*, New York: Oxford University Press.

Irwin, T. (2008) "The Platonic Corpus," in G. Fine (ed.), *The Oxford Handbook of Plato*, Oxford: Oxford University Press.

Jowett, B. (tr.) (1892) *The Dialogues of Plato*, 3rd edn, Oxford: Clarendon Press.

Jowett, B. and Campbell, L. (eds., notes, essays) (1894) *Plato's Republic*, vol. 3, Oxford: Clarendon Press.

Kahn, C. (1981) "Some Philosophical Uses of 'to Be' in Plato," *Phronesis* 26: 105–34.

Kahn, C. (1996) *Plato and the Socratic Dialogue*, Cambridge: Cambridge University Press.

Kahn, C. (2002) "On Platonic Chronology," in J. Annas and C. Rowe (eds.), *New Perspectives on Plato, Modern and Ancient*, Cambridge, MA: Harvard University Press.

Kahneman, D. (2011) *Thinking, Fast and Slow*, New York: Farrar, Straus and Giroux.

Keyser, P. (1991) Review of G. Ledger, *Re-counting Plato: A Computer Analysis of Plato's Style*, in *Bryn Mawr Classical Review*, http://bmcr.bryn-mawr.edu/1991/02.07.03.html.

Keyser, P. (1992) "Stylometric Method and the Chronology of Plato's Works," review of L. Brandwood, *The Chronology of Plato's*

Dialogues, in Bryn Mawr *Classical Review*, http://bmcr.brynmawr.edu/992/03.01.12.pdf.

Kirk, G., Raven, J., and Schofield, M. (1983) *The Presocratic Philosophers*, 2nd edn, Cambridge: Cambridge University Press.

Kosman, L. (1974) "Platonic Love," in W. Werkmeister (ed.), *Facets of Plato's Philosophy*, Assen: Van Gorcum.

Kraut, R. (1984) *Socrates and the State*, Princeton, NJ: Princeton University Press.

Lattimore, R. (tr.) (1951) *The Iliad of Homer*, Chicago, IL: University of Chicago Press.

Lattimore, R. (tr.) (1967) *The Odyssey of Homer*, New York: Harper and Row.

Lane, M. (2007) "Virtue as the Love of Knowledge in Plato's *Symposium* and *Republic*," in D. Scott (ed.), *Maieusis: Essays in Ancient Philosophy in Honour of Myles Burnyeat*, Oxford: Oxford University Press.

Lear, G. (2006) "Permanent Beauty and Becoming Happy in Plato's *Symposium*," in J. Lesher, D. Nails, and F. Sheffield (eds.), *Plato's "Symposium"*, Cambridge, MA: Harvard University Press.

Lear, J. (1998) "Eros and Unknowing," in J. Lear, *Open Minded: Working out the Logic of the Soul*, Cambridge, MA: Harvard University Press.

Lear, J. (2005) *Freud*, Abingdon: Routledge.

Lear, J. (2008) "Mythic Justice," paper presented at the Thirteenth Annual Arizona Colloquium in Ancient Philosophy, Tucson, February.

Lennox, J. (1987) "Kinds, Forms of Kinds, and The More and The Less in Aristotle's Biology," in A. Gotthelf and J. Lennox (eds.), *Philosophical Issues in Aristotle's Biology*, Cambridge: Cambridge University Press.

Lesher, J. (1981) "Perceiving and Knowing in the *Iliad* and *Odyssey*," *Phronesis* 26: 2–24.

Lesher, J., Nails, D. and Sheffield. F. (eds.) (2006) *Plato's "Symposium"*, Cambridge, MA: Harvard University Press.

Lorenz, H. (2009) "Ancient Theories of Soul," in E. N. Zalta (ed.), *The Stanford Encyclopedia of Philosophy*, http://plato.stanford.edu/archives/sum2009/entries/ancient-soul.

Lorenz, H. (2006) *The Brute Within*, Oxford: Clarendon Press.

McCabe, M. (1994) *Plato's Individuals*, Princeton, NJ: Princeton

University Press.

McCabe, M. (1996) "Unity in the *Parmenides*: The Unity of the *Parmenides*," in C. Gill and M. McCabe (eds.), *Form and Argument in Late Plato*, Oxford: Clarendon Press.

McPherran, M. (ed.) (2010) *Plato's "Republic"*. Cambridge: Cambridge University Press.

Madison, D. (2013) *Vegetable Literacy*, Berkeley, CA: Ten Speed Press.

Mann, W. (2000) *The Discovery of Things*, Princeton, NJ: Princeton University Press.

Mason, A. (2010) *Plato*, Abingdon: Routledge.

Mayer, J. (2007) "Whatever It Takes," *The New Yorker*, February 19–26: 66–82.

Meinwald, C. (1991) *Plato's "Parmenides"*, New York: Oxford University Press.

Meinwald, C. (1992) "Good-bye to the Third Man," in R. Kraut (ed.), *The Cambridge Companion to Plato*, Cambridge: Cambridge University Press.

Meinwald, C. (1998) "Prometheus's Bounds: *Peras* and *Apeiron* in Plato's *Philebus*," in J. Gentzler (ed.), *Method in Ancient Philosophy*, Oxford: Oxford University Press.

Meinwald, C. (2002) "Plato's Pythagoreanism: Philolaus and the Program of the *Philebus*," *Ancient Philosophy* 22: 87–101.

Meinwald, C. (2005) "Literary Elements and Dialogue Form in Plato's *Parmenides*," in A. Havlicek and F. Karfík (eds.), *Plato's "Parmenides"*: *Proceedings of the Fourth Symposium Platonicum Pragense*, Prague: Oikoymenh.

Meinwald, C. (2011) "Reason v. Literature in Plato's *Republic*," *Ancient Philosophy* 31: 25–45.

Meinwald, C. (2014) "How Does Plato's Exercise Work?" *Dialogue* 53: 465–494.

Meinwald, C. (forthcoming) "Who Are the *Philotheamones* and What Are They Thinking?" *Ancient Philosophy*.

Moline, J. (1978) "Plato on the Complexity of the Psyche," *Archiv für Geschichte der Philosophie* 60: 1–26.

Morrow, G. and Dillon, J. (trs) (1987) *Proclus' Commentary on Plato's "Parmenides"*, Princeton, NJ: Princeton University Press; paperback edition with corrections published 1992.

Moss, J. (2007) "What Is Imitative Poetry and Why Is It Bad?" in G.

Ferrari (ed.), *The Cambridge Companion to Plato's "Republic"*, Cambridge: Cambridge University Press.

Moss, J. (2008) "Appearances and Calculations: Plato's Division of the Soul," *Oxford Studies in Ancient Philosophy* 34: 35–68.

Mueller, I. (1992) "Mathematical Method and Philosophical Truth," in R. Kraut (ed.), *The Cambridge Companion to Plato*, Cambridge: Cambridge University Press.

Murray, A. (tr.) (1924–5) Homer: *"The Iliad"*, London: William Heinemann.

Nehamas, A. (1975) "Confusing Universals and Particulars in Plato's Early Dialogues," *Review of Metaphysics* 29: 287–306.

Nehamas, A. (1979) "Self-Predication and Plato's Theory of Forms," *American Philosophical Quarterly* 16: 93–103.

Nehamas, A. (1988) "Plato and the Mass Media," *The Monist* 71: 214–34; reprinted in A. Nehamas (1999) *Virtues of Authenticity*, Princeton, NJ: Princeton University Press.

Netz, R. (2009) *Ludic Proof: Greek Mathematics and the Alexandrian Aesthetic*, Cambridge: Cambridge University Press.

Nussbaum, M. (1986) "The Speech of Alcibiades," in M. Nussbaum, *The Fragility of Goodness*, Cambridge: Cambridge University Press.

Owen, G. (1957) "A Proof in the *Peri Ideōn*," *Journal of Hellenic Studies* 77: 103–11; reprinted in R. Allen (ed.) (1965) *Studies in Plato's Metaphysics*, London: Routledge & Kegan Paul and also in *Logic, Science and Dialectic* (1986) Ithaca, NY: Cornell University Press.

Owen, G. (1960) "Eleatic Questions," *Classical Quarterly* new series 10: 84–102; reprinted in D. Furley and R. Allen (eds.) (1975) *Studies in Presocratic Philosophy*, vol. 2, London: Routledge & Kegan Paul; and in G. Owen (1986) *Logic, Science and Dialectic*, Ithaca, NY: Cornell University Press.

Owen, G. (1966) "Plato and Parmenides on the Timeless Present," *The Monist* 50: 317–40; reprinted in A. Mourelatos (ed.) (1974) *The Pre-Socratics*, Garden City, NY: Doubleday; and in G. Owen (1986) *Logic, Science, and Dialectic*, Ithaca, NY: Cornell University Press.

Pappas, N. (2003) *Routledge Philosophy Guidebook to Plato and the "Republic"*, 2nd edn, London: Routledge.

Patterson, R. (1985) *Image and Reality in Plato's Metaphysics*, Indianapolis, IN: Hackett Publishing Company.

Patterson, R. (1991) "The Ascent in Plato's Symposium," *Proceedings of the*

Boston Area Colloquium in Ancient Philosophy 7: 193–214.

Penner, T. (1987) *The Ascent from Nominalism*, Dordrecht: D. Reidel.

Peterson, S. (1973) "A Reasonable Self-Predication Premise for the Third Man Argument," *Philosophical Review* 82: 451–70.

Peterson, S. (1995) *Mental Conflict*, London: Routledge.

Peterson, S. (2009) "Are Plato's Soul-Parts Psychological Subjects?" *Ancient Philosophy* 29: 1–15.

Peterson, S. (2011) *Socrates and Philosophy in the Dialogues of Plato*, Cambridge: Cambridge University Press.

Price, A. (1989) *Love and Friendship in Plato and Aristotle*, Oxford: Clarendon Press.

Reeve, C. (1988) *Philosopher-Kings*, Princeton, NJ: Princeton University Press; reprinted by Hackett Publishing Company in 2006.

Reynolds, L. and Wilson, N. (1991) *Scribes and Scholars*, 3rd edn, Oxford: Clarendon Press.

Rickless, S. (2007) *Plato's Forms in Transition: A Reading of the "Parmenides"*, Cambridge: Cambridge University Press.

Riginos, A. (1976) *Platonica*, Leiden: E. J. Brill.

Robinson, R. (1953) *Plato's Earlier Dialectic*, 2nd edn, Oxford: Clarendon Press.

Ross, W. (1924) *Aristotle's Metaphysics*, vol. 1, Oxford: Clarendon Press.

Rutherford, R. (1995) *The Art of Plato*, London: Duckworth.

Sachs, D. (1963) "A Fallacy in Plato's Republic," *Philosophical Review* 72: 141–58.

Santas, G. (1988) *Plato and Freud: Two Theories of Love*, Oxford: Blackwell.

Sapolsky, R. (1998) "Open Season," *The New Yorker*, March 30: 57–72.

Sattler, B. (2013) "The Eleusinian Mysteries in Pre-Platonic Thought: Metaphor, Practice, and Imagery for Plato's Symposium," in V. Adluri (ed.), *Philosophy and Salvation in Greek Religion*, Berlin: de Gruyter.

Sayre, K. (1978) "Plato's Parmenides: Why the Eight Hypotheses Are Not Contradictory," *Phronesis* 23: 133–50.

Sayre, K. (1995) *Plato's Literary Garden: How to Read a Platonic Dialogue*, Notre Dame, IN: University of Notre Dame Press.

Schofield, M. (2007) "Metaspeleology," in D. Scott (ed.), *Maieusis: Essays in Ancient Philosophy in Honour of Myles Burnyeat*, Oxford: Oxford University Press.

Scolnicov, S. and Brisson, L. (eds.) (2003) *Plato's Laws: From Theory Into*

Practice (Proceedings of the VI Symposium Platonicum), Sankt Augustin: Academia Verlag.

Scott, D. (1999) "Platonic Recollection," in G. Fine (ed.), *Plato 1: Metaphysics and Epistemology*, Oxford: Oxford University Press.

Sedley, D. (1989) "Is the *Lysis* a Dialogue of Definition?" *Phronesis* 34: 107–8.

Sedley, D. (1995) "The Dramatis Personae of Plato's *Phaedo*," in T. Smiley (ed.), *Philosophical Dialogues, Proceedings of the British Academy* 85: 3–26.

Sedley, D. (1998) "Platonic Causes," *Phronesis* 43: 114–32.

Sedley, D. (2006) "Platonic Immortality," paper presented at Chicago Area Consortium for Ancient Philosophy Conference on Philosophy and Religion in Ancient Greece, Chicago, November.

Sedley, D. (2007) "Equal Sticks and Stones," in D. Scott (ed.), *Maieusis: Essays in Ancient Philosophy in Honour of Myles Burnyeat*, Oxford: Oxford University Press.

Sedley, D. (2009) "Three Kinds of Platonic Immortality," in D. Frede and B. Reis (eds.), *Body and Soul in Ancient Philosophy*, Berlin: de Gruyter.

Sedley, D. and Long, A. (2011) *Plato: "Meno" and "Phaedo"*, Cambridge: Cambridge University Press.

Sheffield, F. (2006) *Plato's "Symposium"*, Oxford: Oxford University Press.

Shorey, P. (tr.) (1930) *Plato: The Republic*, London: William Heinemann. I take quotations from version (with Americanized orthography) in E. Hamilton and H. Cairns (eds) (1961) *The Collected Dialogues of Plato*, Princeton: Princeton University Press.

Silverman, A. (2002) *The Dialectic of Essence: A Study of Plato's Metaphysics*, Princeton, NJ: Princeton University Press.

Skinner, M. (2005) *Sexuality in Greek and Roman Culture*, Oxford: Blackwell.

Slings, S. (ed.) (1993) *Platonis Respublica*, Oxford: Clarendon Press.

Smith, N. (2010) "Return to the Cave," in M. McPherran (ed.), *Plato's "Republic"*, Cambridge: Cambridge University Press.

Stone, I. (1988) *The Trial of Socrates*, Boston, MA: Little, Brown.

Strang, C. (1963) "The Physical Theory of Anaxagoras," *Archiv für Geschichte der Philosophie* 45: 101–18; reprinted in D. Furley and R. Allen (eds.) (1975), *Studies in Presocratic Philosophy*, vol. 2, London:

Routledge & Kegan Paul.

Szlezák, T. (1999) *Reading Plato*, London: Routledge; tr. G. Zanker from T. Szlezák (1993) *Platon Lesen*, Stuttgart: Verlag Frommann-Holzboog.

Vernant, J. (1991) *Mortals and Immortals*, Princeton, NJ: Princeton University Press.

Vlastos, G. (1954) "The Third Man Argument in the *Parmenides*," *Philosophical Review* 63: 319–49.

Vlastos, G. (1965) "Degrees of Reality in Plato," in R. Bambrough (ed.), *New Essays on Plato and Aristotle*, London: Routledge & Kegan Paul; reprinted with original pagination in brackets in G. Vlastos (1981) *Platonic Studies*, 2nd edn, Princeton, NJ: Princeton University Press.

Vlastos, G. (1969) "Reasons and Causes in the *Phaedo*," *Philosophical Review* 78: 291–325; reprinted with corrections, and new material in notes in G. Vlastos (1973, rev. 1981), *Platonic Studies*, Princeton, NJ: Princeton University Press.

Vlastos, G. (1973a) "Justice and Happiness in the *Republic*," in G. Vlastos, *Platonic Studies*, Princeton, NJ: Princeton University Press (rev. edn with corrections 1981); parts substantially identical with G. Vlastos (1969) "Justice and Psychic Harmony in the *Republic*," *Journal of Philosophy* 66: 505–21.

Vlastos, G. (1973b) "The Individual as Object of Love in Plato," in *Platonic Studies*, Princeton, NJ: Princeton University Press (rev. edn with corrections 1981).

Vlastos, G. (1983) "The Socratic Elenchus," *Oxford Studies in Ancient Philosophy* 1: 27–58.

Vlastos, G. (1991) *Socrates: Ironist and Moral Philosopher*, Ithaca, NY: Cornell University Press.

Vogt, K. (2012) *Belief and Truth: A Sceptic Reading of Plato*, New York: Oxford University Press.

Whittaker, J. (2007) "A Summit Technology Can't Reach," *New York Times* Op-Ed, March 9, www.nytimes.com/2007/03/09/opinion/09whittaker.html?_r=0 (accessed August 3, 2015).

Wodehouse, P. G. (1922) "Sir Roderick Comes to Lunch," *The Strand Magazine*, March; reprinted in *The Inimitable Jeeves* (1923, London: Herbert Jenkins); *The Jeeves Omnibus* (1931, London: Herbert Jenkins); *The World of Jeeves* (1967, London: Herbert Jenkins); etc.

Wood, J. (2013) "Sins of the Father," *The New Yorker*, July 22: 70–74.

Young, C. (1994) "Plato and Computer Dating: A Discussion of Gerard R. Ledger, *Recounting Plato: A Computer Analysis of Plato's Style* and Leonard Brandwood, *The Chronology of Plato's Dialogues*," *Oxford Studies in Ancient Philosophy* 12: 227–50.

Index

Taylor & Francis eBooks

Helping you to choose the right eBooks for your Library

Add Routledge titles to your library's digital collection today. Taylor and Francis ebooks contains over 50,000 titles in the Humanities, Social Sciences, Behavioural Sciences, Built Environment and Law.

Choose from a range of subject packages or create your own!

Benefits for you

» Free MARC records
» COUNTER-compliant usage statistics
» Flexible purchase and pricing options
» All titles DRM-free.

Benefits for your user

» Off-site, anytime access via Athens or referring URL
» Print or copy pages or chapters
» Full content search
» Bookmark, highlight and annotate text
» Access to thousands of pages of quality research at the click of a button.

REQUEST YOUR **FREE** INSTITUTIONAL TRIAL TODAY | **Free Trials Available** We offer free trials to qualifying academic, corporate and government customers.

eCollections – Choose from over 30 subject eCollections, including:

Archaeology	Language Learning
Architecture	Law
Asian Studies	Literature
Business & Management	Media & Communication
Classical Studies	Middle East Studies
Construction	Music
Creative & Media Arts	Philosophy
Criminology & Criminal Justice	Planning
Economics	Politics
Education	Psychology & Mental Health
Energy	Religion
Engineering	Security
English Language & Linguistics	Social Work
Environment & Sustainability	Sociology
Geography	Sport
Health Studies	Theatre & Performance
History	Tourism, Hospitality & Events

For more information, pricing enquiries or to order a free trial, please contact your local sales team:
www.tandfebooks.com/page/sales

 Routledge
Taylor & Francis Group | The home of Routledge books

www.tandfebooks.com